Buying and Selling

To my husband, Martin and our children Rachel, Rebecca and Benjamin and my clients whose buying and selling law problems never cease to educate me

Buying and Selling

A Legal Guide

E. Susan Singleton

Singletons Solicitors
t: 0181 864 0835
f: 0181 248 3810
e: essingleton@link.org

ICSA Publishing
The Official Publishing Company of
The Institute of Chartered Secretaries and Administrators

First published 1997 by
ICSA Publishing Ltd
Campus 400, Maylands Avenue
Hemel Hempstead
Hertfordshire, HP2 7EZ

Typeset in 10/12pt Palatino
by Hands Fotoset, Ratby, Leicester

Printed and bound in Great Britain by
T. J. International Ltd, Padstow, Cornwall

British Library Cataloguing in Publication Data

A catalogue record for this book is available from
the British Library
ISBN 1–860720–00–5

1 2 3 4 5   01 00 99 98 97

Contents

1 Introduction

This book seeks to provide for the company secretary an overview of the law relating to buying and selling. All companies, except in rare cases, such as charities, are involved in the sale or supply of goods or services as seller, and in the purchase of goods or services, even if this is simply office stationery. This area of the law is therefore of fundamental importance and some knowledge of this field is essential for all company secretaries.

This first chapter provides an introduction and overview of buying and selling law. Its contents are summarised below:

- Requirements for a contract of sale: offer and acceptance, consideration and intention to create legal relations.
- Written and oral contracts: both equally binding for sales of goods or services, but written contracts provide better evidence of the agreement between the parties.
- Incorporation of written terms into a contract: terms on the back of an invoice are supplied too late to be part of the contract, the party whose terms are sent last will usually prevail, how to deal with the so-called battle of the forms.
- Different forms of contract of sale and the distinction between them – sale of goods, supply of services, hire and leasing.

Requirements for contracts

A contract is a legally binding agreement and therefore under the law it will be enforceable only where certain conditions are met. These conditions are examined below. For most company secretaries there will be no problems in practice with proving that a contract exists. For example, if goods have been sold and the customer is refusing to pay, the existence of the contract is rarely in doubt. However, there may be circumstances – such as where a customer claims never to have placed an order, or the

1

other party to a transaction believed the parties were simply in negotiations rather than having reached the position of a formal contract – when the issues described below will be of practical relevance. So some understanding of this area is necessary.

The requirements for a contract are:

- offer
- acceptance
- consideration
- intention to create legal relations.

When a customer picks goods off the shelves in a supermarket and then proceeds to the till to pay, he or she is offering to purchase the goods. The shop may refuse to sell the goods if, for example, the shopkeeper believes the customer is under age and trying to buy cigarettes, or if he or she has been barred from the premises or for whatever reason. The contract is not made until the proprietor or his staff agree to sell the goods to the customer. The display of the goods on the shelves is not the offer. Although, there are various legal provisions which require shops to sell goods at the price displayed, this does not affect the contractual principles in consideration here.

Similarly with a mail order sale, the company selling the goods publishes a catalogue. This is known as a mere *invitation to treat* and is not an offer. The customer returning an order form with his or her cheque is making an offer to buy the goods and the company then decides, using factors such as whether the cheque clears etc., whether or not to accept the offer and thus form a contract or agreement with that customer.

It is important to appreciate, in each part of a business with which a company secretary is involved, when agreements are made because it is much easier to withdraw before the contract is made. Afterwards, although there are rights to reject goods after the contract is made where they are not *accepted* (and this is covered in later chapters), it is simpler to withdraw before a legally binding contract is in place.

There is no clear rule of when a display, such as in a shop or other business premises, amounts merely to an invitation to treat or an offer. A display of car parking rates outside a car park is usually regarded as an offer. The customer driving in accepts the offer: a case called *Thornton v. Shoe Lane Parking [1971] 2 QB 163* made this clear.

In business many contracts are made after an expensive and lengthy tendering process. This can be usefully analysed here in the context of offer and acceptance and contractual requirements. Despite the fact that it is very expensive to prepare and submit a tender document, this is simply regarded as an offer. There is no obligation *per se* on the company seeking the tenders to proceed. It is free to accept any tender it wishes, subject to any other legal rules. For example, tenders under the EU public procurement regime are subject to special requirements to ensure fairness with various bases for evaluation of tenders being set out, and under EU competition law all companies must ensure that they do not engage in collusive tendering. Companies in a dominant position in the EU must act fairly to ensure there is no breach of Article 86 of the Treaty of Rome in choosing a supplier. However, subject to these detailed rules, companies are free to pick and choose from tenders.

In *Carlill v. Carbolic Smoke Ball Co [1893] 1 QB 256*, decided over 100 years ago, and a case with which many company secretaries who have studied contract law will be familiar, an advertisement promised to pay £100 to any user of a carbolic smoke ball who caught influenza. This was held to be an offer, and a user who caught flu sued successfully for breach of contract when promises made were not fulfilled. Company secretaries need to consider each area of the business so that they know whether advertisements, notices at premises, car parks, in newspapers, mail order catalogues, tender advertisements etc. are offers or merely invitations to treat; that is, if a customer accepts or orders, must the company supply?

Practical exercise

Check all company advertisements, materials, catalogues and tender or order procedures: are they offers or invitations to treat? If they comprise formal offers does the company want them to be so or should they be altered by their wording to a mere invitation to treat so that customers can be refused goods or services? Modify procedures accordingly if necessary. In cases of doubt ensure that written materials contain a statement such as 'We reserve the right to refuse any order' or 'Supplies are subject to availability' or some other wording which makes it clear that there is no obligation to supply following receipt of an order.

Conversely, if the company is a buyer, it will want its orders to be met. It should therefore resist clauses in long term distribution contracts which give the supplier the right to refuse to meet any order.

Consideration

A contract will not be legally binding unless there is 'consideration'. This usually means payment. If company A agrees to do a favour for company B for no reward then A can withdraw the practice at any time. For example, A and B may share a site and A may let B's customers use its waiting area. Generally it is preferable to have such arrangements set out in writing even where no money is paid, even if only to make it clear that A can withdraw the favour at any time.

Consideration can be money or money's worth, so if B performs a reciprocal service, a contract may be formed even though neither pays the other. If Mr X agrees with Mr Y to fix his car in exchange for piano lessons that is as much a contract as if money were changing hands. The courts do not look into the sufficiency of consideration which is why many contracts are expressed to be 'in consideration of the payment of £1 receipt of which is here acknowledged'. Sometimes a peppercorn is given, usually in property transactions. If the matter is litigated, the courts will not state that one party did a poor deal or agreed to pay too little or too much for the goods or services and thus the consideration was not adequate. The courts leave the parties to make their own deals, good or bad. The legal issue is simply whether consideration is paid or not.

Consideration must be provided by the party making the promise, known as the requirement that consideration must move from the promisee. However, the other party does not have to gain the benefit of the consideration. For example, the promisee may give up a flat. The detailed rules are much more complicated than the simple statements set out here. In practice, company secretaries faced with a set of circumstances where it is not clear whether consideration is paid for a particular contract should either seek legal advice, include some consideration or ensure the document is executed as a deed.

Execution as a deed is often used in cases where it is not clear if there is consideration. For example, confidential information may be handed over to a third party as part of a technology transfer arrangement. Whilst the third party company will benefit from the arrangement and is probably paying licence fees which are clear consideration, employees of the company are not. Many licensees of such information or knowhow require not only that the company sign a contract, but also that the individual employees who will have access to the information should enter into a separate contract with the licensor or owner of the information, so that there is a direct contract which can be enforced against that individual in the future. However, the employee is gaining no consideration for entering into the contract. He or she is not paid by the licensor. He or she merely performs his or her normal duties under his contract of employment with his or her employer. For this reason such documents are often entered into *as a deed*. This no longer has to be *under seal* with red sealing wax or red stickers. The document simply has to be expressed to be a deed. Where executed by a company it must be signed by two directors or one director and the secretary. The other advantage of a deed is that the limitation period during which actions may be brought under the agreement is extended from the usual six year period to twelve years.

Other circumstances where a lack of consideration may become an issue include where there are three parties to an agreement: they may not all be benefiting from its terms; or a number of different legal entities within the same group of companies is involved; or one party agrees to extend the term of a contract or vary the terms perhaps because a product or service has not been to the satisfaction of one party. Ensure that in all such cases there is consideration for the variation and if there is none, execute the change as a deed – hence, the common legal document *deed of variation*.

Intention to create legal relations

'If you complete the marathon I'll eat my hat' – legally binding? No. There was no intention to create legal relations. Similarly if X agrees to buy Y a pint if he can help him fix a washer on a dripping tap, it is highly unlikely the courts would hold that there was an intention to create legal relations even if there was offer, acceptance and consideration. In practice, in cases of doubt there should be a written contract or letter setting out that the arrangement is to be legally binding; and for most proper contracts with which the company secretary will deal it is quite clear that the parties do intend formal legal relations to be established between them.

One area to watch is so-called *letters of intent* or *heads of agreement*. Most letters of intent are not expected to be legally binding. In practice, to ensure they are not they should be marked 'Subject to contract' quite clearly on the first page. Usually they are a statement of the intentions of the parties, perhaps setting out what has been informally agreed in meetings, but which is intended to be followed up by a written detailed contract. If the parties cannot reach agreement on the detail, they would not expect to be bound by the letter of intent. Indeed it would be dangerous for them to be so bound as the letter will usually address only certain details of the arrangement without much of the legal protection given in general clauses in a contract.

Similarly, heads of agreement usually set out bullet points of agreement reached between the parties which will be formalised in a detailed contract later. Again it is usually preferable that they are expressed to be subject to contract so that the parties can retract their positions later and not be bound if a formal contract cannot be agreed. However, if either of these or any other document does not state that it is subject to contract or that it is not intended to be legally binding then the parties may well be bound by the terms, unless there is no consideration or the terms are so vague as to have no legal meaning. This is why the issue of whether a particular document is to be regarded as legally binding or not should be clearly stated.

Statements made rashly or without thought can sometimes lead to contractual relations being established. In *Weeks v. Tybald (1605) Noy 11* the defendant 'affirmed that he would give £100 to him that should marry his daughter with his consent'. There was held not to be an intention to create legal relations. Whilst this is unlikely to be a typical circumstance for the average company secretary this area of law can be relevant where extravagant claims are made in relation to a company's products by staff or in its advertising. The courts have long held that a mere *puff*, such as a statement that 'ours is the best washing powder in the world', is not binding. Representations and warranties are considered later in this book, but it should be noted here that staff and advertising agencies should be instructed not to make extravagant claims or promises as it can be difficult to establish that the company did not really 'mean it' or that there was no intention to create legal relations.

The question of authority for individual employees of a company arises in this area too. Those dealing with a company are entitled to assume that someone cloaked in *apparent authority* (that is, who looks as though she has authority) can enter into contracts on behalf of the company. It is down to the company to ensure that staff know what their powers are in relation to contracts. Contracts over a certain value may need to be signed by a board director or other senior contracts officer or company secretary to ensure that proper control is exercised over those entering into contracts to which the company will be bound.

Written and oral contracts

Most contracts with which the company secretary will be called to deal will be in writing. However, in practice many companies, often those not well organised, rely on a considerable number of unwritten arrangements. For example, a commercial sales agent may operate without any written contract; or distribution arrangements may arise over time without any formal terms being agreed in writing. Finally, if a company is in the retail trade with high street stores then customers will simply attend at the shop and buy goods without written contracts.

In practice, companies secretaries should always seek to ensure that some written terms are in evidence. For example, if customers use a car park, warning notices disclaiming liability for damage to vehicles should be clearly visible before the customer pays for the use of the car park; otherwise that term will not be part of the contract between the parties.

Every company which supplies goods or services should have conditions of sale which are sent to all new customers before the contract is made. Orders should be accepted in writing or by e-mail and a record kept in case of disputes later.

The law will enforce oral contracts, except in certain special cases where contracts are required to be in writing, such as for the sale of land. However, proving the contract is much harder where there is no written evidence of its terms or even of its existence. So-called gentlemen's agreements are usually not legally binding, though if unlawful they can cause legal problems for the parties – for example, where they comprise an anti-competitive arrangement. In that context, even though the arrangement is not legally binding, there will be a breach of UK and EU competition law which applies to concerted practices and non-binding agreements.

Many contracts are made by telephone. It is wise to ensure that a written confirmation follows.

Electronic offers and acceptances

What are the consequences of new methods of organising company ordering, such as fax and e-mail? The law applies easily to such electronic forms. In proving a contract there is a requirement for some type of contract evidence or trail which can be audited or proved later as showing whether or not a contract was in place. However, this can as easily be by copies of faxes or e-mail messages as by letter. A fax may be wrongly addressed by keying in the wrong fax number, and sometimes a print-out suggesting that the fax has been sent successfully is incorrect because the other party had no paper in the machine or for whatever reason it did not get through. However, the post can be equally unreliable. With e-mail there is a need to ensure that e-mail records of agreements reached by that method are kept for as long as paper records. It may be harder to prove that no-one has subsequently altered an e-mail message or other document stored on computer than it is with a written document, though this is simply a matter of evidence.

Many companies are saving large sums of money by altering their purchasing or supply arrangements so that transactions are undertaken electronically. There is nothing to fear legally from such steps provided thought is given in advance to the legal issues and to ensuring that a record is kept in some form of invitations to treat, offers and acceptances.

Whatever the form of documentation, the parties should ensure that all orders are acknowledged and either accepted or not as the case may be and that the other party is given the terms of business before the contract is made.

Incorporation of written terms into the contract

One of the hardest issues for those involved with contracts of sale is ensuring that their terms of sale or purchase are pre-eminent. With many companies having their own conditions of sale or purchase, there is a real risk that whenever the company sends out its terms of sale to new customers the latter retaliate with their terms of purchase and insist they are used. This is known as the *battle of the forms*, and the legal principle is that the party which sends their terms last will prevail. So every time a customer returns their terms the seller must reject them and insist on its own terms of business. If the contract is important, it may be worth the parties' meeting to discuss what terms are acceptable. There may be much common ground between their respective terms in any event. Areas where there is likely to be significant divergence between conditions of sale and purchase include:

- Testing of products, and rights to reject them.
- When title passes to the goods – on payment or on delivery?
- Is interest chargeable on overdue debts?
- Are delivery dates binding?
- What is the limit, if any, on the liability of the seller?
- Are prior representations part of the contract?

Another difficulty in practice arises if the terms of business appear only on the back of invoices. This means that the purchaser will not see the terms until the goods have already been delivered and payment is to be made. In most cases the contract will already have been made and the terms will not be part of the contract. They are brought to the attention of the purchaser too late. For subsequent sales, where there is a course of dealing between the parties, the terms may be included, but not for the first sale. Company secretaries need to ensure that all acknowledge-ment/acceptance of order forms and order forms themselves, sales catalogues and the like include the terms and that they are brought to the attention of the buyer in time before the contract is made. This can be one problem arising when moving over to faxed orders and order forms. However, if the terms are on the back of the form, all the seller has to do to ensure the purchaser sees the terms is to remember to fax both sides of the paper.

In an ideal world all purchasers would sign the conditions of sale to acknowledge that they agreed to be bound by their provisions. If company secretaries are able to insist on this procedure so much the better. All new customers with whom there is to be a regular course of dealing can be required to return the terms duly signed in advance of a business relationship being established and perhaps in consideration of credit facilities being made available.

Variety of contracts of sale/supply

This book looks at buying and selling goods and services. There are many forms of contract which might be loosely categorised as buying and selling contracts. This book will mention briefly, where relevant, contracts for the *leasing* of goods. Many companies to aid cash flow and for tax and other reasons lease computers, cars and other large value capital equipment rather than buying outright. This book does not examine consumer credit law which will be very relevant to those company secretaries whose companies are involved in offering consumer credit to customers: the Office of Fair Trading offer a series of useful booklets in this area of the law. Nor does it examine in detail contracts for hire or hire purchase, though passing reference is made throughout to these areas.

Most readers will know the difference between a sale and hire contract. Hire purchase results in the customer owning the goods outright when the payments have been completed, usually over a period of years. Other forms of purchase such as contract purchase are usually some hybrid form of leasing and purchase. In practice, all company secretaries should be clear as to which contracts are those of sale and which of hire or leasing. There are different, though similar, terms implied by law into such contracts under the various statutes discussed in detail in this book.

2 The supply of goods and services

This chapter provides a summary of the main Acts of Parliament and other statutory measures which apply to the sale or purchase of goods and services. The statutes are summarised in the table below.

Table 2.1 Main UK statutes relevant to the supply of goods and services

Name of Statute	Summary
Sale of Goods Act 1979 as amended, including by the Sale and Supply of Goods Act 1994, and Sale of Goods (Amendment) Act 1994 and the Sale of Goods (Amendment) Act 1995	Addresses main legal issues of buying and selling law, such as contracts of sale, subject matter of the contract, the price, conditions and warranties, transfer of title, performing the contract, rights of unpaid sellers and actions for breach of contract. In particular it determines when goods will be 'accepted' and implies terms into contracts as to title (s12), compliance with description (s13) and satisfactory quality and fitness for purpose (s14, 14A).
Supply of Goods and Services Act 1982	Implies terms into contracts for the transfer of goods (except sale of goods contracts), such as hire agreements concerning title, compliance with description and satisfactory quality and fitness for purpose. Implies a term the services will be provided with skill and care (s13), time for performance (s14) and consideration (s15) in services contracts.

Table 2.1 (Continued)

Name of Statute	Summary
Unfair Contract Terms Act 1977 and Unfair Terms in Consumer Contracts Regulations 1994	Set out the law on exclusion and limitation of liability. The regulations apply only to consumer sales and implement the EU unfair terms directive, 93/13. They came into force on 1 July 1995. Chapter 5 covers this area in detail.
Consumer Protection Act 1987	Enforces strict liability (liability without fault) on supplier and manufacturers and brand owners who supply defective products which cause physical injury or damage to property. Implemented EU product liability directive, 85/374 in the UK. Imposes a general safety requirement on suppliers and prohibits misleading price indications. See Chapter 5.
General Product Safety Regulations 1994	Requires that all products put on the market are 'safe'. Implemented the EU general product safety directive, 92/59. See Chapter 5.
Misrepresentation Act 1967	Covers damages for misrepresentation even where the misrepresentation was innocent.
Consumer Credit Act 1974 and Consumer Protection (Cancellation of Contracts Concluded away from Business Premises) Regulations 1987	Provides for compulsory licensing for those who supply on credit and gives rights of cancellation during a cooling-off period. The 1987 regulations implement EU directive, 85/577, giving rights to cancel for non-credit purchasers.
Trade Descriptions Act 1968	Makes it a criminal offence to apply a false trade description to goods. Note also the Control of Misleading Advertising Regulations 1988 which implement the EU directive, 84/450 and prevent misleading advertisements.
Unsolicited Goods and Services Act 1971	After stated periods those sent unsolicited goods may keep them

Table 2.1 (Continued)

Name of Statute	Summary
Fair Trading Act 1973	Provides for investigation of conduct detrimental to consumers, investigation of monopolies and mergers, prohibition of pyramid selling and similar schemes.
Resale Prices Act 1976	Prohibits minimum resale price maintenance and refusals to supply goods because of resale prices (unless goods sold as a loss leader).
Restrictive Trade Practices Act 1976	Principal UK competition law applying to agreements. Agreements containing restrictions on two parties must be registered in advance with the Office of Fair Trading and may be referred to the Restrictive Practices Court.
Competition Act 1980	Provides for investigation of anti-competitive practices by the Office of Fair Trading and the Monopolies and Mergers Commission.
EU Public Procurement Directives and UK implementing legislation	Provide that certain large-value public works, supplies and services contracts and contracts with utilities must be advertised throughout the EU and fairly awarded.

Scotland

Many of the statutes covered in this book, including those relating to sale of goods, differ in connection with Scotland. The summary below addresses only the law in England, Wales and Northern Ireland. There are special provisions, for example, under the Sale of Goods Act 1979 in relation to Scotland.

Sale of Goods Act 1979

The Sale of Goods Act 1979 is the main UK statute on sale of goods law. It covers a wide range of legal issues arising from contracts of sale. It implies certain terms into contracts of sale and addresses issues such as when goods will be deemed accepted and when title or ownership to goods passes. The Act deals with many different issues and the short summary below sets out only the principal issues relevant to those who purchase goods for a business.

When the Act applies

The Act applies to all contracts for the sale of goods made on or after 1 January 1894. Goods are defined in s60 as including all personal chattels, but not money, and includes crops and things attached to or forming part of land which are agreed to be severed before sale or under the contract of sale. The Act may also apply to those taking a licence of computer software. In *St Albans v. ICL (1994)* the court suggested that computer software was 'goods' for these purposes. The Act applies to written and oral contracts (s4).

Payment

The Act provides that where a price is not agreed for goods then a reasonable price dependent on all the circumstances must be paid (s8). Few company secretaries would be involved in advising on contracts where no payment has been agreed.

Implied terms about title

In every contract of sale there is an implied term that the supplier has the right to sell the goods, unless it can be inferred that the seller intended only to transfer what title to the goods he had. If there is a breach of this condition, the purchaser has the right to repudiate the contract. The true owner may claim his property. S21 provides that a purchaser from someone who is not the true owner of goods acquires no title to them – let the buyer beware. There used to be an exception for goods bought at certain public markets known as the 'market overt' rule, but this provision of the 1979 Act was abolished by the Sale of Goods (Amendment) Act 1994, with effect from 3 January 1995.

Sales by description

Many contracts are now made and orders placed over the telephone as mentioned in Chapter 1. In these cases the purchaser will not have seen the goods. Most of these sales will be 'sales by description' under s13 of the 1979 Act. There is an implied condition that the goods will correspond with their description. In practice, it is better to include an express term to this effect and for more valuable products to include a requirement that the goods correspond with a full technical specification. This is very common with computer contracts and provides significantly improved protection over a simple agreement to sell named products. However, where the company secretary is advising the supplier then it is wise to exclude this implied term and include an express term properly and carefully describing the goods.

Implied terms of satisfactory quality and fitness for purpose

By s14 of the 1979 Act in every contract of sale there is implied a condition that the goods are of satisfactory quality and fit for their purpose. This applies both to business and consumer sales. In practice most contractual conditions exclude these rights. This is acceptable even for a purchaser, provided there is then some express protection for the purchaser that what has been supplied will meet required standards or descriptions of the products.

The Sale and Supply of Goods Act 1994 from 3 January 1995 brought in the term 'satisfactory quality' replacing the older term 'merchantable quality'. The term merchantable quality is, however, still part of US law; hence its appearance in many US contracts. New sections 2A and 2C are inserted in the 1979 Act.

Goods are of *satisfactory quality* where they meet the standard that a reasonable person would regard as satisfactory, taking account of any description of the goods, the price (if relevant) and all the other relevant circumstances.

If a defect is drawn to the attention of the buyer before the contract is made, if the buyer examines the goods in advance and an examination ought to reveal the defect, and if the sale is by sample and a reasonable examination of the sample ought to reveal the defect, then the implied term of satisfactory quality does not apply. The quality of goods is defined as including their state and condition, including the fitness for the purpose for which goods of that kind are commonly bought, their appearance and finish, freedom from minor defects, and safety and durability.

Acceptance and rejection of goods

The Sale of Goods Act 1979 s35 provides that goods are accepted where the buyer intimates that she has accepted them or when she does any act in relation to them which is inconsistent with ownership of the seller or if after a lapse of a reasonable period of time she retains the goods without intimating to the seller that she has rejected them.

If some of a batch of goods are rejected as defective, the rest may be accepted. The section also applies where the buyer has the right to reject an instalment of goods. Goods will be deemed to be in a breach of contract under these provisions if by reason of the breach they are not in conformity with the contract. If there is a contrary intention expressly or by implication in the contract, none of these provisions apply.

Remedies

S15A covers the situation where a buyer would have the right to reject goods because of a breach of the implied terms under ss13, 14 and 15 of the Act – that goods will correspond to their description where there is a sale by description; the implied term about satisfactory quality and fitness of the goods for their purpose; and for sales by sample that goods will correspond to their sample. Where those rights apply, if 'the breach is so slight that it would be unreasonable for [the buyer] to reject [the goods], then, if the buyer does not deal as consumer, the breach is not to be treated as a breach of condition but may be treated as a breach of warranty'.

This provision came into force on 3 January 1995 and was a substantial change in the law, in particular in relation to the right to reject goods. However, the section applies unless a contrary intention appears in, or is implied from, the contract.

Many commercial contracts contain express provisions concerning rights of termination and the consequences of termination. Typically the contract will give a right to terminate where there is a breach of contract or where the other party is in liquidation or by notice.

These provisions address rights to terminate a contract, not necessarily a right to reject goods. Most sale of goods contracts in relation to which the Sale of Goods Act provisions in this area apply are not long-term contracts where termination of the contract is an issue, but contracts where the concern is whether the goods have been accepted in the first place.

If the company concerned is a purchaser, it will wish to have the widest rights possible to reject goods, even where there is a minor non-conformity with the contract. Many contracts, particularly those for goods which are manufactured on a bespoke basis, will provide for acceptance test procedures, rather than relying on the law in this area as implied by statute. Ensuring that important provisions are conditions (which entitle the party complaining of the breach to terminate the contract) rather than warranties (which simply give a right to sue for damages) is crucial in drafting contracts in this field.

Much depends on the nature of the sale. If the company is simply selling a standard product then acceptance testing may not be appropriate. If the buyer is not a consumer then it is not entitled under the Act to treat any failure of the goods as a breach of condition, with a right to repudiate the contract, where the breach is 'so slight that it would be unreasonable for him to reject the goods'. If the goods are sold to a consumer then a slight breach of contract, such as scratch on the top of a new washing machine, does entitle the consumer to reject the goods. This change in the law and new distinction between consumer and non-consumer sales was introduced by the Sale and Supply of Goods Act 1994.

Under these rules, a company buying a new computer where the screen is slightly scratched would not be allowed to reject the computer entirely and demand its money back where payment has been made in advance *unless* the contract says otherwise. Company secretaries involved in the purchase of goods, therefore, can include a clause in conditions of purchase to ensure that there is a right to reject goods for slight breaches of contract. A clause along the following lines could be included in such cases:

> It is a condition of this Agreement that the goods purchased will comply in every way with the [specification/user requirements] of the purchaser. The purchaser reserves the right to reject the goods, without prejudice to its other rights and remedies, where they fail in any way to meet this condition and/or there is a breach by the supplier of the implied conditions in ss13, 14, and 15 of the Sale of Goods Act 1979 as amended, however slight the failure to meet these requirements and s15A(2) of the Sale of Goods Act 1979 shall apply.

Sales by sample

Where goods are purchased by sample then by s15 there is an implied condition that the bulk will correspond with the sample in quality.

Sales by bulk

Where goods are sold by bulk where the bulk falls below the agreed quantity of goods to be supplied, the goods are automatically the property of the buyer with effect from the 18 September 1995 for contracts made after 18 July 1995 under the Sale of Goods (Amendment) Act 1995. The goods are effectively divided between all purchasers in proportion to their percentage share.

Passing of title

There are detailed rules in the 1979 Act about when title or ownership of goods sold will pass. Where companies have written terms of business they will usually specify when title will pass. In many cases title does not pass until payment is made. Reservation of title clauses of this type are not always enforceable so legal advice should be sought. Another area to cover in contracts is at whose risk the goods are in transit. The international trading terms, *Incoterms 1990*, which are often expressly incorporated into contracts by reference, deal with risk for international supplies.

The Sale of Goods Act 1979 also covers sales by instalment, rights of the seller against the goods where payment is not made and actions for breach of contract. The summary above concentrates on those provisions of the Act which in practice for company secretaries are most important in the negotiation of contracts of sale. However, these statutory provisions are dealt with in more detail in later chapters where relevant.

Supply of Goods and Services Act 1982

The Supply of Goods and Services Act 1982 implies terms into contracts for the transfer of goods except for sales of goods contracts. Sale of goods contracts are covered by the 1979 Act discussed above. The Act implies into contracts for the transfer of goods that:

- The supplier has the right to enter into a hire agreement.
- The goods will comply with their description.
- The goods will be of satisfactory quality.
- The goods will be fit for their purpose.

Implied terms in services contracts

Company secretaries will handle goods and services contracts. The 1982 Act implies the following terms into such contracts that:

- The services will be provided with skill and care (s13).
- Where the time for the performance of the contract is not set out in the contract, the services will be performed within a reasonable time (s14).
- Where no price is fixed a reasonable price will be charged (s15).

What is reasonable is a question of fact and may not always be easy to prove. In practice, the company secretary should set out in writing in the contract when the services will be performed and at what price.

Where the contract is being drafted from the point of view of the service provider then it is important not to be too specific on timing so that any delay does not put the company in breach of contract.

Unfair Contract Terms Act 1977 and Unfair Terms in Consumer Contracts Regulations 1994

The Unfair Contract Terms Act 1977 (UCTA) provides that certain terms in contracts excluding or limiting liability, usually of the supplier, may be unenforceable, often if they are unreasonable. Many contracts contain exclusion and limitation of liability provisions, particularly to exclude liability of the supplier for consequential and indirect loss, loss of profit, revenue and goodwill. In practice, such exclusion of liability is not always enforceable.

S2(2) of UCTA permits an exclusion of liability for negligence which causes economic loss where it is reasonable in the circumstances. S3 provides that contract terms which limit or exclude liability for breach of contract or allow the supplier to perform the contract in a different way or not at all will be valid only where reasonable in all the circumstances.

S3 applies not only to people who deal as a consumer (that is, contract other than in the course of a business (s12)) but also where the contract is on another's standard written terms of business. Many business purchases are undertaken under standard terms of the supplier and thus these provisions are relevant. They are considered in detail in Chapter 5.

S4 provides that contract terms which require a consumer to indemnify another person against liability incurred by the other party for breach of contract or negligence are unenforceable unless reasonable in all the circumstances.

S7 states that liability in non-consumer contracts may be excluded, provided the clauses satisfies the reasonableness test.

S11 provides that in determining whether or not a term is reasonable the question is whether the term was a fair and reasonable one to be included, having regard to the circumstances which were, or should have been, known to the parties when the contract was made.

Schedule 2 of the Act gives some help in assessing whether or not a provision satisfies the reasonableness test, although in theory schedule 2 applies only to ss6 and 7, but the courts are highly likely to have regard to the guidelines in schedule 2 whenever provisions are required to be reasonable under the Act.

The EU directive on unfair terms in consumer contracts (directive 93/13, OJ 1993 L95/29) was brought into force in the UK by the Unfair Terms in Consumer Contracts Regulations 1994 and applies to contracts with consumers. As with UCTA it renders terms unfair, but applies more broadly than UCTA, though not to business-to-business contracts. More detail on these regulations is given in Chapter 5.

Consumer Protection Act 1987

The Consumer Protection Act 1987 implemented into English law the EU product liability directive 85/374, which harmonised consumer protection law throughout the EU. This Act will be of relevance only to those who suffer physical damage to persons or property and is covered in Chapter 5. For the Act to apply it is necessary to prove that there is a defect in goods which has caused the damage of which complaint is made.

Misleading price indications

The Act also makes it a criminal offence to put a misleading price indication on goods. Company secretaries at companies which supply goods into retail stores need to consider carefully the way prices are indicated under this and other legislation in this field.

General Product Safety Regulations 1994

The General Product Safety Regulations 1994 came into force on 3 October 1994 and are of relevance to all suppliers of products intended for consumers or likely to be used by consumers. The regulations implement the general product safety directive 92/59. Not all commercial companies with which company secretaries are involved are engaged in the supply of consumer goods. The regulations are covered in Chapter 5 and require that goods placed on the market be safe.

Misrepresentation Act 1967

An essential part of many supplies of goods or services is persuasion of the customer, whether through the statements of salesmen or through advertising. Representation will be made about whether a product can fulfil a particular function. Salesmen, many of whom depend on sales for their personal income, tend to speak over-enthusiastically about the goods or services they are selling. Misrepresentation law seeks to curb these excesses and ensures that damages can be claimed in appropriate cases.

Is the representation part of the contract?

Most standard terms and conditions of sale make it clear that no prior representations about the goods sold are part of the agreement. If there are no written terms then the general law, as described below, applies. This will also be the case where the purchaser does not see the terms of sale until after the contract is made, so that they do not form part of the agreement.

In addition, some express representations are so strongly made that they override any exclusion (see the *Purnell* case described below). In those circumstances it will be a question of fact as to whether or not the representation is part of the contract. In practice, company secretaries of purchasing companies should avoid all problems in this area by simply including an express term in all contracts setting out what features or performance is expected of the goods purchased.

The tort of misrepresentation

A misrepresentation is a statement of fact made by one party to another before the contract is entered into which is not a term of the contract and which induces the other party to enter into the agreement. In *Oscar Chess v. Williams*, [1957] 1 All ER 325, the purchaser was told that a car was a 1948 Morris. The court found that this was not a term of the contract. If a statement is a *term*, there is a right to reject the goods. However, as it was an untrue unequivocal statement it was a misrepresentation and there was a right to claim damages. Had the seller intimated that he simply *thought* that the car was a 1948 Morris, there would have been no misrepresentation at all. The statement would have been an accurate description of his state of mind, unless one could have expected the seller to have investigated the matter. This might arise where a seller of a new vehicle describes it to potential customers, who ought to be able to assume that the seller has some knowledge of the products on sale.

Reliance

Even if a misrepresentation is found to have been made, an action in tort can be brought only where the purchaser relied on the misrepresentation in deciding to purchase the goods; so, if the purchaser knew the statement was wrong but went ahead with the purchase anyway, no action would lie; nor would it where other factors, such as an independent report or the purchaser's own judgement were the reasons why he or she made the purchase. Where there are a number of reasons why the sale went ahead, an action for misrepresentation will still be available, provided one of the reasons was the representation by the other party.

Fraudulent and negligent misrepresentation

A misrepresentation can be made either fraudulently or negligently. In *Hedley Byrne v. Heller*, [1964] AC 465, the court accepted that a careless statement which caused loss, even simply financial loss, where a duty of care was owed to the person to whom the representation was made, could lead to an action in tort for misrepresentation.

The Misrepresentation Act 1967 in s2 provides that where a person has entered into a contract after a misrepresentation has been made to her by another party and, as a result, she has suffered loss, then, if the person making the misrepresentation would be liable to damages in respect of that loss had the misrepresentation been made fraudulently, that person shall be so liable, notwithstanding that the misrepresentation is not made fraudulently. This is the case unless he proves that he had reasonable grounds to believe, and did believe up to the time the contract was made, that the facts represented were true.

It is necessary in each case to assess whether or not the party making the representation was fraudulent and, if not, negligent in making the statement of which complaint is made.

Remedies

Remedies for the tort of misrepresentation include damages which will put the plaintiff in the same position as she was in before the contract was made. Actions for damages for breach of contract result in the plaintiff being put into the position she would have been in had the contract been properly performed, which is not the same.

Rescission

There is also a right to rescind a contract on the grounds of misrepresentation. S2(2) of the 1967 Act gives the courts the right to award damages instead of requiring that the contract be rescinded.

Case example

In *Lease Management Services Ltd v. Purnell Secretarial Services Ltd* [1994] Tr.L.R. 337 the Court of Appeal had to consider a misrepresentation as to the parties to a transaction in a case involving a replacement photocopier by the company which supplied the copier. However, the contract of sale was with a finance company. The decision also considered other relevant areas of consumer law such as unfair contract terms and exclusion clauses.

Purnell had bought photocopiers for years from a company in the Canon Group, Canon (South West) Ltd. It was made clear to the company's representative that any new model purchased must make paper plates. The representative had no understanding of this function and simply suggested that a demonstration model be tried to see if it complied with the requirement. The demonstration model did make the plates, but not all models in the series did and the model ultimately purchased did not. As soon as this was discovered, the plaintiff demanded the return of its old copier which had been traded in, and it made no payment of monthly hire for the new machine.

The position was complicated by the fact that although the contract appeared to be with Canon (South West) Ltd it was, in fact, with a wholly unrelated company trading as Canon (South West) Finance. The judge found it hardly surprising that the plaintiff thought she was hiring the machine from the first company. Only in small print on the documentation was there a reference to the real lessor. In the contract the finance company had excluded its liability widely.

The judge held that the plaintiff had been deliberately misled into thinking that she was contracting with Canon (South West) and that the finance company was *estopped* from denying (i) that it was a different body and (ii) that the representative who intimated that the machine fulfilled the function required had no authority.

The judge restated the doctrine of estoppel by representation. If A misleads B about an existing state of facts intending B to act accordingly and B does so in reliance on A's misrepresentation, A is estopped (prevented) from asserting the true facts.

The defendant argued that the finance company had not given any misrepresentation about the product. The court held that the finance company had fostered and encouraged the mistaken belief of the plaintiff that it was contracting with Canon (South West) Ltd, not the finance company. Due to the misrepresentation of contracting parties any representation by a representative of Canon could not be escaped by the finance company.

The finance company had a contract with Canon (South West) Ltd, which stated that Canon warranted that the equipment accorded with all the warranties given by Canon to the customer. The judge referred to the finance company possibly having recourse against Canon in this case. In practice, company secretaries should ensure that contracts between manufacturers or suppliers and finance companies contain such protection where they advise the finance company.

Company internal regulations should require that staff with authority to enter into contracts always ask with whom the contract is to be made and look at the conditions early in the negotiations. Include any important prior representations into the contract so that there is no doubt that they are express contractual conditions.

Consumer Credit Act 1974 and Consumer Protection (Cancellation of Contracts Concluded away from Business Premises) Regulations 1987

There is a considerable body of law relating to consumer credit which may apply to sales of goods handled by the company secretary. The consumer credit field is regulated by the Consumer Credit Act 1974 which provides for compulsory licensing for those who supply on credit. In August 1995 the Department of Trade and Industry (DTI) published a consultation document proposing change in this area. This proposed various deregulation measures, particularly in relation to unincorporated businesses, altering monetary limits; hence the latest position should always be checked.

Although as a general rule of law once a contract has been entered into the parties must stick to its terms, the Consumer Credit Act 1974 and the Consumer Protection (Cancellation of contracts concluded away from business premises) Regulations 1987 give purchasers a right to cancel agreements. Contracts of hire are also regulated in a similar way.

Regulated agreements

The Consumer Credit Act 1974 applies to 'regulated agreements'. A regulated agreement is any agreement under which credit, which does not exceed £15,000, is provided to an individual (which can also be a sole trader or partnership as well as an individual customer). Those buying business goods on credit are within the 1974 Act only if they are a sole trader or partnership. In addition, the agreement must not be 'exempt'.

There are a number of categories of exempt agreements: normal trade credit; low-cost credit; finance of foreign trade; land transactions repayable in four instalments or fewer; certain mortgage lending; and certain loans and insurance policies.

Cancellable agreements

Agreements which are regulated consumer credit agreements, as described above, will either be cancellable or non-cancellable. In both cases there must be a written agreement signed by both parties and there are requirements that certain headings appear, the name and postal address of the trader and customer should appear and certain financial particulars must be included.

For companies who are involved with regulated agreements, some of which are cancellable and some non-cancellable, it may be simpler to have one agreement applying to both categories. In those circumstances it is possible for a company to choose to give cancellation rights to customers where they would not otherwise be cancellable.

A cancellable agreement is one where, before the agreement is entered into, a trader (which can be a creditor, credit broker or supplier) in the presence of the customer discusses the prospective agreement or the credit transaction provided under it *and* the agreement is signed by the customer off the trader's premises.

Cooling-off periods

Cancellable agreements give the debtor a 'cooling-off' period where, after the agreement has been signed, he or she may change their mind and 'get out of' the contract. This period expires on the end of the day following the day on which the debtor receives a statutory copy of the agreement under s63(2) or a notice under s64(1) or (where regulations remove the need for a copy) fourteen days from the day on which the debtor signed the unexecuted agreement.

One copy of the agreement should be given or sent to the customer when the original agreement is given to her for signature. It is also necessary to give the customer a second copy in the post within seven days of making the agreement, unless the trader has already signed the agreement and the customer is therefore the final signatory whereupon the agreement becomes executed by both parties. The purpose of this legislation is to protect individuals who may have signed an agreement for credit on the spur of the moment without giving it proper thought.

Cancellation

Customers can cancel such agreements by sending a written notice to the trader at any time in the cooling-off period whereupon both parties should take steps to ensure that the position between them is as far as possible the same as if the agreement had never been made. The customer must return the goods, but has a right to keep them until the trader has repaid any money due. There is no obligation to return perishable goods or goods such as fuel and there is no obligation to pay for them either. Where goods such as fitted furniture have been installed by the customer, he does have to pay for those goods on cancellation, unless the trader installed them during the cooling-off period.

It is therefore essential that goods are not installed by the trader until after the cooling-off period has expired or else the trader must be prepared to suffer the consequences of cancellation.

Customers who have been given a loan as part of the arrangement do not have to pay any interest or any other charges whatsoever where they cancel before first repayment of the loan is due. On cancellation the trader must return any sums received, such as a deposit. The cancellation will also cancel 'linked' transactions or contracts (that is, other contracts entered into as part of the same transaction) but not insurance. Goods supplied in part exchange should be returned unless this is impracticable, in which case the trader should make payment for those goods. The Consumer Credit (Linked Transactions) (Exemption) Regulations 1983 (SI 1983/1560) exempt any contract of insurance which is a linked transaction in relation to a cancelled regulated agreement.

The EU directive on doorstep selling

The EU directive of 20 December 1985 to protect the consumer in respect of contracts negotiated away from business premises (85/577, OJ 1985 L 372/31) covers contracts concluded during an excursion organised by the trader away from his business premises or during a visit by a trader to the consumer's home or consumer's place of work where this is not at the express request of the consumer. Article 4 requires member states to bring in laws giving consumers a written notice of their cancellation rights by sending a notice within a period of not less than seven days from receipt by the consumer of a required notice stating particulars enabling the contract to be identified.

Member states had to implement the directive into their own national law by 23 December 1987. In the UK this was effected by the Consumer Protection (Cancellation of contracts concluded away from business premises) Regulations 1987 which came into force on 1 July 1988.

These regulations give protection to many *non-credit* customers who make contracts away from business premises in a similar fashion to those who are buying on credit. The regulations have brought within the scope of cancellation rights many more transactions than was previously the case. Food and drink supplied by regular roundsmen is excluded, as are contracts where payments do not exceed £35. There are also other exclusions.

There is a seven-day cancellation period (as required in the directive) and the contract is unenforceable if the consumer is not informed of her right to cancel. Other exclusions include contracts in connection with land or construction or extensions to buildings; certain contracts the terms of which are contained in the trader's catalogue; insurance contracts; and investment agreements.

Application of the 1974 Act and the 1987 Regulations

Where an agreement can be cancelled under the 1974 Act then it is not cancellable under the 1987 Regulations. Some suppliers of agreements will not fall within the 1974 Act, for example, because they are above the £15,000 limit for the application of the Act. In those cases the agreement may be cancellable if it falls within the 1987 Regulations.

The effect of cancellation under the 1987 Regulations is very similar to that under the 1974 Act. The contract is treated as if it had never been entered into by the customer and sums paid under the contract are repayable. Customers may retain goods until repayment of money is made to them and there are similar provisions as those under the 1974 Act in relation to the return of goods by the consumer after cancellation and the treatment of goods taken in part exchange.

There are similar rules in connection with agreements under which goods are hired or rented where the hire can last for more than three months and the consideration is no more than £15,000. Again, for there to be a right to cancel there must have been representations made in the presence of the hirer and the contract must be signed by the hirer off the premises.

Traders can apply to the Director General of Fair Trading for a determination exempting them from the requirement for a separate notice of cancellation rights to be sent to a customer within seven days of an agreement being made. This will be appropriate where the goods can be returned to the trader within fourteen days without liability; or there will be continued contact between the parties; or where catalogues and advertisements have been circulated beforehand containing prominent notices and information concerning credit and repayment terms; or where the credit is used to finance a supply of goods by the trader to the customer. Usually only catalogue mail order traders can successfully apply for such an exemption which costs £95.

Traders can apply individually for a direction exempting them from some of the requirements generally, but such exemptions are very limited. The applicant would have to show that it was impracticable to meet a requirement; and inconvenience to the trader will not be sufficient to result in the Director General exempting the trader from the requirements as to the form and contents of agreements. The European Commission has also proposed a distance selling directive which may have implications for purchasing managers. However, the text of this directive has not yet been agreed.

Further information

Further information concerning all these requirements is obtainable from the Office of Fair Trading, Field House (Room 306) 15-25 Bream's Buildings, London EC4A 1TR. The Office of Fair Trading (OFT) issues a number of helpful booklets in connection with legislation under the Consumer Credit Act which include appendices giving examples of notices of cancellation rights in various circumstances, forms of signature box, forms of statements of customers' protection and remedies and so on which are extremely useful to those who are involved in ensuring that their agreements comply with the requirements of the legislation. These booklets include *Cancellable Agreements* (5th edn, November 1990), *Non-cancellable Agreements* (5th edn, 1990), *Hire Agreements* (7th edn, December 1992) and *Regulated and Exempt Agreements.* These and other relevant booklets are available free from the OFT on tel. 0171 242 2858.

Trade Descriptions Act 1968

The Trade Descriptions Act 1968 provides in s1 that anyone who applies a false trade description to goods or supplies such goods is guilty of an offence. The Act is a criminal statute and should be used by those buying goods who wish to have traders prosecuted where a false trade description is applied to the goods purchased. Local trading standards officers enforce the provisions of the Act. A trade description by s2 is any indication by any means about matters such as the quantity of goods, their method of manufacture or production, fitness for purposes, approval by any person or conformity with any type approved by any person and the identity of the manufacturer of the goods.

A purchaser, for example, may find that genuine branded computer hardware is, in fact, reconditioned or has foreign parts inside or is a straight counterfeit or pirated product. Trading standards officers can be alerted, as well as consideration given, after taking legal advice, as to whether there has been a breach of any contract term. There may be a breach of intellectual property rights or the tort of passing off over which the genuine manufacturer may wish to litigate.

Unsolicited Goods and Services Act 1971

The Unsolicited Goods and Services Act 1971 applies where goods are sent which were not requested by the recipient or someone on his behalf and they were sent to him with a view to his acquiring them. Where the conditions of the Act are met the recipient may deal with the goods as if they were an unconditional gift if nothing happens for six months. If the recipient would like to have the goods sooner, then he or she may write to the sender, stating that the goods were unsolicited and giving an address where they can be collected within the next thirty days. If the seller does not claim them in that period, they can be treated as an unconditional gift.

Criminal offences can be committed where a seller demands payment for unsolicited goods. In practice, purchasing managers need to be careful to ascertain whether goods received apparently unsolicited fall within the 1971 Act before keeping them. This is one reason why it is crucial to keep proper records of what is ordered and what is received within an organisation.

Fair Trading Act 1973

The Fair Trading Act 1973 provides for investigation of conduct detrimental to consumers and prohibits pyramid selling. It also provides for investigation of mergers and monopolies by the Monopolies and Mergers Commission (MMC). Public mergers where a 25% market share is exceeded or the value of the assets acquired exceeds £70m can be referred to the MMC. Companies need not wait to be asked, but should write to the OFT if they have concerns about mergers or abuse of monopoly power. Similar complaints can be made to the European Commission. Large EU mergers with a 'Community dimension' must be notified in advance to the EU Mergers Secretariat.

Resale Prices Act 1976

The Resale Prices Act 1976 prohibits minimum resale price maintenance. Such activities may also be contrary to Article 85 of the Treaty of Rome where there is an effect on trade between EU member states. A purchaser may be buying goods for resale and the seller requires that the goods be resold at a stated price. Any condition in a contract with a supplier and a dealer which stipulates a minimum resale price for goods will be unenforceable. In addition, refusing to supply goods because of the resale price of the dealer is unlawful under the 1976 Act except where the goods are being sold as a loss leader.

Restrictive Trade Practices Act 1976

The Restrictive Trade Practices Act 1976 potentially applies to every commercial agreement or arrangement, whether written or oral and whether binding or not. It requires prior registration at the OFT of all agreements within its scope. Such agreements are scrutinised and may be put on a public register and referred to the Restrictive Practices Court. Breach of that court's orders is contempt of court and fines can be imposed and individuals jailed. In August 1995 eighteen ready-mixed concrete companies were fined a total of £8m under these provisions and several directors were personally ordered to pay fines of up to £20,000.

The Act is technical in scope and legal advice should be sought in cases of doubt. If company secretaries believe that suppliers operate a cartel or price fixing or market sharing agreement, they can sue for damages and/or report the matter to the OFT. The November 1994 *DGFT v. Pioneer* decision of the House of Lords, (1995) Tr.L.R. 355, held that companies will infringe the Act even where they have forbidden their employees from entering into arrangements of the type caught by the Act.

Group or joint purchasing arrangements and joint ventures, tripartite second sourcing deals, distribution agreements and blatant cartels, price exchange agreements and trade association recommendations may all infringe the 1976 Act. The Act will apply only where there are restrictions on two parties to the agreement of the sort set out in s6 (for goods restrictions) and s11 (for services restrictions).

For many technical infringements which are not restrictive the OFT puts the agreement on the register and no further action is taken under s21(2) of the Act. However, registration must take place before the restrictions take effect. The Deregulation and Contracting Out Act 1994 which came into force in part in November 1994 permits some secret particulars such as pricing to be kept off the public section of the register but a special application has to be made, otherwise all of the agreement notified will be open to public access. Certain non-notifiable agreements avoid the Act too by virtue of the 1994 Act, including where they are not significant (except for pricing agreements) and where they are exempt by an EU block or general competition law regulation.

The consequences of infringing the Act are that the restrictions are void, proceedings before the Restrictive Practices Court may be brought and third parties can bring actions for damages where they have suffered loss.

Such arrangements where they affect trade between EU member states may also infringe Article 85 of the Treaty of Rome. Fines of up to 10% of world-wide annual group turnover may be levied by the European

Commission under Regulation 17. The Commission has powers to carry out searches of premises, unannounced.

Competition Act 1980

The Competition Act 1980 gives powers to the OFT and MMC to investigate anti-competitive practices. Companies with a turnover of less than £10m *and* a market share of less than 25% cannot be investigated under the Act by virtue of the Anti-Competitive Practices (Exclusions) (Amendment) Order 1994 (SI 1994/1557), which came into effect on 14 August 1994.

Some practices by large suppliers may amount to anti-competitive practices; for example, requiring purchasers to buy other products they do not want (ties), either unrelated products or spare parts, consumables, or requiring purchasers to take maintenance from the supplier. Such tying provisions *may*, however, be justifiable. Some ties are void under s44 of the Patents Act 1977 where the products are patented. Except for s44 which renders such ties void, other ties may simply be grounds for the OFT to investigate, so there is no immediate remedy for the purchaser. However, the OFT actively investigates complaints and this can result in the tie being dropped.

Other such practices by dominant suppliers include refusals to supply, where the purchaser is setting up in competition; or offering worse terms to one purchaser for anti-competitive reasons; or predatory pricing below cost and excessive pricing. These types of activities when carried on by companies dominant in a substantial part of the EU market can also infringe Article 86 of the Treaty of Rome, so complaints to the European Commission are also possible for aggrieved purchasers. Under EU law fines of up to 10% of turnover can be imposed for breaches of Article 86. Large suppliers are often very concerned about being brought to the attention of the UK and EU competition authorities, so a complaint to the company concerned may be sufficient to result in the anti-competitive practice ceasing.

EU Public Procurement directives and UK implementing legislation

Those involved in the public sector and within utilities need to have great familiarity with the EU public procurement regime. HM Treasury issues various leaflets and booklets on the law in this field and there are substantial legal textbooks commercially available in this specialist area. This short section simply summarises in very brief outline the law in this area. There are various EU directives most of which have been brought into force in the UK which require that public works, services and supply contracts and contracts with utilities must be advertised in the EU official journal and be available for tender throughout the EU. Strict rules to ensure fairness are imposed and the rules apply only to contracts above certain stated thresholds; that is, to large value contracts. The table below summarises the legislation in this field.

Table 2.2 Public procurement: EU directives and UK implementing legislation

Name of measure	Directive No.	UK SI No.	Dates
Public works directive	93/37 of 14.6.93 (Consolidated earlier directive 71/305 amended by 89/440)	Public works Contracts Regs. 1991 SI 1991 No.2680 (will not be amended to reflect the consolidated 1993 directive)	SI in force in UK since 21.12.91
Public supplies directive	93/36 of 14.6.93 (Consolidated and amended earlier directive 77/62 amended by 80/767,88/295	The Public Supply Contracts Regulations 1995 (SI 1995/201) repealed (SI 1991 No.2679)	In force from 21.2.95
Utilities directive	93/38 (replaces directive 90/531 of 17.9.90 from 1.7.94)	SI being drafted to replace Public Procurement, Utilities, Supplies and Works Contracts Regulations 1992 (SI 1992 No.3279)	New SI due in 1996, old SI in force since 1.1.93. In November 1994 the Treasury circulated draft regulations for comment by 16 January amending the existing SI. The regulations will be known as the Utilities Contracts Regulations 1996
Remedies/ compliance directives	89/665 (remedies general) and 92/13 (utilities)	SI 1991 No.2679 and 2680 Part VII; SI 1993 No.3279, Part VII	General, in force since 21.12.91. for works, 1.1.93 for utilities, 1.7.93 for services
Public services directive	92/50 of 18.6.92	Public Services Contracts Regs 1993 (SI 1993 No.3228)	In force since 1.7.93

The threshold values for contracts are set out in Ecu and summarised on the table below (1.29 Ecu = £1).

Table 2.3 Threshold values for contracts in Ecu

	Works	Supplies	Services
Public sector	5m	200,000 (125,576 for GATT bodies, central Government, health authorities and certain other public bodies)	200,000
Utilities (not telecoms)	5m	400,000	400,000
Utilities (telecoms)	5m	600,000	600,000

The rules set out what type of tender procedure should be used in different areas: open, restricted or negotiated procedures are the three means of tendering. Those whose purchases fall within the rules need to ensure that they follow the requirements carefully. The remedies directives can result in contracts having to be re-advertised. Companies which do not think they have been treated in accordance with the rules can complain to the European Commission, which may investigate such complaints and require remedial action to be taken. These rules run alongside the EC competition laws (discussed above) which also apply to ensure fairness in the tendering process. The enlarged Government Procurement Agreement negotiated at the Uruguay Round of trade talks at the end of 1993 will result in further changes to the law in this field; so the latest position should always be checked. HM Treasury handles legislation in this field in the country (tel. 0171 270 1649).

Local Government Acts 1992 and 1988 and Local Government, Planning and Land Act 1980

The requirement for local authorities to subject their purchase of services to 'compulsory competitive tendering' (CCT) involves a complex series of legal rules, which cannot be summarised in any depth here. Those employed by local authorities charged with complying with the rules in this field need detailed knowledge of the legal requirements in this area, and various specialist legal textbooks are available. The principal statutes are the Local Government Acts 1992 and 1988 and the Local Government, Planning and Land Act 1988 (LGPLA 1988). The 1988 Act regulates matters such as the advertising process, invitations to tender and time limits. Special procedures must be followed and, when consideration is given to local authority services in-house being used, particular tendering processes must be followed.

These rules mainly affect local authorities, but also authorities in charge of urban development, new towns, police, fire services and metropolitan transport. The rules apply in England, Wales and Scotland and there have been proposals to extend CCT to Northern Ireland.

3 Payment, price and delivery of goods

Buying and selling law in relation to payment and price is straightforward. In general terms English law leaves the parties to a commercial contract free to set the price and method of payment that applies to a contract by agreement between themselves. This chapter looks at the implied provisions in contracts of sale dealing with price, payment and delivery. It also examines in some detail EC competition law as it affects pricing, particularly by dominant companies and the international trade terms, Incoterms, frequently used in international contracts for the sale or purchase of goods, but not always understood by those using such terms.

Sale of goods law

If the parties to a transaction do not agree a price then, under s8 of the Sale of Goods Act 1979, a 'reasonable price' may be charged. What is a reasonable price is a question of fact dependent on the circumstances of each particular case. Similarly if work is done and no price or contract agreed then the supplier is entitled to claim the value of the work done on what is called a *quantum meruit* claim. In practice, few sales of goods or supplies of services are agreed without the parties agreeing the price. Under the Supply of Goods and Services Act 1982 s15, where the contract for the supply of a service does not determine the consideration (or payment) for the service or contain some other method of working out the price, there is an implied term in the contract that the party contracting with the supplier will pay a reasonable charge. What a reasonable charge might be is a question of fact in each case.

In an international forum, the Vienna Convention on the international sale of goods also deals with this issue. Article 57(1)(a) provides that, where the parties to a contract have not agreed a price, the price is that which is generally charged at the time of conclusion of the contract for goods sold under comparable circumstances in that sector of trade. The Convention does not apply to sales to consumers.

In practice it is much better to deal with pricing issues in detail in all contracts for the sale or purchase of goods or services. The conditions of sale contained as an Appendix to this book include detailed provisions in this area.

Every company secretary should ensure that there is a clear company policy in the following areas. Whether a provision listed below is desirable depends on whether the company is buyer or seller.

- Decide whether interest is charged on overdue debts and at what rate. (There is no general right to charge interest unless legal proceedings are issued unless the contract says so.)
- Restrict customers from holding back money owed to offset it against other debts. Remove any right to what is called in legal terms 'set off' by an express clause in the contract.
- State how payment should be made: for many international sales payment is required by letter of credit. If this is the required method of payment, details about the form of the letter should be set out in the contractual documentation (for example, whether it should be an irrevocable letter of credit payable at sight and when payable; and a requirement that the purchaser pay any bank charges arising from a letter of credit being incorrect). In practice, banks often reject letters of credit because of mistakes made in relation to the documentation by the supplier.
- If any deposit is paid by the purchaser in advance, details concerning deposits should be included in the documentation. In a sale to a consumer, the unfair terms directive requires that, where the contract allows the supplier to forfeit the deposit if the customer cancels, the purchaser should have a similar right to a payment by the supplier where the supplier cancels, otherwise the clause may be void.
- State if interest is payable on the deposit and in what circumstances it is repayable and whether interest is paid in such circumstances. What is the position if the customer cancels because of late delivery of the supplier? Deal with all issues such as this in the documentation.
- For goods, particularly those of high value, where there is a long delivery lead time, the supplier may want to alter the price before delivery. An express right to do so is needed in the agreement. For sales to consumers, the EU unfair terms directive provides that the consumer must have a right to reject the goods in such circumstances.

Quality and price

Price is also very relevant to issues of quality. Under the 1979 Act, as amended by the Sale and Supply of Goods Act 1994, one of the factors in assessing whether goods are of satisfactory quality is their price. The quality of vintage champagne, for example, should be better than that of fizzy wine.

Misleading Prices

Those advertising their goods or services to consumers need to consider the Misleading Prices Act which proscribes the application of misleading prices to goods. Company secretaries of retailers need to be particularly careful to ensure that the company follows all legal requirements for their particular sector, such as ensuring that prices are visible and that they are selling the goods at the price marked on the product, even if it is marked in error.

Freedom to price

Suppliers of goods or services are largely free under English law to determine at what price they will sell their goods or supply services. However, there are exceptions. Companies in a dominant position on the EC market or a substantial part of it (which can comprise part of a member state, provided it is large enough) may abuse their dominant position by unfair, predatory or discriminatory pricing. One advantage of enjoying a dominant position is that companies are, to some extent, free from market constraints and are more easily able to raise prices without needing to be concerned about their competitors; hence, the need for competition law to step in to control pricing.

Excessive pricing

There have been few EC competition decisions concerning excessive pricing and none which held that this alone, without other abuses, comprised an abuse of a dominant position. It is difficult for the Commission to establish that prices are excessive, as the evidence which it would require is not readily available. Generally if consumers will pay a high price then companies are free to make supplies on that basis. Indeed, the EC unfair terms directive and UK implementing regulations provide that the price cannot be challenged in a consumer contract on the grounds that it is unfair. Consumers are left free to strike a bad bargain.

In *United Brands* [1978] ECR207, the court made it clear that charging prices which have no reasonable relation to the economic value of the product supplied would be an abuse, but overturned the Commission's finding of excessive pricing in its decision in this case. In assessing whether pricing is excessive the Commission will examine the relationship between the cost of the goods and their selling price. Difficulties arise where goods are sold at widely different prices in different EC member states. The market may be able to bear higher prices in some states. Is this difference in pricing an abuse? Where such a pricing policy results in geographical market partitioning then an abuse may be found; however, there have been few cases in the excessive pricing field, and the risk of infringement is perceived as being small.

Different prices in different EC member states

The issue of whether dominant companies operating within the EC can be obliged to charge the same price for their goods throughout the EC was addressed in the *Tetra Pak II* Commission decision upheld by the Court of First Instance on appeal at the end of 1994, where the Commission stated:

> Tetra Pak's charging of selling prices for its cartons varying considerably from one Member State to another, is discriminatory and constitutes an abuse within the meaning of Article 86 of the EEC Treaty.
>
> It has been demonstrated that the relevant geographic market in this case, bearing in mind that transport costs are negligible, is the Community as a whole. The price differences observed cannot be explained in economic terms.

This was particularly the case, in this decision, as the raw materials for the cartons made up 70% of the cost. The price differences were made possible by other measures of Tetra Pak's to compartmentalise markets.

It must be stressed that there is no general requirement to impose uniform prices throughout the EC. Many companies are moving towards such a single pricing policy in the single market for a number of reasons, not least to discourage the parallel importation of their products across EC boundaries. Such harmonised pricing does remove the risk of allegations that differing pricing policies infringe Article 86. However, different prices may be justifiable, even for dominant companies, where, for example, national regulations have a significant influence on prices. This is often the case for pharmaceuticals, the price of which is kept deliberately low for political reasons in a number of member states. Wine will always be cheaper in the village near the vineyard than in the upper reaches of northern Europe after allowance has been made for transport costs.

The relevant question in assessing whether pricing policy infringes Article 86 will be whether there are economically justifiable reasons why prices differ throughout the EC. Can a dominant company justify differing prices on the grounds that consumers in particular member states are simply prepared to pay more for goods for historical reasons or perhaps because wages are higher there? Provided a company does not seek geographically to partition the EC market and prevent the parallel importation of its goods in such circumstances, such differential pricing is unlikely to amount to an abuse of a dominant position. The safest position, therefore, is to achieve single European pricing.

Predatory pricing

Article 86 proscribes unfair pricing. Dominant companies selectively reducing prices to prevent competitors establishing or consolidating their position in the market may be acting abusively. This will be directly relevant to consumers only in that the price war may result in only one dominant supplier remaining, and thus in less consumer choice. There is no offence in pricing competitively and, in practice, it can be difficult to distinguish predatory pricing from a normal competitive response. *Discriminatory pricing* may also be an abuse of a dominant position, where for the purposes of restricting competition a dominant company offers better or worse prices to a third party than are offered in relation to comparable transactions. The *Akzo v. Commission* decision of the European Court of Justice of July 1991 (Case C-62/86, [1991] I ECR 3359) assists in making the distinction between predatory and acceptable pricing.

Akzo Chemie was held to have attempted to drive its small competitor, ECS, out of the market when ECS proposed to use its profits from its UK flour additives operation to expand into the organic peroxides market in the EC. Akzo was alleged to have threatened to reduce its prices in the UK flour additives market unless ECS agreed not to enter the organic peroxides market. When ECS did not capitulate, Akzo was accused of adopting uneconomic prices.

Akzo alleged that, as it made a profit on all sales, it could not be accused of predatory pricing. Its prices were above average variable cost. The price, however, covered the costs of the item sold but made no contribution to other necessary overheads of the company, such as running a factory. It could not, therefore, maintain prices at that low level over the full range of its products.

This was the first decision of the European Court of Justice (ECJ) on predatory pricing. The ECJ upheld the Commission's decision almost entirely, though it reduced Akzo's fine to Ecu7.5m.

In determining whether a company has been guilty of predatory pricing the *Akzo v. Commission* decision has the effect that there will be an abuse where:

- A company charges prices below its average variable costs (average variable costs are direct costs and vary with the level of output; in transport the cost of fuel would be a variable cost, whereas labour would be a fixed cost); or
- A company charges prices above average variable cost, but below average total costs where there is a plan to eliminate a competitor (an exclusionary intention).

A company can ascertain how much it costs to produce a product A. There will be the cost of materials (a direct cost), for example. This may give a figure of £20 per unit as an average variable cost. If it resells the unit at £15 to drive a competitor out of the market, this may be an abuse of its dominant position. The price is below average variable cost. If it feeds into its calculations the overhead cost too, such as the costs of labour in producing product A, then the costs are higher. This may give a figure for average total costs of £22. If it resells the product at £21, this may also be an abuse. It has covered its fixed costs, but not the total costs.

In practice, it is not at all easy to ascertain these figures in undertaking cost/price analysis. For many companies, parts of a business are more profitable than others and subsidisation of a more profitable line for a less popular product is common.

Pricing may be unfair where a purchaser is not allowed a sufficient price margin to allow it to compete in a downstream market against the supplier, as in the *National Carbonising Company v. Commission* ([1975] ECR 1193, [1975] 2 CMLR 457) case.

Discounts and rebates

Companies in a dominant position need to ensure that they do not abuse their strong market position in the way that discounts and rebates are given and to which companies they are available. It should be clear that the discount or rebate is not discriminatory, clear and transparent and related to cost.

Dominant companies offering rebates to customers who take all of their requirements for a particular product from the dominant company will abuse their dominant position. These are known as fidelity or loyalty rebates.

In the *Hoffman-La Roche* [1979] ECR 461 decision the court held that:

> An undertaking which is in a dominant position on a market and ties purchasers – even if it does so at their request – by an obligation or promise on their part to obtain all or most of their requirements exclusively from the said undertaking abuses its dominant position within the meaning of Article 86 of the Treaty whether the obligation in question is stipulated for without further qualification or whether it is undertaken in consideration of the grant of a rebate.

The court also held that an informal system of fidelity rebates would infringe Article 86, such rebates occurring where discounts are offered which are conditional on the customer obtaining all or most of its requirements from the dominant company (ties).

The Commission has also held that target rebates – where the purchaser obtains a rebate based on his purchasing particular quantities over a long reference period, perhaps of the order of twelve months – can amount to an abuse of a dominant position. The purchaser is put under considerable pressure to continue to purchase from the supplier towards the end of the reference period.

Companies which do not enjoy a dominant position will be entirely free to set what prices they choose, provided that they do not enter into collusive arrangements with competitors, suppliers or purchasers concerning prices.

Other competition law

In the UK, unfair pricing of this type may be an anti-competitive practice under the Competition Act 1980 and subject to investigation under that Act by the OFT and then the MMC. Price cartels, of course, will always infringe UK and EC competition and resale price maintenance is prohibited under the Resale Prices Act 1976.

Price is the main means of free and fair competition. It is not surprising that the law steps in to ensure that fairness is achieved.

Incoterms

Most companies involved in the export or import of goods use the international trade terms, Incoterms. There is no legal requirement to do so and, given the misunderstanding of these terms, their use is sometimes unfortunate and can be misleading; for example FOB Leeds

(FOB = Free on board) is nonsensical as Leeds is not a sea port. However, the value of Incoterms when properly used is that they are a form of legal shorthand. The use of three letters such as CIF (CIF = Cost, insurance, freight) can save a page of clauses in a contract dealing with issues covered by Incoterms such as where delivery is made, who insures and who bears the risk of loss in transit.

Terms of trade or other contracts which refer to Incoterms should refer to Incoterms 1990, the latest version. References to older versions are still legally valid, but confusing. It is sensible to retain older Incoterms in case they are still in use by some companies. It is wise to buy a copy of Incoterms, which can be purchased for £20 in the UK from the International Chamber of Commerce, (tel. 0171 823 2811) so that the precise meaning of trade terms used can be ascertained.

Incoterms do not replace entirely the need for conditions of supply and in many cases the parties may not want to use an Incoterm. It may not be in their commercial interests to do so. However, many standard conditions of sale incorporate terms such as ex works or CIF without problem.

The sections that follow look at the Departure (Group E), EXW (ex works) and Main carriage unpaid (Group F) terms; FCA, FAS and FOB. Then other Groups are considered: Main carriage paid (Group C): CFR, CIF, CPT and CIP; and Arrival (Group D): DAF, DES, DEQ, DDU and DDP.

Departure

Ex works

Ex works is one of the most commonly used Incoterms. Most people in business know that this means that the supplier simply makes his goods available at his premises. It is the responsibility of the purchaser to arrange to collect the goods. Under ex works the seller does not have to load the goods on to the buyer's vehicle or clear the goods for export. If the parties want to provide otherwise, their contract must say so. This term requires the least effort by the seller, but should not be used where the buyer cannot carry out export formalities (when FCA should be used: see below).

The Incoterm ex works implies many other obligations too. For example, the seller must provide goods in conformity with the contract and render assistance to the buyer in obtaining export licences. The goods should be made available for delivery at the place and time agreed, giving the buyer sufficient notice of when this will occur. The seller must also arrange packing of the goods at its own expense for their transportation, and packaging should be marked appropriately. The buyer must pay the price, obtain any export and/or import licences required for the goods and bear the risk of damage to the goods once they are placed at his or her disposal.

These are much fuller obligations than many people understand in using the term ex works, which is why a copy of Incoterms should be acquired. These terms go into more detail than many conditions of sale and cover areas many companies might forget. For this reason alone the incorporation of Incoterms into conditions of sale is sensible.

Main carriage unpaid

The terms FCA, FAS and FOB cover twenty pages of Incoterms which cannot be summarised in detail here. FCA (Free carrier – named place) means that the supplier hands the goods to a carrier arranged by the buyer after they have been cleared for export. This is the usual term for ship transport where the goods are not loaded over the ship's rail in the traditional manner.

FAS (Free alongside ship – named port of shipment) means the supplier delivers the goods alongside the ship. The *buyer* clears the goods for export. It can be used only for sea or inland waterway transport methods. It cannot be used where the buyer cannot carry out export formalities.

FOB (Free on board – named port of shipment) means that the seller completes his or her obligations where the goods pass over the rail of the ship at the named port of shipment. The seller clears the goods for export and pays the cost of export formalities. The term can be used only for sea or inland waterway transport. The buyer is responsible for import formalities. If there is no such thing as a ship's rail (such as in roll-on/roll-off vessels or container traffic) then FCA is the term to use (see above).

In all these terms the buyer makes the contract with the carrier and the seller hands the goods over to the carrier by some means. The *buyer* chooses the carrier.

Main carriage paid

The next set of terms are the main carriage paid terms (Group C in the Incoterms) which are CFR, CIF, CPT and CIP. This group provide for the *seller* contracting for carriage on usual terms at his own expense, whereas the departure terms considered above, including the well known ex works term, should be used where the *buyer* arranges transport of the goods. There are similarities between those two sets of terms, however, as in both the seller completes its performance of the contract in the country of sale.

Incoterms are not a substitute for contracts with carriers and there may be circumstances where buyer and seller prefer to draft their own terms or expand upon or modify Incoterms.

Cost and freight (CFR)

The first term in this category is CFR (cost and freight). This means that the seller pays the costs and freight charges needed to bring the goods to the port of destination. However, the risk of loss or damage to the goods and other costs relating to events after the goods are delivered on the vessel are transferred to the buyer when the goods pass over the ship's rail in the port of shipment.

Various obligations listed on the Incoterms are implied into CFR contracts. The seller is responsible for export licences and for ensuring that the goods conform with the contract requirements. There is no obligation on the seller to take out insurance and the seller enters into the contract of carriage at his or her own expense to transport the goods to the port. This term should not, therefore, be used where goods are being transported abroad by air, roll-on/roll-off container traffic and rail (such as through the Channel Tunnel).

The seller must give the buyer sufficient notice that the goods have been put on board the vessel so that the buyer has time to make his or her own arrangements to collect the goods. If the contract allows the buyer to specify when goods must be delivered then the buyer must tell the seller in sufficient time of the date and time required. The seller must supply transport documentation and provide packaging at his or her own expense, unless it is usual to ship the type of goods involved unpacked.

Cost, Insurance, Freight (CIF)

CIF is perhaps the best known term in this category, but is not always the best term to use. CFR (above) should be used if the seller does not wish to insure the goods and the goods are sent by sea and loaded over the ship's rail. This term means the same as CFR except for an additional requirement that the seller must take out marine insurance to protect the goods for the benefit of the buyer against loss or damage to the goods during carriage. It is the seller who enters into the contract of insurance, but the seller may choose minimum coverage.

The buyer may wish to have a higher level of cover and should obtain this. Under this term the seller must clear the goods for export. As with CFR, the term CIF can be used only for sea and inland waterway transport and not for rail or roll-on/roll-off or container transport. The key issue in determining whether these two terms may be used is whether the goods are loaded over the ship's rail in traditional fashion.

Carriage paid to (CPT)

Carriage paid to (CPT) provides that the seller pays the freight charge to the country of export. Once the goods are given to a carrier the risk of loss passes from seller to buyer. This term can be used for any method of transporting goods. The seller clears the goods for export and there is no obligation on the seller to take out insurance, though this would be prudent at least up to the point where the goods are handed over to the carrier when the seller's liability ceases in this respect.

Carriage and insurance paid to

Carriage and insurance paid to (CIP) is the same as CPT (above) except that the seller must take out cargo insurance against loss during carriage (similar to the insurance obligation under CIF contracts discussed above). This term, unlike CIF, may be used for any type of transport or where a mixture of different means of transport are used.

As with CIF, the level of insurance cover which the seller must take out is minimum coverage and the buyer may want to take out additional insurance or state in the contract that the seller must take out a fixed level of cover, notwithstanding the incorporation of the Incoterm into the contract.

In practice, there is much misuse of Incoterms. Using the term CIF for a contract where the goods are transported by a roll on/roll off ferry, for example, is wrong. CIP should be used instead. Ensuring that both parties understand the meaning of the Incoterms on which they have contracted ensures that these types of mistakes do not occur.

Arrival

The next set of terms are Group D, Arrival. They are: DAF, DES, DEQ, DDU and DDP. If the parties require that the *seller* be responsible for the arrival of the goods at their destination then the Group D terms should be used. The seller bears all costs and risks of transporting the goods. The Group C terms conversely are evidence of shipment contracts. The D terms split into two halves: DAF, DES and DDU where the seller is not required to deliver the goods cleared for import; and DEQ and DDP where the seller is responsible for this.

The DDU term was added for the first time in the latest (1990) version of Incoterms and is used where the seller delivers the goods in the country of destination without clearing them for import and paying the duty. This is particularly useful in the EU where clearance of goods for import is not normally problematic.

Which term to use, as has already been seen with the other Incoterms, is partly dependent on what type of transport is used for the goods and it is important that the correct Incoterm is used and that the parties know their precise meaning. It is preferable to have a reference copy of Incoterms, or to use terms fully described in the contract which cover the same areas as Incoterms. In the Group D category DAF, DDU and DDP may be used for any type of transport and DES and DEQ should be used only for sea and inland waterway transport.

Delivered at frontier (DAF)

This term means that the seller has performed his or her obligations to deliver the goods where they have been made available, cleared for export at the named port and place at the frontier, but before the customs border of the adjoining country. 'Frontier' may be used for any relevant frontier, including the frontier of the country of export, not just the frontier where the goods are destined. That is why it is vital in the documentation to define what is meant in each case by 'frontier' for the particular contract concerned. This term is mainly relevant where goods are sent by rail or road, but could be used for other means of transport.

Delivered ex ship (DES)

Under DES terms the seller must deliver the goods to the buyer on board the ship uncleared for import at the port of destination. The seller pays all the costs of taking the goods to the port of destination and is responsible for the goods until that time. This term should be used only where goods are transported by ship or inland waterway transport.

Delivered ex quay (duty paid) (DEQ)

Under this term the seller makes the goods available at the quay at the port of destination, cleared for importation. The seller pays all the costs of transport and taxes and delivery charges. DEQ should be used only where the seller is able to obtain directly or indirectly relevant import licences.

If, instead, the *buyer* is to clear the goods for import then the words 'duty unpaid' may be used instead. Some contracts will require that the seller will not pay all the costs of importation, such as value added tax; this can be made clear by using words such as 'delivered ex quay, VAT unpaid . . . [named port of destination]'. Again this term may be used only for contracts where the goods are sent by sea or by inland waterway transport.

Delivered duty unpaid (DDU)

Under this term (DDU) the seller fulfils his or her obligation to deliver when the goods have been made available at the named place in the country of importation. The seller pays all costs except duties, taxes and other official importation costs. The buyer carries out customs formalities under this term unless the parties' contract states otherwise. This term may be used for any type of transport.

Delivery duty paid (DDP)

The final term in the Arrival class is delivery duty paid (DDP). The seller must deliver the goods to a place in the country of destination, so if the purchaser wants no responsibility for delivery at all, DDP can be used to ensure that the goods are sent to his or her own premises. The seller bears all risks and costs of transport. This term is the opposite of ex works. DDP is the maximum obligation which can be imposed under the Incoterms on the seller.

If the seller cannot obtain an import licence this term should not be used: DDU would be better. Like DDU, DDP may be used for any form of transport.

Delivery in general

The Incoterms described above are frequently used in international commerce. However, in the UK most supplies are simply made on the basis of the parties' terms of business.

S27 of the Sale of Goods Act 1979 provides that it is the duty of the seller to deliver the goods and that payment of the price and delivery are concurrent obligations, unless there is agreement to the contrary. In practice, there is always some express term of a contract, written or oral, dealing with these issues. S29 sets out rules for delivery. It provides that who delivers depends in each case on the contract, express or implied, between the parties. If that contract has not addressed the issues, s29(2) provides that the place of delivery is the seller's place of business. If the contract says that the seller must deliver and no date is agreed, s29(3) provides that delivery should take place within a reasonable time. A delivery at an unreasonable hour can be treated as non-delivery.

In practice, these issues should be addressed specifically; so, for example, if the seller wants to deliver out of normal working hours then he or she should inform the purchaser and agree what is to occur.

If the contract does not say so, the costs of putting the goods into a deliverable state must be borne by the seller. Issues such as packaging, particularly for expensive items, need to be addressed. Which party pays for the packaging? Is the seller to apply any special marks or logos on the goods for the benefit of the purchaser? (See Chapter 8 on intellectual property rights for more detail on this.)

A purchaser cannot be forced to accept delivery by instalments under s31(1) unless there is agreement to the contrary. Delivery to a carrier by the seller in goods contracts under s32 is treated as prima facie delivery to the buyer, though the seller is obliged to make a 'reasonable' contract with the carrier, having regard to all the circumstances.

This chapter has considered issues of pricing, the Sale of Goods Act provisions in that area in particular, and the impact of EC competition law for dominant companies in their pricing policies. It has also considered issues of delivery of goods, in particular examining the commonly used Incoterms for international transactions. The most crucial point however is that reliance on the statutory provisions is not sensible. In most cases much greater detail on the responsibilities of the parties should be given. For example, the law may imply that in the absence of an agreed delivery date goods must be delivered in a reasonable time. Purchasers need to ensure delivery dates are binding and that 'time is of the essence' in connection with such clauses. Conversely suppliers, particularly of custom-made or bespoke products or who are themselves at the mercy of suppliers or sub-contractors may want it made clear in the contract that any delivery dates are *not* binding. Estimated times for delivery, which the supplier undertakes to use its reasonable endeavours to meet, can be given, with the back up of a tight *force majeure* clause excusing any failure to perform on the part of the supplier through the fault of others.

4 Title

This chapter considers the all-important topic of transfer of title. A sale contract is of no use if the purchaser does not acquire good right and title to the goods sold. Most company secretaries will know the legal slogan, let the buyer beware or caveat emptor, but what is the strict legal position in relation to those who buy and those who sell goods which are not theirs?

The Sale of Goods Act 1979 is the starting point. S12 provides that in a contract of sale there is an *implied condition* on the part of the seller that in the case of sale she has a right to sell the goods and in the case of an agreement to sell, she will have a right to sell the goods at the time when the property is to pass. This is not the same as a condition that the seller owns the goods. The seller may have bought the goods under terms which contain a retention of title clause which permits a resale by the seller before payment and before title is transferred. In those circumstances compliance with s12(1)'s condition is still achieved because the seller has a right to sell even though she does not own the goods.

There is also an *implied warranty* that the goods are free from any charge or encumbrance not disclosed to the buyer or known to him before the contract is made and that the buyer will enjoy quiet possession of the goods except so far as may be disturbed by the owner or someone else who benefits from the charge disclosed to or known by the buyer.

The most obvious example of a breach of s12 is if the seller does not own the goods which she is selling; in other words, a straightforward sale without title. Many sales are effected without any written terms and this term is implied into all contracts. Notice also that the first provision concerning title is a 'condition'. A breach of a condition entitles the other party to reject the goods and claim back any money paid or, at the other party's option, keep the goods and claim damages. The provisions concerning the goods being free from charges etc. are warranties, so breach of such provisions entitles the purchaser simply to sue for damages and not to repudiate the contract.

The Niblett case

In *Niblett v. Confectioners' Materials Co Ltd* [1921] 3 KB 387 the court held that the seller had no right to sell the goods because they were labelled with a trade mark of a third party without its consent. As the third party could have obtained a court injunction restraining sale then the seller had no right to sell. If a vendor can be stopped by a process of law from selling he or she has no right to sell.

Exceptions

There are exceptions to these rules in s12(3) – (5) which address sales with limited title. In a contract where the contract or circumstances suggest that the seller intends to transfer only that title which he has, there is an *implied warranty* that all charges known to the seller and not known to the buyer have been disclosed to the buyer before the contract is made. There is also an implied warranty that the buyer's quiet possession of the goods will not be disturbed by the seller, by a third party to whom the parties agree the goods should be sold and by anyone else claiming through the seller, except for anyone whose charge was disclosed in advance.

Excluding terms as to title

S12 of the Unfair Contract Terms Act 1977 provides that liability under s12 cannot be excluded or restricted by reference to any contract term (s6(1)). This term may not be excluded in any contract. Some commercial companies' exclusion of liability provisions do not take account of this provision with potentially difficult consequences. Many such clauses are very broad excluding virtually all liability of the supplier to the buyer. They should always make it clear that no exclusion is intended of the implied provisions as to title in s12.

Practice Point

Check the company's terms of sale to ensure that the exclusion of liability clause does not expressly or by implication exclude liability where the seller is in breach of the implied condition that it has title to the goods. If the terms make no reference to this provision, but exclude all terms implied by law then amend the term as soon as possible.

This provision may not be avoided by a choice of law provision by virtue of s27(2). The limits on contracting out do not apply to international supply contracts (s26). If the parties make it clear that the seller is only transferring such title as he has, then s12(1) can be excluded because of the specific wording in subsections (3) – (5) which deal with those circumstances. It may still be possible to limit the liability of the seller for breach of that warranty, say to the contract price or the level of its insurance or some other figure.

Summary

To summarise the points above:

- All sales, consumer or otherwise, contain an implied condition that the seller has the right to sell the goods.
- Any exclusion of such condition will be void.
- Exclusion of liability clauses in contracts should not therefore exclude such liability in a contract of sale.
- Liability could, however, be limited to a fixed sum.
- Breach of the condition entitles the purchaser to repudiate the contract and claim damages, usually with no reduction in damages to take account of use of the goods which the purchaser has enjoyed up until such repudiation or, at the buyer's option, a right to claim damages instead and continue with the contract.
- Practical issues should also be considered, such as the bad publicity which can flow from making a sale without title. Efforts should always be made in contracts with suppliers to ensure that they give proper express warranties as to title.
- Goods to be bought should be examined for evidence that they might be stolen, and checks made in advance of any agreement to buy as to whether there is any evidence of the products being pirated or counterfeit. Check for holograms not appearing or packaging looking strange.

Buying from a thief

Most company secretaries will know that the rule known as *market overt* was abolished recently. Since the dark ages, probably originating in Medieval times, goods bought at certain markets were an exception to the usual contract rule, let the buyer beware. Good title to stolen goods could be obtained at such markets, including all shops in the City of London, Bermondsey market and the like, even if the goods were stolen. This was known as the rule in *market overt*.

The Sale of Goods (Amendment) Act 1994 came into force on 3 January 1995 and abolished the *market overt* rule. This means that thieves have fewer outlets for goods and those buying at markets will run the risk that the 'true' owner of the goods turns up later and claims title, even though the purchaser was entirely innocent. The Sale and Supply of Goods Act 1994 can be bought from HMSO, price 60p.

If a sale is made to a consumer by someone who is not the owner of goods or has no right to sell them, a right to repudiate the contract as described above, for breach of the condition in s12, is often of little use. If the seller was dishonest he probably already has his money and has disappeared. Cases arise regularly in this area. In October 1995 a horse breeder recognised one of 'her' ponies which had been sold by a thief to another family. DNA tests on the owner's animals proved the pony was from her stables and she was able to claim the pony back. The purchasers sought to argue that the *market overt* rule applied as they bought the pony at a market before the law changed, but they were not successful. In those circumstances the legal argument is often between two innocent parties – the buyer in possession of the goods and the original owner.

S21 of the 1979 Act provides that a buyer acquires no better title to the goods than the seller had, unless the owner of the goods is by his conduct precluded from denying the seller's authority to sell.

Remedies

In such circumstances the owner of goods has a right to possession of the goods and can retake them without action or bring an action for their delivery or claim damages. There are many exceptions to this rule including:

- Estoppel.
- Sales under the Factors Acts.
- Sales under certain special powers of sale.
- Sales under a voidable title.
- Sales where the seller who sold the goods has possession after the sale.
- Sales where the buyer has bought the goods and is in possession of them.
- Sales of a motor vehicle under the Hire Purchase Act 1964.

Seller in possession

The seller in possession exception is particularly important. S24 of the Act provides that where goods are sold and the seller or his agent still has the goods and then resells them to a third party who buys in good faith, the effect is the same as if the owner had authorised the sale. In other words, if A sells a car to B to be delivered next week and then agrees to sell it to C and supplies it to C, C will own the car not B unless C had been in cahoots with A or had other reasons to doubt B's ownership of the car. In practice therefore it is important to take possession of goods which are bought in this way straightaway so that the seller in possession provisions never apply, or not to part with any money until delivery. It does not matter in what capacity the goods remain at the premises of the seller: provided the goods are on the seller's premises these provisions will apply.

In *Pacific Motor Auctions Pty. Ltd v. Motor Credits (Hire Finance) Ltd* [1965] AC 867 a dealer remained in possession of cars sold to them by the plaintiffs and used them for display. They then sold the cars as agents of the plaintiffs. The agency authority was revoked and after that the dealer sold the cars to the defendant who bought as a bona fide purchaser. The defendant got good title under an identical section to this provision despite the fact that he was not holding the goods as owner. This case has been followed in others. The seller does not have to be in possession of the goods with the consent of the buyer. For example, a buyer may say delivery must take place that evening as soon as a cheque clears. If the seller does not comply with the contract and next day sells to an innocent purchaser then the second contract of sale will be valid and the first purchaser will lose out.

Buyer in Possession

The buyer in possession provisions of the Sale of Goods Act 1979 are another exception to the buyer beware rules in the area of transfer of title. S25 of the 1979 Act provides that where a person has bought or agreed to buy goods and has possession of the goods or documents of title to the goods, the delivery of the goods or documents to

> any person receiving the same in good faith and without notice of any lien or other right of the original seller in respect of the goods, has the same effect as if the person making the delivery or transfer were a mercantile agent in possession of the goods or documents with the consent of the owner.

The effect of this provision is that a seller who has agreed to sell goods to a buyer and retains title to goods until payment is made, and yet who lets the buyer take possession of the goods, may lose title if the buyer sells the goods to an innocent purchaser.

Applying this to a normal commercial sale, company X supplies tractors and agrees to sell one to an agricultural machinery dealer, company Y. Before Y makes payment but after Y obtains possession of the tractor, Y resells the goods to which it does not have title to an innocent purchaser, and then fails to pay. Company X cannot reclaim the goods from an innocent purchaser. X could, of course, sue Y for damages, but that remedy may be of no use if Y is insolvent.

Retention of title clauses

This exception to the buyer beware rule leads on to the area of express contractual provisions concerning title in contracts of sale. Most company secretaries will be familiar with the retention of title clause used by many companies in the UK, under which the seller continues to own the goods until the purchaser pays. It is a useful protective measure against the purchaser going into liquidation and many goods have been recovered under such provisions, the details of which are considered below.

The first issue for company secretaries in this area, however, is whether such a clause is needed at all. If payment is made in advance (rare, though not unknown, in some industries) then the clause is not needed. Some exporters, for example, require that payment be made by letter of credit, and some mail order companies require cheques with the order. Where this is the case, it may not be strictly necessary to have a retention of title clause. However, remember that sometimes exceptions are made for particular customers and it can do no harm to have such a clause even if it rarely applies. As with other promises, retention of title clauses need to be made part of the contract. If the purchaser is not sent the terms until he receives an invoice after delivery, the term is not a part of the contract. The purchaser may send its own conditions of purchase – the so-called battle of the forms – and they may supersede the conditions of sale containing the reservation of title clause.

Finally, such clauses do not always work: for example, those where the purchaser incorporates the products into other goods where they cannot easily be detached or where the purchaser will be reselling the goods before paying for them. Under English law sometimes a 'charge' is inadvertently created which must be registered under the Companies Act 1985 and, because it has not been, it is void. There are lots of English cases in this area (see below). This is not a reason to leave out a retention of title clause, but consideration should be given to the particular goods and contractual arrangements of the parties first, rather than adopting a clause without any thought to these issues. Careful drafting may ensure that an enforceable clause is prepared.

For exporters there are two other important preliminary issues. First, if the customer does not pay, what in practice can the UK supplier do to recover the goods? He may have a presence in the relevant country. Some agency agreements with local agents require the agent to assist in enforcing retention of title clauses. He may have some sort of branch office or a good relationship with a local lawyer or make regular visits to the country concerned. However, there may be cases where the sum at stake is just not worth a visit to a local lawyer or an aeroplane fare to the country in question.

The second issue for the foreign exporter is that of local law. Although the contract may state that it is subject to English law and under the Rome Convention on choice of law, signatory countries generally respect choice of law in contracts, it is not always easy to persuade some local courts to allow enforcement of such a clause. A review of the law of retention of title in many European states reveals a surprising conformity of laws, however. Many contain similar requirements for such clauses as under English law, such as clauses not working where the goods have lost their physical form or where they are mixed with other goods or cannot be identified as the property of the supplier.

For further information on foreign retention of title clauses in Europe see *Debt Recovery in Europe*, the title of two books covering this topic with contributions from the various EU/EFTA states, one by Bermans (published by Jordans, 1995) and the other by KPMG, edited by James Richardson (published by Blackstone, 1993).

Legal issues

In practice, it is not always easy to enforce clauses of this sort as mentioned above. Liquidators and their foreign equivalents have an obligation to maximise funds realised for creditors of the company and this applies as much abroad as in the UK. It is their duty to resist claims under such clauses unless they can be properly proven. There are three main legal difficulties with these clauses.

The clause is not part of the contract
Ensure that the terms of supply are brought to the attention of the purchaser before the contract is made. A written order confirmation which contains the terms is best and if this is faxed ensure the terms are on the back fax.

The goods cannot be identified
One of the hardest parts of enforcing retention of title clauses in practice

is in proving to the liquidator that the goods at the premises of the purchaser are:

- the supplier's goods; and
- those of the supplier's goods for which no payment has been made.

Retention of title clauses should require the purchaser to keep the goods separate and name them as the goods of the supplier. This may not be practical in all industries, but the supplier can add labels with its name and address to aid subsequent identification. In many cases companies will have been supplying goods on credit over a long period. The liquidator will not allow the goods to be reclaimed unless the supplier can prove that the goods at the premises of the supplier have not been paid for. This is not as simple as it sounds. There may be stocks of the supplier's products at the purchaser's premises some of which are paid for and some not. The liquidator will not helpfully split the goods.

The supplier should ensure that a batch or other identification number appears on invoices which also appears on the goods themselves or on a label, so that the liquidator can be shown the relevant unpaid invoice and taken to the goods identified as those for which no payment has been made.

The clause does not work

The most difficult area in relation to retention of title clauses arises from the legal enforceability of clauses. Although the English courts have upheld many simple clauses, many more complex clauses have been struck down. The courts have held that some clauses are a charge over the goods and as such clauses are virtually never registered under the Companies Act 1985 at Companies House, they are void for want of registration. For big deals there is nothing to stop a cautious supplier sending the charge to Companies House with the relevant registration form. Indeed, for no fee and only a slight administrative burden companies can significantly increase the chances of enforcing more complicated clauses. However, in practice, companies do not have time to register each sale of goods contract with Companies House.

A clause which retains title until payment will be unlikely to comprise a charge and will not require registration, unless the goods are mixed with others or cease to exist. It should be clear that the supplier continues to own the goods, despite possession by the purchaser. Any provision which suggests that the purchaser has taken title is likely to be construed by the courts as reflecting the fact that the supplier has transferred title and simply obtained a charge.

Proceeds of sale

The best clauses will restrict the purchaser from selling the goods until payment has been made. Such a restriction goes a long way to proving that the purchaser still owns the goods.

Case example

In *Compaq Computer Ltd v. Abercorn Group Ltd*, [1991] BCC 484, the seller claimed that it had a right to the proceeds of sales made by the purchaser of goods sold under a retention of title clause which permitted such resale before payment. The contract said that Compaq sold as Abercorn's *bailee and agent*. The court held that the provision was a charge. In reality Abercorn had only a limited interest in the proceeds of sale by way of a security.

What was fatal to the claim was the fact that the seller could resell the goods for its own profit and was entitled to retain some of the profit. If the purchaser must be allowed the right to resell the goods before payment to the seller, the clause should require that the seller resell the goods other than in its ordinary course of business. The original seller should be entitled to all the proceeds of sale and the original purchaser should be required to keep the proceeds of sale in a separate account. In those circumstances a proceeds of sale clause of this type may be upheld, but unless these cumbersome provisions are acceptable it is better to restrict sales altogether until payment is made.

Mixed goods

Finally, clauses should always be drafted bearing in mind the nature of the products concerned. It was established in the *Clough Mill* case, [1984] 3 All ER 982, that where the goods become inextricably mixed with other goods, either of the purchaser or of other suppliers, then a retention of title clause will not work. All the seller achieves is a charge over the finished or mixed product. Such charge must be registered. A restriction on the purchaser mixing the goods until payment is made, where practicable, should assist some suppliers. Where goods can be easily detached from others then a clause may be enforceable too.

Guidelines for clauses

- Incorporate retention of title clauses into contracts carefully.
- Require that goods be kept separate.
- Give the seller the right to enter premises to take the goods back on demand.
- Ensure that the clause does not comprise a registrable charge.

5   Faulty goods and excluding liability

This chapter looks at buying and selling law as it affects faulty goods. Chapter 1 set out the many statutes which apply in this area. The principal legislative provisions are the Sale of Goods Act 1979 which implies various terms concerning quality into sale of goods contracts; the Consumer Protection Act 1987 which renders manufacturers and suppliers strictly liable without proven fault for defective products which cause damage to persons or property; and the General Product Safety Regulations 1994 (SI 1994/2328) which require that goods placed on the market must be 'safe'.

The principal implied terms: quality and fitness for purpose

Chapter 1 sets out in detail the provisions of the Sale of Goods Act 1979 as amended, that goods will be of satisfactory quality and fit for their purpose. This chapter concentrates on what the contract says. In practice, there may be many implied terms in relation to a contract, but most agreements exclude or severely limit terms implied by law. The extent to which companies can lawfully exclude such liability, particularly in relation to a failure of the goods to correspond to the contract or their description is a subject which much exercises the company secretary.

Unfair Contract Terms Act 1977

S2(2) of the 1977 Act permits an exclusion of liability for negligence which causes economic loss where it is reasonable in the circumstances. S3 provides that contract terms which limit or exclude liability for breach of contract or allow the supplier to perform the contract in a different way or not at all will be valid only where reasonable in all the circumstances.

S3 applies not only to people who deal as a consumer (that is, contracts other than in the course of a business, s12) but also where the contract is on another's standard written terms of business. So, the section applies not only to consumer contracts, but to some business contracts too, where standard terms are involved and is thus of much wider impact in a business context for company secretaries than the new UK unfair terms law described below, and which are derived from the EU unfair terms directive, which applies only to consumer contracts.

S4 provides that contract terms which require a consumer to indemnify another person against liability incurred by the other party for breach of contract or negligence are unenforceable unless reasonable in all the circumstances.

Finally, s7 provides that in non-consumer contracts (those between businesses) terms as to description, sample, merchantability and fitness for purpose may be excluded, provided the clause satisfies the reasonableness test. (In consumer contracts such exclusions of those implied terms would be void.)

Practice Point

Ensure that all terms of business which may be used in contracts with consumers make it clear that no exclusion of the implied terms as to quality, conformance with description and fitness for purpose is implied. Words such as 'Save in so far as the buyer is dealing as a consumer . . . ' 'XY&Z is excluded' can be used.

These, then, are the principal provisions of the Act which import the so-called 'reasonableness' test. Those involved in drafting exclusion and limitation clauses in contracts need to ensure that such clauses are reasonable or else the clause will be unenforceable.

Although there may be some commercial merit in drawing up a draconian clause to frighten customers off when making claims, it is unlikely that the advantages of such strong-arm tactics outweigh the disadvantages of producing a clause which would not be enforceable in court.

'Reasonable'

S11 provides that, in determining whether or not a term is reasonable, the question is whether the term was a fair and reasonable one to be included having regard to the circumstances which were, or should have been, known to the parties when the contract was made.

Schedule 2 of the Act gives some help in assessing whether or not a provision satisfies the reasonableness test. Although in theory schedule 2 applies only to Ss6 and 7, the courts are highly likely to have regard to the guidelines in schedule 2 whenever provisions are required to be reasonable under the Act. The schedule offers 'guidelines' comprising a list of matters to which regard should be had:

- Strength of bargaining power between the parties, including whether the customer had any alternative source of supply.
- Whether inducements were offered or the customer could have entered into a similar contract with someone else without accepting the onerous provision.
- Whether the customer knew or should have known about the term (Here it can help if terms and conditions are legible and exclusion clauses appear in block letters. The latter must, of course, form part of the contract; that is, be provided in time).
- Where the term restricts liability if a condition is not complied with, it is relevant to assess whether it was reasonable to expect compliance with such a condition.
- Whether the goods were a special order from the customer.

The burden of proving that a clause is reasonable lies with the supplier who is relying on the clause.

Case law

In *George Mitchell (Chesterhall) v. Finney Lock Seeds* [1983] 2 All ER 737, the defendants, who were seed merchants, supplied the plaintiff farmers, with 30lbs of Dutch winter cabbage. With the delivery came an invoice which contained a term excluding all liability for consequential loss. The wrong seed was supplied which was wholly unsuitable, so that the plaintiff's entire crop failed. The House of Lords held that the defendant was liable for the value of the entire crop and reliance could not be placed on the exclusion clause.

Of particular importance to the judges in reaching their decision was practice in the seed trade. When similar problems occurred in the industry suppliers usually made a substantial payment to aggrieved purchasers in compensation. Also the supplier was held to be in a better position to take out insurance against these types of loss. 'Without hesitation' the court held that it would not be fair or reasonable to allow the defendants to rely on the clause.

A contrasting case, where the court upheld a clause was in *White Cross Equipment v. Farrell* [1983] TrL 21 . A waste compactor machine was sold to the defendant salvage company. A six-month guarantee was given with the machine, but all liability thereafter was excluded. After the guarantee period had expired the machine began to cause problems and the defendant, therefore, refused to make any further payments under the agreement for the purchase of the machine. He argued that the exclusion clause was invalid.

There were a number of reasons why the court upheld the clause:

- The parties were dealing at arm's length and the defendant could have negotiated away the term if he had wished.
- Six months would generally be long enough a period in which any defects in relation to the machine would emerge.
- These machines had very rough treatment, both from the people who operated them and the materials (waste) fed into them. It was quite fair to say that after six months no further claims could be made.

The court viewed the matter simply as a question of allocating risk between two commercial parties of equal bargaining power, taking all the circumstances into consideration.

The issue of which of the parties could best insure against the liability concerned can be an important factor in assessing whether a clause is reasonable. This was the case in the leading House of Lords' judgement in *Photo Production v. Securicor* [1980] AC 827 which did not relate to the Unfair Contract Terms Act, but was a case addressing the broader issue of reasonableness. For this reason many exclusion clauses contain a statement that the purchaser acknowledges that it is easier for him or her to effect insurance. How effective such acknowledgements are, where they do not honestly reflect commercial realities, remains to be seen.

The St Albans v. ICL case

In a Court of Appeal judgement on 26 July 1996 in *St Albans City and District Council v. International Computers Ltd* (not yet reported) the court confirmed an award to St Albans of over £1.3m damages arising from the supply of a computer system to handle the Community Charge. The court considered the extent to which software was 'goods'. The defendants argued that neither the Sale of Goods Act 1979 nor the Supply of Goods and Services Act 1982 applied to their contract with St Albans. The judge in the court below pointed out that software is a supply of goods for the purposes of value added tax and is treated as plant and machinery, like a book, for the purposes of capital allowances. In *Toby Construction Products Ltd v. Computa Bar (Sales) Pty Ltd* [1983] 2 NSW 48, an Australian case, the court came to the conclusion that the sale of a computer system, comprising hardware and software, was the sale of goods.

The court of appeal stated that if software is sold on disk the disk is goods under the Sale of Goods Act 1979 and the Supply of Goods and Services Act 1982. If a disk is sold or hired and the program is defective such that it will not perform its purpose this is a defect on the disk. In this case though the software was not sold or hired on a disk. An ICL employee had installed the software. In that case the implied terms did not apply. Common law was used. The court held that common law terms of fitness for purpose and that the program would fulfil its purpose were implied. In this case it does not appear to have been argued that the writing of bespoke software was the supply of a service. The first instance decision has been reported at [1005] FSR 686.

The judge at first instance found that an error of the defendants resulted in the plaintiffs incorrectly estimating the number of people who would be liable for Community Charge. St Albans therefore fixed the level of its charge too low and lost a total of £1,314,946. The software supplied, a COMCIS package, operating the plaintiffs' system produced the relevant statistical error.

The facts of how the contract terms were agreed in this case were revealing. As often happens, detailed discussion of the terms and conditions relevant to the contract appear to have been left too late for proper consideration. The judge refers to a draft agreement based on one the chief of St Albans had used when he was at London Transport. The judge said that this individual had no legal qualification and 'in my judgement was out of his depth'. Those terms were not incorporated into the contract.

The advice of the in-house solicitor was not sought on this draft contract either before or after it was agreed. In practice, it is often a complaint of in-house lawyers that commercial staff and IT managers do not seek their advice when they should. The judge said that the defendants fully exploited the concerns of the plaintiffs in agreeing the contract quickly, effectively forcing them to accept ICL's terms – its standard terms.

The terms were examined on a clause-by-clause basis in meetings at the time and an indication was made by the plaintiffs that they were not happy with the £100,000 limit of liability in the defendants' standard terms. The plaintiffs were told that if the contract was not signed by the following Monday there was a risk that partly constructed hardware would be lost and could not be reserved for them after that date. These provisions therefore remained untouched.

ICL said that 'these standard ICL conditions are accepted by over 250 local authorities and in no way detract from the business partnerships'. Suppliers frequently quote other companies who have accepted their terms as if that makes the terms suitable. This case should serve as a warning to company secretaries and others that terms should always be considered carefully. St Albans' staff were also told that if they objected, any revised terms would have to be considered by the defendants' legal department (another popular tactic) and that this would cause delays. It probably would have done, but had discussion of the terms begun earlier, the time pressure would not have been so great.

When the tender was priced, ICL had insurance cover against product liability claims of £50m in total. ICL said it would have had to increase the price if the limit of liability were higher than the £100,000 figure. The relevant clause, which came from the ICL, 1985 conditions (which, in fact, had been superseded by some 1988 conditions which increased the limit of liability to £125,000 and were not used for this contract) read as follows:

> In all other cases ICL's liability will not exceed the price, or charge payable for the item of Equipment, Program or Service in respect of which the liability arises or £100,000 (whichever is the lesser). Provided that in no event will ICL be liable for:
> (i) loss resulting from any defect, or deficiency which ICL shall have physically remedied at its own expense within a reasonable time; or
> (ii) any indirect or consequential loss or loss of business of profits sustained by the customer or
> (iii) loss which could have been avoided by the customer following ICL's reasonable advice and instructions.

S3 of the Unfair Contract Terms Act 1977 requires such clauses to be 'reasonable' either where one party deals as a consumer or on the other's written standard terms of business. St Albans was not dealing as a consumer, despite not being in business, but it had dealt on ICL's standard terms, so s3 applied. The fact that some of the terms are negotiated will not prevent this provision applying. The conditions remained 'effectively untouched'. The burden of proof in establishing whether the terms were reasonable lies on the defendant by s11(5). The judge at first instance, confirmed in the Court of Appeal, examined the five matters relevant to reasonableness in Schedule 2 of the Act – in particular, the strength of bargaining position of the parties, whether the customer received an inducement to agree to the term and whether the customer knew of the existence of the term.

1. *ICL's financial status*. In assessing these facts the judge examined ICL's status as an international company, a wholly owned subsidiary of STC plc, a company with record profits for the first half of 1988 of £100.2m on a turnover of £1,109m.

2. *ICL's Insurance Cover.* He then examined ICL's insurance cover of £50m worldwide, which bore no relation to the £100,000 limit.
3. *The Bargaining Position.* Other companies who could have supplied the plaintiffs had similar conditions. St Albans was some way between a consumer and a business. Local authorities often do not insure and they are not generally run by 'businessmen'.
4. *Inducement.* There was no opportunity to enter into a better contract with others.
5. *Knowledge of the term.* The plaintiffs were aware of the term.

The judge quoted the Salvage Association case (unreported) and held the following to be the relevant points:

1. The parties were of unequal bargaining power.
2. The defendants had not justified the figure of £100,000 which was small, both in relation to the potential risk and the actual loss.
3. The defendants were insured.
4. The practical consequences of the decision – it was better for this loss to fall on a rich international company than the individual council tax payers of St Albans.

The court held that the software contained an error which put the defendants in breach of contract. The software did not correspond with the description in the tender documents and was not of merchantable quality or fit for its purpose. There had been an innocent misrepresentation and negligence and the plaintiffs were not at fault in failing to discover the error earlier. The limitation of liability provision was unenforceable under the 1977 Act and damages of £1,314,846 were ordered.

There are many other cases under the Act, but those above illustrate how the courts have interpreted the reasonableness test.

Wording of clauses

For those involved in drafting exclusion clauses the reasonableness test should always be considered. The following points may assist in ensuring that a clause is held to be reasonable, though no assurance can ever be given that a particular clause would always be held reasonable in all circumstances by all judges. A question mark over enforceability remains with all exclusion clauses.

1. Ensure that the other party has the clause drawn to their attention before the contract is made. Make sure that the clause is legible, perhaps in block letters or bold type.

2. Split the clause into sub-clauses so that if a judge finds parts unenforceable the rest of the clause has a better chance of survival on its own, applying English law rules of 'severance', the so-called 'blue pencil' test. Add a severance clause to the general provisions of the contract.

3. Exclude various forms of liability by name, such as the various implied terms and categories of consequential loss. A broad, sweeping exclusion may not be as likely to be upheld, whereas a clause which spells out to the other party exactly what is excluded is more likely to be regarded as reasonable.

4. Consider alternative provisions, though these can look rather strange. Some companies exclude all liability, and then provide that if such a provision is held unenforceable then liability is, in any event, limited, perhaps to the value of the contract or a sum set out in the contract.

5. Consider offering the purchaser two prices – one with one level of liability and another higher priced contract where the supplier accepts a higher limit of liability so that a court can see that the other party was offered a choice.

6. Consider including acknowledgements by the other party (a) that the provisions are reasonable and (b) that the other party is better able than the first party to insure against the liabilities excluded.

7. As a final point, make the clause as 'reasonable' as is commercially justifiable. Good guarantees help sell products. Consider the limits of any insurance policy and perhaps accept liability up to those limits. In Germany, for example, it is common to provide that the limit of liability is the level of the supplier's insurance cover and such a provision is highly likely to be enforceable in this country.

Consequential loss

Many commercial contracts provide that the supplier excludes all liability for consequential and indirect loss, including loss of profit, opportunity, revenue and goodwill. Such an exclusion is sensible and usually justifiable. However, ensure that for all contracts the wording is read carefully. Some clauses are so widely drawn that they exclude all liability under the contract, even for direct loss, and the purchaser has no effective legal recompense if there is a breach of contract, except, perhaps simply to invoke a clause giving the supplier the right to try to correct the relevant problem. Ensure that all parties are clear as to what is a direct loss and what is indirect. If it is not clear in a particular instance, set out in detail in the contract which losses are classed as which.

Consequences of breach of contract

In commercial contracts the statutory implied terms are often irrelevant, unless it is possible to render a clause void under unfair terms law. What is more important is the inclusion of express warranties and obligations on the supplier. The company secretary may be on either side of a trans-action. As a supplier, warranties should be kept to a minimum and staff should be informed that alterations to standard wording in exclusion and limitation of liability provisions, guarantees and warranties and indemnities must always be checked first with the company secretary, the in-house legal department or an outside lawyer.

When advising a purchaser the opposite is true. The supplier's terms usually exclude most liability. They should be amended to ensure a fairer balance between the parties. Where goods or services are being provided which are being made or provided specifically for the purchaser it is particularly important to test them before full payment has been made. The contract should also set out the consequences of a failure of the supplier to perform the obligations set out and in particular provide goods or services of the right description.

Both parties will wish to avoid litigation for breach of contract, so some escalation procedures and/or liquidated damages provisions can be included. If a breach of warranty concerning performance is found, the supplier should attempt to correct the fault. Many suppliers make that their entire liability. From a purchaser's perspective that may not be sufficient. There should be limits on the time taken to correct the fault and if the fault is not corrected in time, purchasers will want a right to sue for damages.

It is relevant to consider here the provisions of any exclusion or limita-tion of liability clause (as discussed above). If the limitation clause excludes all liability under the agreement then the warranty is worthless, unless the exclusion clause is void. A typical compromise is to accept liability for direct loss, such as the cost of replacing the system with another, and to exclude liability for indirect loss, such as loss of profit or goodwill.

Both parties should insure and each should ensure that their liability is capped under the contract to a stated figure.

Acceptance testing

Who decides whether the goods or services are acceptable or not is crucial. Suppliers want acceptance tests they can follow. Purchasers need to have an assurance that they can reject the goods if they fail agreed tests and will wish to withhold money until final acceptance. In practice, much depends on the negotiating position of the parties. In addition, for many contracts such tests are not appropriate. As a rule of thumb all contracts for bespoke products, including computer software and hardware, should have acceptance testing provisions.

Many contracts provide for acceptance testing, but simply say that the sole remedy where the test is failed is that the supplier will make various attempts to correct the error. From the purchaser's perspective a right to reject and have any advance payments repaid is crucial. The issue is particularly important where the product is customised for one particular user.

Bespoke software and warranties

Important issues concerning bespoke software are first that it may be untried and second who will own copyright in it. Consider whether the purchaser wants to go into the business of copyright ownership or whether a licence would suffice.

Unfair terms law: consumers and the EU directive

The EU directive on unfair terms in consumer contracts had to be brought into force throughout the EU by the end of 1994. The directive was adopted on 5 April 1993, bearing the number 93/13/EEC. The DTI had to issue two consultation papers on the implementation of the directive in the UK, owing to the controversy surrounding the measure. The *Unfair Terms in Consumer Contracts Regulations 1994* (SI 1994/3159) came into force on 1 July 1995, which leaves open the interesting question of the rights of those who suffer through a failure of the Government to implement on time. They could sue the Government for damages, but not have rights as against private individuals.

Most companies have printed terms and conditions of sale or purchase. All standard terms in consumer contracts should have been revised to take account of the law.

UK regulations

The Unfair Contract Terms Act 1977 (UCTA, discussed above) is the principal UK statute relevant to this area, and it remains unamended. From July 1995 there have been two laws in operation. Many people commented to the DTI that this would be impracticable. In its last consultation paper the DTI decided that it was not even possible to 'align' the two measures. However, the DTI believe that the test of fairness in the directive is very similar to the test of reasonableness in the Act, although the two tests are not the same.

UCTA is broader than the directive in some respects; for example, the directive applies only to consumer contracts. The directive is broader in other ways; it is not, for example, confined only to goods agreements. The reason for this proposed approach is because there was not time to revise UCTA and implement in time.

UCTA forbids the exclusion and limitation of liability for negligence except where the relevant term satisfies the requirement of reasonableness. S3 addresses contracts where one party deals on the other's standard terms of business or one deals as a consumer. For such contracts, under existing law, clauses excluding or restricting liability for breach of contract or enabling the supplier to render a different contractual performance from that which would have been reasonably expected of him, or no performance at all, must satisfy the test of reasonableness set out in the Act.

Those terms which do not satisfy this test will be void. UCTA addresses a number of other issues too, such as unreasonable indemnity clauses. The directive covers similar, but not identical, ground to UCTA.

Exclusions

The DTI take the view that the directive applies only to contracts for the supply of goods or services and not to contracts for the creation or issue of financial securities. Contracts for the supply of commodity futures and options are regarded by the DTI as contracts for the sale of goods and within the directive where they are consumer transactions. It would appear that a contract between an individual and his or her broker or financial adviser would come within the regulations. The impact on financial services business could be significant in an industry already weighed down by regulation. It does not appear that the directive applies to the creation or issue of financial securities as the security is simply evidence of indebtedness and the service is provided after the consumer provides the money.

Employment contracts are not included, nor contracts relating to succession rights or under family law or relating to incorporation and organisation of companies or partnership agreements.

Terms in insurance contracts which define and limit insured risk and the liability of the insurer are excluded. Other provisions in insurance contracts will be within the regulations. Under UCTA all such contracts are excluded. Oral contracts are included within the directive.

It has been argued by some legal commentators that where a bank lends one person money on the basis of a guarantee from a third party consumer, arguably the guarantee must be 'fair' even though the guarantor does not him or herself receive anything from the bank. If a business rents a house from a private individual it could even find the lease contract assessed for fairness.

Also excluded by schedule 1 is any term which is incorporated: to comply with or which reflects –

(i) statutory or regulatory provisions of the United Kingdom; or
(ii) the provisions or principles of international conventions to which the member States or [sic] the Community are party.

'Consumer contracts'

The directive applies to terms in consumer contracts. Companies which make no sales to individuals will not be affected by the directive. A consumer is defined in Regulation 2 (1) as 'a natural person who, in making a contract to which these Regulations apply, is acting for purposes which are outside his business'. A consumer is defined in the directive as a natural person who 'in contracts covered by this directive, is acting for purposes which are outside his trade, business or profession'. Many businesses do sell products to end users other than for business purposes. Under existing English law they may have protection under UCTA as in the *R&B Customers Brokers Ltd v. Dominions Trust Ltd* [1988] 1 WLR 321 case. The directive will not apply but protection will still be available under existing English law.

Contracts between two consumers are not caught. There must be a sale between a business seller and a consumer before the directive applies.

Individual negotiation of contracts

The directive applies to contractual terms which have not been individually negotiated. Regulation 3(3) of the UK Regulations provides that a term will always be regarded as not having been individually negotiated where it has been drafted in advance and the consumer has not been able to influence the substance of the term. The directive provides that terms which have been drafted in advance, where the consumer has not had the chance to influence 'the substance of the term, particularly in the context of a pre-formulated standard contract', are caught. The burden of proving that a term has been individually negotiated falls on the supplier.

The regulations may apply to a contract issued by a house builder's solicitor to the solicitors of the purchaser where the house builder insists his standard terms must be used, though it is doubtful whether a contract for the sale of freehold land is a sale of goods. Tenancy agreements, mortgages, take-over offers, foreign exchange transactions and others may also be covered by the regulations as many such contracts may be contracts for the supply of services. However at the date of writing the regulations had been in place in the UK for only four months and no case law had then emerged on the ambit of the regulations.

UCTA applies to business-to-business contracts only where they are concluded on standard written terms, but to all consumer contracts, even if they are not on standard terms and are negotiated.

Given that UCTA will continue to apply, companies falling within both measures will have two tests to apply. Imagine the following example. Consumer A receives goods under standard conditions which are not negotiated. The directive applies. Consumer B argues about the terms and negotiates several. He will not be caught by the directive, but UCTA will apply. The directive, unlike UCTA, is not confined to exclusion clauses.

An overall assessment of the contract is undertaken in order to ascertain whether as a whole it is a pre-formulated standard contract. The fact that one term has been individually negotiated does not mean that the supplier is able to avoid the application of the UK Regulations. Where one term is negotiated or part of a term, the UK Regulations make it clear that the regulations will be applied to the other terms of the contract.

Unfair terms

The principal provision of the directive and the UK Regulations is to state what terms in such pre-formulated contracts with consumers will be regarded as unfair. Unfair terms will not be 'binding on the consumer', but the contract will continue to bind the parties if the other terms can stand alone. The penalty is, therefore, that the term drafted to protect the supplier fails. Article 3(1) (Regulation 4(1)) defines a term as unfair where it causes a significant imbalance in the parties' rights and obligations arising under the contract, to the detriment of the consumer. This must be 'contrary to the requirement of good faith'. The nature of the goods or services are considered in determining whether a term is unfair, together with all the circumstances at the time.

Good faith

The requirement of good faith has not, to date, existed in this context under English law. This is a concept now implied in many commercial agency contracts, as set out in Chapter 7, below. Recital 16 of the directive goes into this area and provides that regard is had to the strength of the bargaining power of the parties; and whether the consumer had an inducement to agree to the term; and whether the goods or services were sold or supplied to the special order of the consumer; and the extent to which the seller has dealt fairly and equitably with the consumer. The UK regulations contain these provisions in Schedule 2. Good faith can be shown where the supplier 'deals fairly and equitably with the other party whose legitimate interests he has taken into account'.

The DTI was pressed to define 'unfair terms' more clearly than in the directive, but has not done so. It comments generally that if it were to implement the directive inaccurately it would be open to individuals to look behind the UK regulations to the directive in any event. Some wanted the schedule to include where the individual has taken legal advice. However, the DTI believe that even if someone has taken legal advice that should not preclude them from arguing that the term is unfair.

Examples of unfair terms

The directive sets out in an annex a non-exhaustive list of unfair terms. These are mirrored in Schedule 3 of the regulations and called an 'Indicative List'. This list is worth careful scrutiny. It sets out similar matters to those found in the guidelines for the application of the reasonableness test in UCTA. The terms in the list are not the only terms which might be unfair and they are not automatically unfair, nor deemed unfair unless proved fair.

The DTI point out in their consultative document that some of the terms are already governed by English law in the annex. For example, term 1(a) would be regarded as unfair in all circumstances. This does not make the situation very straightforward for those in practice. The DTI state:

> For those annex terms which fall within the scope of the Act, either the Act or these Regulations could be invoked. Under the Act it is for the person wishing to rely on the term to show that it satisfies the test of reasonableness. In the case of the annex terms which do not fall within the scope of the Act, it will be for the consumer to demonstrate that the term is unfair according to the test in Article 3(1).

In May 1996 the Office of Fair Trading published a report of its action to date in enforcing the law in this area which provides useful information and examples for company secretaries.

The directive lists relevant unfair terms, including:

1. Excluding or limiting liability of the seller where the consumer dies or is injured, where this results from an act or omission of the seller. This is very similar to existing law, except that it does not require that the seller be negligent. It will no longer be possible to exclude liability for death or personal injury where the seller was responsible, even unwittingly.

2. Exclusions or limitations allowing a total, partial or incomplete performance of the contract by the seller. This is similar to existing law under UCTA.

3. Making a contract binding on the consumer, where the seller can avoid performing the contract by some term in the contract. Both parties should, therefore, be bound to perform or neither.

4. Allowing the seller to retain sums if the consumer terminates the contract where the consumer does not have a right to compensation where the seller terminates the contract.

5. Requiring consumers to pay disproportionately high sums in compensation where the consumer terminates the contract.

6. Allowing the seller to terminate the contract at will, where the consumer has no such right, or allowing sellers to retain sums paid for services not yet supplied at the time of termination.

7. Allowing the seller to terminate a contract of indeterminate duration without reasonable notice except where there are serious grounds so to do.

8. Automatically extending fixed term contracts unless the consumer indicates by a stipulated deadline that he does not wish to continue with the contract.

9. Irrevocably binding the consumer to terms which he had no chance to become familiar with before the contract was entered into. The issue here will be whether or not the consumer had a 'real opportunity', to quote the words in the annex to the directive, to become acquainted with the terms. This appears to go further than simply requiring that the consumer be supplied with the terms before the contract was entered into. Becoming familiar with standard terms is not something many consumers ever achieve. It may be necessary to provide that consumers have a right to reject or modify terms after they become part of the contract or ensure that companies institute a procedure whereby the consumer is told about terms well in advance and asked to sign a piece of paper acknowledging that the consumer is now acquainted with the terms. Even such an acknowledgement may not be sufficient.

10. Enabling the seller unilaterally to alter the terms of the contract without a valid reason stipulated in the contract. It is not clear what a valid reason might be. Contracts could specify that terms may be

varied to reflect changes in the law, for example, but, presumably not simply to accommodate changed business objectives, such as reducing a payment period from sixty to thirty days.

11. Allowing the seller unilaterally to alter the characteristics of a product or service, without a valid reason. Many sets of terms give the seller rights to change the specification of the product. The difficult issue will be when such a change will be valid in future. Most consumer contracts are one-offs so many of these provisions which deal with on-going relationships will not arise in the context of contracts with consumers. However, where there is such a term, a change in design of a product may be effected because of changes in customer preference or due to a change in Government or industry regulations. The former may not be a sufficient reason to change the nature of the product. The latter may be. In drafting terms, the fuller the clauses are as to the reasons why changes to products or services may be made the more likely the term will be upheld.

12. Determining the price at the time of delivery or increasing the price later without giving the consumer a right to reject the goods.

13. Giving the seller the right to decide if the goods conform to the contract or the exclusive right to interpret contract terms. Clauses stipulating that allegedly defective goods must be returned to the seller who will assess whether or not there are defects could be unenforceable under this provision. The provision does not state that the consumer must be free to decide if goods conform to the contract. An objective test is therefore the best compromise.

14. Limiting sellers' commitments to actions undertaken by agents or making the commitments of the seller dependent on a particular formality.

15. Requiring that consumers fulfil all their obligations where the seller does not fulfil his.

16. Allowing the seller to transfer his rights under the agreement, where this may reduce the guarantees for the consumer, without the consumer's consent. Where the seller proposes to assign all contracts to a third party it is conceivable that where the third party is not in such a strong financial position as the seller, such a transfer may be held to reduce guarantees. The phrase 'reducing guarantees' is not very clear. The provision does not mention reducing the 'value' of guarantees.

17. Limiting rights of the consumer to bring legal actions. The provision specifically refers to requiring the consumer to take disputes exclusively to arbitration not covered by legal provisions.

The UK Regulations contain in the annex at schedule 3 some indication of the scope of paragraphs 7, 10 and 12 above.

1. Financial services suppliers may still terminate a contract of indeterminate duration unilaterally without notice where there is a valid reason, provided that the supplier is required to inform the other contracting party or parties immediately.
2. Suppliers of financial services may alter the rate of interest payable by the consumer or due to the consumer or the amount of its charges without notice where there is a valid reason, provided that the supplier is required to inform the other party at the earliest opportunity and they are free to dissolve the contract immediately.
3. A seller may reserve the right unilaterally to alter the conditions of a contract of indeterminate duration, provided that he is required to inform the consumer with reasonable notice and the consumer is free to dissolve the contract.
4. Paragraphs 7, 10 and 11 (above) do not apply to transactions in transferable securities, financial instruments and other products or services where the price is linked to fluctuations in a stock exchange quotation or index or a financial market rate that the seller or supplier does not control *or* to contracts for the purchase or sale of foreign currency, traveller's cheques or international money orders denominated in foreign currency.
5. Paragraph 12 (above) – allowing price increases without a right to cancel – is without 'hindrance' to price indexation clauses 'where lawful' provided that the method by which prices vary is explicitly described.

Assessing unfair terms

The provisions set out at length above are not the only provisions which may be rendered non-binding by the new measure. Unfairness is to be assessed taking into account the types of goods or services supplied and looking at all the circumstances surrounding the formation of the contract, as mentioned above. Whether the price is fair cannot be the subject of challenge except where the price terms are not in intelligible language.

Choice of law

The provisions of the directive cannot be avoided by choosing the law of a non-member country. US companies, for example, will find themselves subject to the directive even where their contracts specify a particular US state law as applying. This will be the case wherever the consumer has a 'close connection' with the territory of a member state.

The UK Regulations in Regulation 7 state that the regulations apply notwithstanding any term which applies the law of a non-member state if the contract has a close connection with the territory of the member state.

Plain intelligible language

The directive requires that terms be written in plain and intelligible language. Few terms are. The only penalty is that where the terms are unclear, they will be construed against the seller. However, that could be a major incentive for improving the drafting of terms of business with consumers. The UK regulations contain this provision in Regulation 6. They do not say that terms must be in plain English, which raises the question of whether, say, a French company operating in the UK must use English or whether French can be used or Welsh in Wales and so on. To whom must the term be intelligible? For example, in some parts of the country it may be necessary to produce terms in English and the most commonly spoken immigrant languages in the relevant areas.

These provisions reflect the position under existing English law. There is much to be gained for both consumer and seller in ensuring that terms are easily understood. Breaking clauses down into numbered sections and adding headings, as well as using a legible typeface assist in achieving this objective.

Court actions

Member states must enact legislation giving persons and organisations interested in consumer protection rights to bring actions before the courts for a decision on whether terms are unfair. Such actions may be against a number of sellers for the same economic sector or their associations which recommend or use the same general contractual terms. This measure could have a significant effect in reducing the number of unfair terms in consumer contracts. However, the DTI stated in their first consultation document that:

> UK law at present contains no general provision for representative actions: only the party to a contract may sue under that contract. Thus according to the national law concerned (i.e. that applying in the UK) this provision has no effect.

This seems to amount to ignoring obligations under the directive, and arguably the Government could be sued for damages by a consumer who has lost out because a body with more funds, such as the Consumers'

Association, was not given the rights it should have been. Similarly, Article 7(3) has been ignored. This article is 'with due regard for national laws' and provides that remedies referred to under Article 7(2) may be directed separately or jointly against a number of sellers or suppliers from the same sector or their associations.

Due to strong criticism by independent lawyers and consumer organisations that the DTI approach would result in improper implementation of the directive, in the last consultation paper the DTI decided to place an obligation on the Director General of Fair Trading to consider any complaint made to him that any contract term or terms drawn up for general use are unfair and, where appropriate, to bring proceedings for an injunction to secure that the use of that term or terms is discontinued. These provisions are now included in the regulations – Regulation 8. Notwithstanding this, the Consumers' Association has been given leave by the court to apply for judicial review in connection with the omission of the representative action provisions of the directive in the UK Regulations, so the Government's hand may ultimately be forced to implement the directive as it stands in due course.

The DTI will not empower consumer bodies to bring actions as there is no general right of representative action in the UK. Nor do the DTI accept that breach of the provisions of the directive should bring criminal sanctions in the UK. The directive allows member states to keep more stringent laws in this field.

Timing

Member states had until the 31 December 1994 to amend national law to comply with the directive. The UK regulations, as we have already seen, have applied from 1 July 1995. There are no express transitional provisions in the UK regulations. There is nothing in the regulations restricting them to contracts made after that date; however, the directive states that 'These conditions shall be applicable to all contracts concluded after 31 December 1994'.

It has been suggested in one legal article that the validity of a twenty-year-old mortgage contract could now be challenged. However, the directive is quite clear that it applies only to new contracts, and as the UK Regulations do not address the issue (surprisingly) it should be reasonably safe to leave existing contracts untouched if this is administratively possible – running two sets of terms of business, for example, could be difficult. It is not clear what a new contract would be in many cases.

As any term which allows contract terms to be varied unilaterally will be void under the new law, it will be hard for some companies to comply with the law by forcing changes to conditions upon the other party.

The cost of compliance with the directive

The DTI's latest consultation paper contains a compliance cost assessment. The British Bankers' Association predicted the cost for a large bank to examine its terms and conditions under the new law, to reprint and circulate them to all branches at between £500,000 and £1m. One member bank spent £250,000 on ensuring that guarantees are in plain English. It was also expected that banks may have direct costs of £100,000 – £200,000 per annum in dealing with increased complaints arising from the regulations.

The Council of Mortgage Lenders estimated costs of £2m for building societies – about £23,000 per member. The Association of British Insurers estimated that if they were to instruct a solicitor charging £125 per hour to look at five contracts spending five hours on each contract, the bill for 1,675 contracts of its members would be over £1m. ABTA estimated costs of between a few hundred pounds and £6000 per member for their 3,500 members.

General Product Safety Regulations 1994

The General Product Safety Regulations 1994 (SI 1994/2328) implement the EU general product safety directive in the UK. They require that only safe products be put on the market in the EU. Regulation 2(1) provides that products which are used 'exclusively in the context of a commercial activity even if . . . used for or by a consumer' do not come within the regulations. The regulations do not apply to second-hand products which are antiques (but they do apply to other second-hand products and there is no definition of antiques) and products which are supplied for repair or reconditioning before use, provided that the supplier clearly informs the person to whom he supplies the product to that effect. Most purchasing of goods within companies will therefore fall outside these regulations.

The Consumer Protection Act 1987 s10 already imposes a general safety requirement, providing that an offence is committed where consumer goods are supplied which are not reasonably safe, having regard to all the circumstances. The 1994 Regulations, by Regulation 5, disapply s10 to the extent that it imposes a general safety requirement for products to be placed on the market by producers or sold or offered for sale or possessed by distributors. The two safety requirements are not identical, so in practice there may be cases when it is crucial to determine which general safety requirement applies.

S7 of the 1994 regulations is the principal provision. It states that no product shall be placed on the market unless the product is a 'safe product'. There is a definition of 'safe product' for these purposes. This will be any product which under normal or reasonably foreseeable conditions of use, including duration, does not present any risk or only minimal risks compatible with the product's use, considered as acceptable and consistent with a high level of protection for the safety and health of persons.

In determining whether or not a product is 'safe' the following factors are taken into account:

- The characteristics of the products, such as its composition, packaging and instructions for assembly and maintenance.
- The effect on other products, where it is reasonably foreseeable that the product will be used on other products.
- The presentation of the product, the labelling, any instructions for its use and disposal and any other indication or information provided by the producer.
- The categories of consumers at serious risk when using the product, in particular children.

Distributors are required, by Regulation 9, to act with due care in order to 'help' ensure compliance with the producer's obligations under the general safety requirement and information provisions above. A distributor must not supply products which he knows, or should have presumed on the basis of information in his possession and as a professional, are dangerous products. Distributors must also, within the limits of their activities, participate in monitoring the safety of products placed on the market; in particular, by passing on information on the product risks and cooperating in the action taken to avoid those risks.

'Distributors' are defined as any professional in the supply chain whose activity does not affect the safety properties of a product. A company buying goods and storing them in unsafe or wet conditions may, thus, become a producer rather than a distributor, as the company's activities (storage) affect the safety of the product (assuming wet causes the product to become unsafe). Distributors who repackage goods where this activity affects product safety may also be producers under these definitions.

The regulations contain a defence of due diligence where someone has taken all reasonable steps and exercised all due diligence to avoid committing an offence. The defence cannot be used when relying on information provided by someone else, unless it was reasonable in all the circumstances to place reliance on that information. Dealers should not assume that suppliers' statements about safety are accurate. There is an obligation to verify information or attempt to do so.

The regulations are enforced by means of prohibition notices and notices to warn, and other provisions under the 1987 Act. No producer or distributor shall sell or offer to sell dangerous products or possess them. Breach of the regulations can lead to a fine of up to £5,000 in the Magistrates' Court and/or a jail term of up to three months. Directors, managers, secretaries or other similar officers of companies may also be subject to these penalties if the offence is committed with their consent or connivance or attributable to any neglect on their part.

This chapter has examined some issues at the heart of contracts of sale – in particular, issues of liability for defective products and clauses limiting and excluding such liability and the extent to which unfair terms law has an impact in that area. In practice, it is unwise to accept unreasonable exclusion or limitation of liability clauses in the hope a court might find them invalid. Most cases are settled out of court and proceedings are expensive. It is much better if the parties can thrash out a compromise acceptable to both sides and their insurers before the contract comes into force.

6 Contracts and lawyers

Knowledge of the law is of crucial importance in the buying and selling field, but, in practice, it is what is included in commercial contracts which is of greater significance. One of the principal strengths of the Anglo-Saxon common law system is its lack of interference in the freedom to contract enjoyed by business people. Many of the statutory provisions in relation to sale of goods can be altered by contract – though with certain notable exceptions, covered in earlier chapters, such as exclusion and limitation of liability and implied terms as to title.

This chapter looks at practical issues in relation to contracts, such as negotiation, preparation and sources of contracts, and how to find and work well with an external lawyer. To an extent, it deals more with psychology than with law and also includes issues to negotiate with a lawyer.

Sources of contract terms

Many company secretaries have their own contracts with which they are familiar, though most realise that no contract is ever perfect and all can be improved in some respect. However, others are just starting in the business or are not happy with the precedents they have cobbled together over the years as the occasion arose. The best source of new contracts specific to one company is usually a solicitor familiar with the industry and relevant area of law. Directories such as *Chambers and partners: the legal profession* and Legalease's *The legal 500* seek to recommend and list solicitors particularly well known in this area of law.

However, some company secretaries may prefer to work up their own contracts. They have extensive industrial/legal expertise and now require assistance from an outside solicitor. What then is the best starting point? In some respects this question is unlikely to arise except for a start-up company. Most companies already have contracts which they use and there are advantages in ensuring that all customers contract on the same or similar terms. Indeed, offering one customer worse terms than another at around the same time for the same products could infringe EC competition law if the company is in a dominant position in a substantial part of the Common Market. Discrimination without justifiable reason in such circumstances can be an infringement of Article 86 of the Treaty of Rome. In addition, there are administrative costs in reprinting contracts and re-educating sales staff.

However, assuming a decision has been made to modify, update or replace an existing contract, the question of which terms to use arises.

CCTA

The Government Centre for Information Systems, CCTA (Central Computer and Telecommunications Agency), publishes *Model agreements for purchasing information systems and services*. These conditions, produced with the assistance of Theodore Goddard, solicitors, were originally devised to replace the various forms of *standard* terms and conditions previously used for IS procurement in government. They are not designed as standard terms and conditions and are principally for government departments and could be of use for local government IS contracting. They cost £90, come on two diskettes with a user guide and can be obtained from HMSO (tel. Bob Hall on 01603 694406). Seventeen main areas are covered, including facilities management agreements and product and software supply. A review of the terms, and a comparison with terms issued by the Chartered Institute of Purchasing and Supply (CIPS) was published in *Purchasing and Supply Management*, April 1994.

CIPS

The CIPS model forms of contract also contain publicly available terms, covering many areas including computer contracts. Their computer contracts are described as *single usage models* protected by copyright. This means that each time a company wishes to use these terms it must buy a new copy, whereas the CCTA terms are a model which can be used repeatedly and tailored to one's own needs. There are three sets of terms and conditions relating to computer hardware: supply and installation for the purchase of hardware; servicing for maintenance and hire; and servicing for maintenance. The CIPS forms can be obtained from the CIPS bookshop (tel. 01780 56777).

Some model terms are drafted to be reasonable, representing a form of middle ground and, as such, are not always an appropriate basis for tough negotiations. Like all forms, precedents or examples, they are a useful starting point for drafting. No two companies have the same requirements and the danger of using a model form is that users assume that they need not even read all the provisions, never mind revise them to reflect their needs. However, they certainly provide good legal protection and clear drafting to a much greater degree than many poor attempts at contractual terms in use.

Legal books

Croner Publications' *Model Business Contracts* contains various contracts which can be used. Increasingly books on law are being produced in hardcopy and diskette format, with a licence for the purchaser of the book to use the diskette. In December 1994 *Computer Contracts* by Michele Rennie (Sweet & Maxwell, £99, ISBN 0 421 490505) was published with twenty-eight computer contracts on diskette. Also in 1994 Michael Henry's *Publishing and Multimedia Law* (Butterworths, £75, ISBN 0 406 03768 X) was published with 52 precedents on diskette, covering media and multi-media law.

Using competitors' contracts

Many people use competitors' contracts as a base for theirs. This is not generally to be recommended. The danger of using any existing contract is that provisions are included for a reason of which the user is not aware. Any precedent should always be used intelligently and every word read and considered to ascertain whether or not it is relevant for the company concerned. Virtually every contract will need to be modified to reflect the individual circumstances of the user. Blind use of lengthy precedents – with managers alleging that they do not understand the provision themselves, but the lawyers included it so it must be right – is silly.

In addition, taking the terms of another company is breach of copyright. It is no defence that everyone in the industry steals each other's terms. Most legal books and CCTA contracts (see above) come with a copyright licence to the user to use the terms. That does not mean that the purchaser/licensee may incorporate the terms into a set of precedents and sell them. The scope of the use will be set out in the contract which is usually provided with the book or diskette.

In addition to copyright problems and the fact that a competitor's contract has been produced for them with their own requirements and business practices, another disadvantage of using someone else's terms is embarrassment. Most companies are aware of the terms of business which their competitors use and companies can look foolish if they begin using a set of terms which looks very like those of another company in the industry.

Exchanging terms with competitors; and trade association recommendations

The exchange of business terms with competitors, so that each party knows the others terms, may appear harmless enough but is highly likely to infringe EC competition law in Article 85 of the Treaty of Rome. In *Fiatgri UK, Ford New Holland and John Deere v. Commission* (Cases T-34, T-35/92, CFI, 27 October 1994) the European Court of First Instance upheld a ruling by the Commission that exchange of information by tractor dealers infringed competition law rules.

Some trade associations tread on very shaky ground in recommending terms to members. Specific recommendations of terms by trade associations, even if not binding on members, must be registered with the OFT under the Restrictive Trade Practices Act 1976 under UK competition law. Members of associations must be free to set their own terms of business and this should be undertaken independently of competitors - though having regard to terms which are common in the industry is not forbidden, of course, if no collusion is found.

Plain English and the unfair terms directive

Contracts should be in clear plain English. Indeed the UK unfair terms law implementing the EU unfair terms directive, requires contracts with consumers to be 'intelligible' (see Chapter 5). This will encourage companies drafting contracts for use by consumers (such as for packaged games and home software) to use contract terms which can be understood. It is not clear if the UK Regulations, mean that terms in the UK must be in English. Is French or Welsh, for example, unintelligible for this purpose? The issue is unlikely to arise as most companies doing business in the UK use contracts in English.

Drafting and negotiating contracts

In considering contractual issues, the first question should be which party will draw up the contract. The tempting answer for the overworked company secretary is to suggest that the other side produce the agreement: there will be much less work that way round. However, this means control is lost over the provisions. Being in charge of production of the contract gives control and power over the other contracting party. However, it is only rarely that a purchaser is in a strong enough negotiating position to be able to dispense with the contracts of the supplier and start from scratch with its own documents drafted heavily from its point of view. Although it is more expensive to pay for the legal costs of producing documents from scratch, rather than commenting upon existing documents of the supplier, it does give the purchaser a significant advantage in that it is working from the standpoint of conditions which favour it, rather than vice versa, as is often the case. Conversely, for suppliers their own terms should be used. With suppliers it is much easier to insist that their terms are used. That is the normal practice and many customers simply sign on the dotted line without any amendment to the conditions. In some cases there is absolutely no alternative but to start again, as the documents produced are so badly drafted that all the principal legal issues are not addressed.

The supplier may employ a solicitor in-house or use outside lawyers for the production of its contracts, and where the purchaser wishes to engage a solicitor to advise on any necessary amendments to the contractual documentation, the supplier may wish to involve its own outside lawyer in any contractual negotiations.

As is expected, standard form contracts are usually one-sided in their drafting. Where the company secretary is acting for the purchaser they should not be afraid of suggesting major modifications to the contractual terms to improve their position and, indeed, should approach the negotiations by suggesting amendments which favour them considerably, so that there is room left for subsequent negotiation.

Those contemplating using a solicitor should think about this early on in the negotiation, so that a proper careful choice can be made. In invitations to tender or request for an estimate, the purchaser should be asked to send their contract conditions. It is at that stage, provided the requirements of the purchaser are known, that initial advice from a solicitor should be obtained. If the documents are fundamentally flawed there is no point in beginning months of negotiation directly with the purchaser in the hope of minimising legal costs if at the last minute, when the contract is sent to a solicitor for a final check, it is found that major aspects have to be changed. It is much better, even if the legal budget is tight, to have a solicitor give an initial overview, even if he or she is not then involved for several months.

It is quite common for wholly inappropriate documents to be put forward by companies which may have had contracts prepared by experienced solicitors in the past, but where the contracts have been changed out of all recognition over the years without proper consideration of the effect of such changes. Also companies sometimes end up using contracts for purposes for which they were never designed.

Some deals will result in several contracts, particularly where a number of different elements are purchased or sold. For computer contracts, for example, a purchaser may be presented with software licence conditions of the supplier and also licence conditions for specific parts of the software which require a direct licence to be signed with the software proprietor. In addition, there may be contracts for the supply of hardware, some standard terms and conditions of business and various maintenance contracts.

The company secretary should make sure they understand the commercial objectives of the deal rather than try to give advice in a vacuum with only a draft contract for guidance. Once it is clear what the objective is, the parties can work towards achieving that objective through the contracts. In practice, it may not matter how complicated and lengthy the documents are as long as the provisions of all the documentation dovetail with each other. In other cases there will simply be one contract. The company secretary needs to ensure that it is clear which documents comprise the contract. Where there are a number of different suppliers involved with whom contracts will be entered into, the company secretary should be able to advise about the respective responsibilities of each and the way the contracts will operate in practice.

Provisions in contracts can be divided quite easily between those which are principally commercial and those which are legal. There is absolutely no point in a solicitor being present during negotiations over the price to be paid for the product which can comprise an important part of the discussions, nor in relation to technical discussions about the products to be purchased or sold and what the products are capable of doing – although, given the enthusiastic and sometimes untrue statements made by salesmen, it is useful to advise them on the law of misrepresentation from time to time.

Areas where the company secretary may wish to issue an instruction to employees that he or she should be involved in include:

- Exclusion or limitation of liability provisions.
- Clauses concerning the ownership of intellectual property rights and an indemnity in relation to losses arising through third party actions for breach of intellectual property rights.
- Warranties.
- Incorporation of additional documentation into the contract.
- All the so-called 'boilerplate' clauses such as choice of law and jurisdiction.

Negotiation styles

If a solicitor is familiar with contractual negotiations then he or she will be familiar with the necessity to reach a compromise, but it is important to establish at the outset (perhaps even before instructing a particular solicitor, – that is, an individual rather than the firm for which he or she works) what negotiation style the company expects from the solicitor and, indeed, employs itself.

Some companies will have a hard-hitting corporate ethos which permeates the whole company. They may agree never to deviate from their standard contracts and stick to that position even if they lose a deal. Others may have a more flexible approach. Neither approach is right or wrong, but all companies should ensure that the company's policy is consistently followed throughout all parts of its business. The company may require any solicitor used to take issue with every point and be prepared to abandon the transaction where the required fundamental contractual provisions are not accepted. However, companies with this view of negotiations should be wary of a negotiation where every small point becomes a battle: this is unlikely to result in a smooth working relationship with customers or suppliers. There will be major issues upon which it will be imprudent to give way, but other more minor issues should be capable of concession on both sides.

Other firms will have at the outset an understanding of the legal position which they hope to reach and be prepared to concede points in a greater spirit of cooperation. What is needed is a firm negotiator who has the practical experience necessary to understand which points are fundamental and which can be conceded. Ensuring that the individual charged with the negotiation is a good communicator, gets on well with people, smiles, shakes hands, employs basic human psychology in his or her dealings with the other side in meetings should assist negotiations.

Running contract negotiation meetings

Set an agenda in advance and agree the proposed duration of the meeting. Where meetings become protracted, preparing a list of the major outstanding points to be returned to at the end of the meeting can ensure that greater progress is made on a larger number of issues. It should always be clear who is in charge of a meeting, who is chairing it. The concentration of the parties will not last over too extended a period and therefore it may be preferable to adjourn the meeting until the following day or break for lunch.

A break also enables both sides to discuss sticking points internally, and cast a fresh eye over protracted negotiations or even seek permission from a senior member of the company to alter a supposedly unalterable term.

Caution should be exercised where one party keeps having to refer to a third party for instructions so that no points are actually settled. It is important that all people who are needed from the company with authority to negotiate are present at the meeting.

If drafts of an agreement have been exchanged between the parties over a period of weeks or months and then a meeting is held, it will be quite clear what the major stumbling blocks are; and it is sensible to concentrate upon those first. If, however, there has not been much discussion of the contract, the meeting can be used as an opportunity to go through the contract(s) from beginning to end, in the order in which the points appear, arguing and agreeing the points as they come up. It is essential that one party (and preferably both) keeps a note of the changes agreed; and, where possible, minutes of the meeting should be taken to clear up any disputes later about what exactly was agreed. One way of dealing with contracts efficiently in long meetings is to have a solicitor or company secretary with a lap-top or other computer system available at the meeting into which the amended text can be inserted, but only if there is time to give careful thought to the amendments later.

Where a contract has been drawn up by an outside solicitor, ensure that the text is downloaded to the company where the final negotiations are taking place so that there is no delay for the corrections to be undertaken. The amended version of the contract can be taken away at the end of the meeting and the parties can consider it before signature.

It may be tempting to sign a contract as soon as agreement appears to have been reached, but it is best to think about it finally over night. In meetings, although all parties will be trying hard to ensure that all points are addressed, there will be times when, because of the length of the meeting or the number of points which have arisen, issues will be overlooked or not addressed at all.

Contractual negotiations are in many ways a negative process. They involve looking at how the parties will be protected under the contract if things went wrong. This is not the spirit in which both parties are usually entering the agreement, but it is important to focus on these issues which the contract is there to cover. The contractual issues should also draw out some of the practical limitations of the product being sold or licensed and the concerns of the supplier. If the supplier is not prepared to warrant a particular function of the software, that suggests that there may indeed be a problem with that function.

Using solicitors to sue

Solicitors are not chosen and instructed only in connection with non-contentious (non-litigation) matters, such as the preparation of contracts. Those using solicitors to litigate should ensure that the solicitors have experience of litigation of the type concerned. Personal recommendation and commercially available guides should give some assistance in choosing a competent firm to litigate (see below). Involve the solicitor early. Where the matter is going to court, a barrister will usually also be instructed. The company secretary should be involved in the process of choosing an appropriate barrister, who will usually be instructed by the solicitor. All company secretaries will know that it is particularly important to ensure that the costs, which can mount substantially, do not begin to reach a level at which it becomes uneconomic in relation to the prospects of success and the likely level of damages which might be recovered. Requiring regular details of the accumulated solicitors' costs and barristers' fees should enable a check to be made in this area.

Use litigation only as a last resort. Taking legal proceedings is expensive. It should be considered only where there is a good likelihood of success, where there is certainty concerning the solvency of the party to be sued and where the company is able to fund its legal costs whilst the action is going on. Even if successful only a proportion of the legal costs of the plaintiff are recoverable in this country. Solicitors' and barristers' fees are not the only costs. Significant amounts of management time needs to be devoted to the management and successful conclusion of litigation. It is clearly preferable to pursue all avenues of compromise first and avoid becoming emotionally involved in the dispute and avoid regarding matters as being matters of principle whatever the cost. Virtually all legal proceedings which are begun are settled before they reach the court.

As well as the cost in terms of management time there may also be bad publicity. For these reasons, alternative forms of dispute resolution should be considered, including senior members of each party sitting down and discussing what the real areas of dispute are or more formal mediation.

Most contracts provide that disputes will be litigated in the courts and that is often cheaper than formal arbitration. The advantage of arbitration is that the proceedings are confidential, but unlike with court proceedings where no payment is made to the judge or for the hire of the court room, the venue and arbitrator have to be paid. It is generally best, therefore, not to include an arbitration clause in a contract.

Giving advice to Shakespeare's rebel-leader, Jack Cade, Dick the butcher urges 'The first thing we do, let's kill all the lawyers' (Henry VI Part 2). Solicitors, however, should not be regarded as a necessary or even an unnecessary evil, but rather a useful business tool in achieving efficient and effective contracts which properly protect the commercial interests of the parties.

Seeking and obtaining legal advice

The extent to which a company secretary uses an outside solicitor will depend on many factors, including whether the company has its own in-house legal department, the legal training and experience of the company secretary and the culture and background of the company itself.

This section looks at how to obtain legal advice and work well with outside solicitors. Managers and company secretaries may not have the time available nor the interest nor inclination to read difficult legal contracts. A specialist solicitor could do so much more quickly, provided he or she has looked at such contracts in the past. This section considers later the question of the cost of engaging solicitors and how to make effective and efficient use of them. Cost is one important element in determining whether or not legal advice should be obtained. There may not be sufficient funds in the relevant budget to allow for incurring any legal costs.

Finding solicitors

Many companies will already have solicitors so the question of how to find one is not relevant. However, this is not always the case. The legal profession in England and Wales is divided between solicitors and barristers. Barristers, in general terms, have rights of audience in court, though audience rights are increasingly being given to solicitors known as solicitor advocates. Traditional sources of free legal advice such as the Citizens Advice Bureau, the Law Centre and the Legal Aid scheme are unlikely to be available to companies. However, trade associations and other professional bodies may be able to provide at least first line legal advice.

It is important to pick a firm which has experience in the relevant field. The best way to find a solicitor is on personal recommendation from a colleague or a competitor who has already used the firm in connection with the same type of matter. Some solicitors advertise their expertise, but advertisements should always be treated with caution. Firms which give public lectures and seminars or produce newsletters in connection with a particular area of law are likely to have some experience in that area. Solicitors may be members of professional interest groups such as the Society for Computers and the Law or the Solicitors European Group, Institute of Export or Licensing Executives Society. There are a number of legal directories which contain some quasi-independent listings of solicitors' practices according to specialisations including the Chambers and partners' directory, *The Legal Profession* edited by Michael Chambers, published annually. It contains full details of specialisations and commentary on solicitors' practices and names individuals who are expert in this field (tel. 0171 606 2266).

Engaging a solicitor

Having ascertained the names of several practices which might be suitable for giving advice, a choice needs to be made. A pre-instruction meeting is sensible. If little legal work is likely to be placed with that firm, it is unlikely to be worth either parties' while to hold a pre-instruction meeting of this sort. Questions to ask any firm include what experience the firm has, what other clients they represent in the same field, how they work in practice, which individual within the firm would do the work and what the cost is likely to be.

Fees

Most solicitors principally charge in accordance with the time spent on the matter; but obtaining estimates or even binding quotations is sensible to ensure that costs are kept under control.

Appointing solicitors

Solicitors should tell clients the name and status of the person responsible for the day-to-day conduct of a matter and the 'principal', (that is the partner) responsible for its overall supervision. The Law Society also recommends that a letter be sent to a new client summarising their relationship or 'retainer'. This letter will typically set out:

- Who is responsible for the work and the partner in overall charge.
- Details of how fees are calculated, perhaps including an estimate.
- Whether any money is required in advance on account of costs, when bills are rendered and when payment is expected.
- To whom any complaints should be directed.
- The nature of the work to be undertaken.

Where a solicitor does not despatch such a letter, it is advisable to request that he or she does so. Where no such letter is forthcoming even after a request, there is no reason why the client cannot write to the solicitor setting out some of the terms and describing the work which the parties have agreed will be done. Such a letter lessens the opportunity for misunderstanding and failure of communication which are responsible for most disputes with solicitors.

How to work effectively with solicitors

Although many solicitors offer practical commercial advice, because of their legal training and the requirements of their profession, they need to be concerned with detail. It is therefore important to appreciate this point and set out as much information as possible in writing which will assist the solicitor. Summaries of the deal which is proposed and lists of the clauses which might be included in a draft contract can be supplied. This not only removes the necessity for the solicitor to make a number of additional enquiries after the original instructions are received, but also ensures that there is a formal record of what is required, ensuring that the document produced adequately reflects the requirements of the client.

Maintaining the balance between close contact and continuing pestering of a solicitor can be difficult. The more time spent on the matter the more expensive it will be to the client, generally; but there is no doubt that regular communication facilitates and speeds transactions and ensures that the solicitor has adequate instructions. Set out clearly the timescale in which tasks should be undertaken, but ensure that this is realistic. If the solicitor suggests that a particular timescale cannot be achieved ask for his or her reasons. It is much better to delay an installation, for example, in order to ensure that a proper contract is in place in advance. Many solicitors are prepared to work overnight and weekends where there is a demonstrable urgency; and with the information technology, fax machines and word-processing facilities which are available in most specialist solicitors' offices these days, advice and communications can be extremely quick.

The extent to which a solicitor is involved is entirely up to the client. Some companies have an extremely limited legal budget and are only able to send the draft contractual documentation to the solicitor, requesting a quick telephone call or fax in response, asking the solicitor to set out any major legal problems. Others will want a thorough job undertaken by the solicitor in producing revisions and improvements to the contract on a regular basis and then request comments on the reaction by the supplier to the amendments proposed. In many cases it can be extremely cost effective, once a contract has been exchanged once or twice between the parties, for the solicitors of both sides and the clients to attend a meeting to agree the difficult legal issues which are outstanding.

A point of contact

In working effectively with solicitors, ensure that one individual within the company – perhaps the company secretary – is the point of contact, with a deputy in case of absences. Where there is no clear point of contact within the company, the solicitor may receive different instructions from different people. One point of contact makes it easier to keep a close check on the amount of time which the solicitor is engaged on the matter, and should also ensure that the company is aware of who within the solicitors' practice is undertaking work on behalf of that client.

Ensuring that one individual is a 'driving force' also has the effect that transactions proceed to completion at a reasonable pace. Although a thorough job may take some weeks, a transaction which takes months or almost a year to negotiate in terms of the contractual documentation will often not be as well done as one that is done in a timescale of weeks where a solicitor is able to concentrate on that one matter. It can be much more expensive for a solicitor to have to familiarise him or herself with the details of a transaction after periods of a month or so when they are not instructed than if the contractual negotiations take place over a relatively short timescale.

The professional relationship should be one of informed trust. Getting on well with the solicitor is obviously important if there is to be a day-to-day personal relationship, and it is important to be honest with the solicitor. There is no advantage in keeping one's legal adviser in the dark in connection with a contract negotiation or dispute. Keeping in touch between transactions also ensures that the solicitor is up to date with developments in the general business of a company and is ready when a new transaction arises. The relationship can also be enhanced by the prompt payment of bills, although bills should always be checked carefully to ensure that any estimates or agreed rates are reflected in the bill or else any discrepancies can be justified.

US companies and their lawyers

Finally, many developments in the USA are often followed in the UK. The US is more advanced in relation to having detailed contractual requirements in place between company and attorney.

Fee agreements

Many US companies have formal fee agreements which they impose on their lawyers. Some UK companies have such agreements already. These deal with issues such as what information must appear on bills, what is the smallest unit of time which can be charged (a tenth of an hour is suggested, with the definite conclusion that a minimum fifteen minute unit, as some US firms have used, is unreasonable), what class of air or rail travel can be used on client business, whether copying is charged in addition and at what rate, what cap, estimate, hourly rate and so on has been agreed, and when rates can be increased.

Sample fee agreements for different types of company are available from Word of the Law, Manchester legal conference organiser (tel. 0161 728 1778).

Litigation guidelines

US lawyers sometimes spend several hours with an in-house lawyer agreeing and estimating how much time would be likely to be spent undertaking particular litigation. Every stage of the litigation is mapped out, described and discussed in detail to test whether the attorney's off-the-cuff estimate is accurate. Litigation management programs are available for different types of companies with in-house law departments of varying sizes from US lawyers and Word of the Law (see above). These would specify requirements such as only one or two named lawyers to work on a particular matter.

Over-manning is regarded in the US as one of the worst billing practices, with lawyers also often spending far too much time on non-specific internal meetings discussing matters with other colleagues which may not be necessary and does not result in any proven product to show that the time was actually spent properly on the client's business.

Beauty contests

In the US, lawyers will be expected to undertake substantial research before attending a pre-instruction meeting and may be paid for their attendance. This is not usual in the UK.

Analysis of legal bills

Analysis of legal bills is also an industry for some US firms dedicated to seeking savings for their clients. Requiring lawyers to specify each item of work each day helps cut out over-billing. Some specialist US firms apply computer programs which will break the bills down into the work done by particular lawyers, so that the main workers on the case can be identified and a full legal audit of bills can be undertaken. Few cases are litigated. Most firms are prepared to settle and reduce bills accordingly. The time and effort required to undertake a formal auditing process of this type is usually not justified where the bill is under $100,000.

Other means of keeping the bills down include requiring monthly billing, which also shows costs to date for a particular piece of litigation, and putting the initials of each lawyer undertaking work on the bill and the hourly rates of all lawyers. Ensuring that where fixed hourly rates are agreed they are complied with is crucial too, particularly where the associate who agreed the fixed rate has left and the new partner taking over the case may not have been briefed on that topic.

Check who is doing the work for a company. In the US paralegals may be used to prepare indices, put papers in binders and undertake, at a reasonably high hourly rate, work which could be done by low grade clerical staff. A rule of thumb was proposed that anyone undertaking work should not be personally paid more than a third of the rate at which they are charged to the client. The example of an auditing report given included the following:

> Paralegal DRC billed 478 hours at the rate of $60.00 per hour for tasks which were primarily secretarial and janitorial. DRC billed a substantial number of hours cleaning a room, organizing documents, filing, indexing, etc. We have reduced DRC's rate to $30.00 per hour to reflect a more reasonable charge for these services. This reduction amounts to $14,340.

If internal photocopying is going to cost too much per page for larger jobs the client should insist it is sent to an outside copying bureau and the fee agreement should specify that no mark up should be allowed for copying. In one reported case a US firm charged a 175% mark-up of over $50,000 for the cost of accessing a legal database for research. Those types of charges should be passed on at cost.

Alternative billing

Alternative billing methods are common in the US too: for example, fixed rates, retainers and use of estimates. Worst US billing abuses include over-manning, mark-ups on telephones, copying and the like, charging more hours than are actually spent, general vague wording on bills ('Reviewing', 'Research', 'Consultation with colleagues' often mask time not properly spent), and not settling litigation early enough. A law firm may, for example, refuse to use new technology which would reduce the time spent by a paralegal sifting through depositions to find references to named individuals, a task which would take, say ten chargeable hours manually and three minutes by computer. Not to use the technology available in such circumstances might amount to professional misconduct. The question of who should pay for and who should own technology purchased for the client's litigation is an issue which should be settled in advance too.

Getting value from professional advisers (Kogan Page, 1993, £12.95) by Catriona Standish deals with many of the issues raised here.

7 Buying and selling through agents

Many companies maximise sale of their products through the use of commercial agents; others use distributors. The distinction is very important and not always properly understood. This chapter considers the commercial law of agency and, in particular, competition law in relation to distribution agreements.

The distinction between agents and distributors

Agents find customers and usually receive a commission on sales. The contract of sale, however, is between the supplier (known as the *principal*) and the customer. The agent never owns the goods. *Distributors* buy goods from suppliers and resell them for their own profit. They take the risk on the transaction. This chapter looks at using agents. These may be purchasing as well as sale agents. Some companies are able to make use of collective purchasing to ensure best prices are achieved.

It is not appropriate in a book on buying and selling law to summarise the whole of the law of agency. There are many excellent legal textbooks available on the subject. English law of agency has developed over the years through the common law. The agent is treated as an organ of the principal and the principal can be bound by the actions of the agent where the agent is given sufficient authority or appears to have such authority (ostensible authority). Other agents are undisclosed agents where the customer does not know of the agency of the agent. There are special categories of agent too where the agent takes the risk of bad debts, known as *del credere* agents and Crown agents.

In practice, the standard commercial agent does not usually fall within any of the special categories above. The agent may be an individual, partnership or company, and their authority will either be set out in a written contract or implied by law under the rules of agency, and, where the agent operates in the European Community under the commercial agents directive. This directive has fundamentally altered the legal

94

relationship between agent and principal and is the main subject matter of this chapter. It was brought into force in the UK from 1 January 1994 and many of its provisions, dealing with issues such as the obligations of the principal and agent and providing for payment of compensation to the agent on termination of the agency agreement or on death or retirement, cannot be altered by any contract term.

The directive

The Commercial Agents (Council Directive) Regulations 1993 (SI 1993/3053) implemented in Great Britain, with effect from 1 January 1994, the EC commercial agents directive 86/653 (OJ 1986 L382/17). There are virtually identical regulations for Northern Ireland, SR 1993 No.483. There are no material differences between the two sets of rules except that the regulations for Northern Ireland came into force on 16 January 1994.

The regulations have been in force in the UK for nearly two years at the date of writing and in that period many companies have stopped using commercial agents. Instead, they have either taken on distributors who do not have rights – in particular, to claim compensation on termination of their agreements – or they use employed representatives whom they can control to a greater extent than agents.

This directive sought to harmonise the law of agency within the EU. Such laws differed widely. Some EU member states compensated agents when the contract was terminated. Others, as in the UK, left the parties in general terms free to determine between themselves the terms and conditions which would apply.

For companies operating in the single market the variety of rules made the appointment of agents difficult. The implementation of the directive has not achieved a single set of rules throughout the EU. The directive did not require that. Indeed it contains several provisions where member states are able to choose alternative provisions which might apply in their own national law, including, in particular in the field of compensation and indemnity.

The original aim, conceived in the 1960s when discussion on this measure began, has therefore not entirely been achieved. However, in broad terms the law is more harmonised than before. Most member states had until 1 January 1990 to implement the directive into national law. Italy was given until 1 January 1993 and UK and Eire until 1 January 1994. In addition, since 1 January 1994 the European Economic Area (EEA) was in existence, linking Austria, Finland, Iceland, Norway and Sweden with the EU. Now Austria, Finland and Sweden have joined the EU from 1 January 1995 and Liechtenstein has joined Norway and Iceland in the

EEA. Virtually all those countries have also implemented the directive, so it provides EEA-wide harmonisation. Switzerland voted by referendum not to join the EEA and has not implemented the directive. This section describes the main provisions of the UK regulations. The position in other EU states is considered later in this chapter.

For each contract or agency proposal it is important that it is first determined whether the regulations apply at all. There is no point in drafting a contract giving the agents rights to which he or she is entitled under the regulations when the regulations do not apply. The agent may be appointed for Australia or may principally be involved in distribution activities or be an agent only for the supply of services.

The Government has slavishly copied the wording of the directive to avoid being sued. The consequence is that all the defects in drafting in the directive have been transferred to the regulations. Little clarification is given.

Which agents are caught?

The directive applies to agents, not distributors. Individuals, partnerships or companies which buy and sell goods on their own account and for their own profit are not covered by the directive. An agent is a self-employed intermediary, a category which can include a corporate agent, who has continuing authority to negotiate, or negotiate and conclude, the sale or purchase of goods on behalf of another person, known as a principal. The following are excluded from the definition of 'agent' in Article 1:

- Agents for the supply of services.
- Unpaid agents.
- Receivers and liquidators.
- Agents operating on commodity exchanges.
- Crown agents for overseas governments.
- Officers of companies or partners entering into commitments on behalf of the company or partnership.
- Where member states so choose, agents whose activities are 'secondary' – a measure which may differ between member states.

Some countries have extended their laws to agents for the supply of services, as well as goods, though not the UK, so it is necessary to consider in each case the relevant national implementing legislation, not just the directive.

There has been some doubt cast on whether the regulations and the directive apply to companies as well as individuals. The definition of *commercial agent* in Article 2 refers to a *self-employed intermediary*, and companies are not generally regarded as being self-employed; however, corporate agents in the rest of the EC have been able to exercise their rights under the directive and the view of the DTI and the European Commission is that the directive applies to corporate agents, so company secretaries should assume that the directive does apply to such agencies for the purposes of drafting agency agreements.

Continuing authority to negotiate

The definition of commercial agent requires that the agent has continuing authority to negotiate the sale or purchase of goods on behalf of the principal, or negotiate and conclude the sale or purchase of goods. It is quite clear that the agent does not have to conclude transactions to be caught. Many agency relationships work by the agent sending leads or requests for supplies of products to the principal.

There has been some debate about what authority the agent needs for the regulations to apply. Many agents have no latitude to vary a fixed price list of the principal and are required to sell goods on the terms and conditions of the principal without variation. Have such agents any authority to negotiate at all? Certainly if one is litigating the issues it would be worth raising this issue, but it is highly likely that the courts would use Euro-type interpretation of the measure and look at the spirit and intention of the directive which the regulations implement. In those circumstances the agent is likely to be held to have such authority simply be virtue of issuing terms to a customer and having the right to bring in sales.

Secondary activities

A schedule to the regulations describes when the activities of an agent are 'secondary' and thus where the agent is outside the regulations. Transactions concluded on one occasion must be likely to lead to further transactions with that customer for the same goods or to other customers in the territory or group of customers to whom the goods are sold. So, one-off agencies for one project, for example, will not bring an agent within the regulations.

Also, the goods concerned must be such that transactions are individually negotiated and concluded on a commercial basis. It is not at all clear what this paragraph means, but since the word "negotiated" is used, it suggests that the agent must have some role in obtaining the sale, making efforts to procure it. It must be in the interests of the principal to develop a market in the goods. The agent should be devoting effort, skill and expenditure from his or her own resources to that end.

What this schedule is really trying to say is that the directive applies to agents who are appointed for the future, for a number of potential transactions, to develop a market in the usual way. There will be cases where lawyers will be able to use the definition of secondary activities to ensure that an agent does not have the benefit of the regulations for unusual projects. A principal may appoint an agent for a large project already identified: 'Go to Glasgow as our agent for the X construction project and buy the materials necessary for the deal'. In that example, there will not be any future sales to customers found.

The regulations list indications of whether the agent's activities are secondary and thus within the regulations or not:

1. The principal is the manufacturer, importer or distributor of the goods.
2. The goods are specifically identified with the principal in the market, rather than with someone else.
3. The agent devotes substantially the whole of his or her time to representative activities for the principal, or for a number of principals whose interests do not conflict.
4. The goods are not normally available in the market in question other than by means of the agent.
5. The arrangement is described as one of commercial agency.

The most useful of these indicators is the factor that an agent who devotes most of his or her time to agency activities will be counted as an agent: hence, an agent who spends most of his or her time on distribution activities is not caught. The activities do not have to be activities within the regulations, so an agent who mostly is a services agent could be caught for a goods contract which amounts to only 1% of his or her activities.

There is also a list of contrary indications:

1. Where the principal or a third party supplies promotional materials direct to potential customers, so the agent is not handing out leaflets etc.
2. Where people are appointed agents without reference to existing agents in a particular area or in relation to a particular group; this is an interesting provision. Many industries operate in this way. Do the regulations apply? It seems unlikely that simply to have non-exclusive agents who service all types of customers renders agencies outside the regulations on this factor alone.

3. Customers normally select goods for themselves and merely place their orders through the agent. There may be an agent who runs a shop. Customers come in and place orders through looking at the principal's catalogue. The agent does no real *selling*.

There is also an exclusion for mail order catalogue agents for consumer goods and consumer credit agents.

In order to benefit from the regulations, agents which also act as distributors may form a separate limited company to ensure that their agency activities are separate and thus covered by the regulations.

Practice tip

Always ask new agents what other activities they undertake at the time the agency is offered and keep a written record of this. Also check what other activities the agent takes on over time: this could prove useful if later the company is trying to maintain that the regulations do not apply to the agent whose activities are secondary. Include provisions in agency agreements requiring the agent to keep the principal informed of other activities. Many principals, keen to ensure the agent does not take on too many other agencies even in non-competing areas, will require the agent to take on no more than, say, six agencies in total and obtain permission from the principal in advance.

Goods and services

In most cases it is clear whether the agent 'sells' goods or services; but this will not always be the case. Services are not covered by the regulations, but a number of other EC states provide that their equivalent statutory provisions apply to agents whether their principal supplies goods or services. Difficult examples include contracts for both goods and services: double glazing installation, for example. Many agents supply goods and services. The courts may look at the proportion of the time, effort and expense incurred on the goods and services elements respectively.

Where the agent supplies a washing machine and then has it plumbed in or a TV and adjusts the aerial the contract is principally for goods. Where the service element is large it is likely that the regulations apply but the compensation payable on termination, for example, might reflect only the termination in relation to the goods element. Case law will have to determine how this area is addressed.

'Goods' is not defined in the regulations, but the DTI, in their guidance notes issued in September 1994 recommend the use of the definition in s61 of the Sale of Goods Act 1979. Contracts of hire are not sale of goods and would not be caught by the regulations.

Computer software

There is some doubt as to whether agents for the supply of computer software, usually supplied by way of a copyright licence rather than a sale of goods transaction, fall within the directive. Where software is supplied on diskette, there is some physical media. Where title in the diskette is transferred, there is a sale of goods. Providing in software contracts that title in the goods is not transferred should assist in arguing that the regulations do not apply. In any event, the goods element (the diskette), is worth about £3, so arguably the compensation should be much less.

Rights and obligations

The directive requires agents to act in good faith, make proper efforts to negotiate transactions and supply necessary information to the principal. The agent should comply with the reasonable instructions of the principal (Article 3 of the directive, Regulation 3 of the regulations). The contract should not derogate from this obligation. It is preferable to set these obligations out in the contract. Not every obligation should necessarily be included in the contract. In practice, the agent may not be aware of his or her rights and including them in the contract simply alerts the agent. However, there should be no merit in including provisions which would be void under the regulations.

The principal similarly must act in good faith, providing 'necessary' documentation and information to the agent, including informing the agent where the volume of transactions is likely to be less than the agent normally would have expected and where a commercial transaction procured by the agent will not be executed (Art. 4, Reg. 4). Both these obligations on principal and agent may not be removed by any contract term.

The obligation of good faith can be quite onerous as it is a very general term and might, for example, result in a principal not being able to delude the agent about any rights to compensation. Giving the agent necessary documentation might be open to dispute. In some contracts the documentation could be referred to. Similarly informing the agent about the expected volume of orders can be hard. Often agents have a better idea than the principal about this, but it is the principal who must inform the agent. Agents often have hugely optimistic expectations so will always be disappointed by the volume of orders.

The principal must inform the agent within a reasonable period of acceptance or refusal of or failure to execute a transaction procured by the agent. The principal may find by a credit check that it cannot supply a potential customer. The agent must now be told. What is a reasonable time is not clear and there may be some merit in setting this out in the contract. This provision cannot be modified in the contract.

Payment

One of the most important commercial issues in any agency agreement is how much commission the agent is paid and when it is payable. Whereas before the agency directive the parties were free to determine these matters themselves, now the law implies certain obligations in this regard. However, some of these provisions can be modified by contract which is a good reason amongst others for having written agency agreements. By Article 6, where the parties to any agency contract have not agreed the remuneration, which in practice would be extremely rare, the agent is entitled to the level of remuneration that agents appointed for such goods would customarily be allowed in the relevant territory. Most agents are paid by commission (that is, a percentage of the net sales which they achieve); however, even where the agent is not paid by commission, the directive may apply. The provisions discussed below concerning the detail of remuneration payable, apply only where the agent is paid by commission.

Commission is payable:

- On transactions concluded through the efforts of the agent.
- On repeat orders (that is, where the agent in the past has acquired a customer for the principal for transactions of the same kind, and that customer places an order again, even where the agent was not instrumental in the placing of the subsequent order.

Member states were given the option in the directive of choosing whether commission would be payable to an agent on all orders from his or her non-exclusive, or his or her exclusive, territory. In the UK Regulations it is provided that where an agent is given an exclusive geographical territory or exclusive group of customers, commission is payable on all orders from such territory or group of customers, even when the customer was not found by the agent. Non-exclusive agents do not have to be paid such commission.

Regulation 7(2) gives the agent a right to commission in any exclusive territory. This provision raises questions about the extent to which it can be modified by agreement. Certain provisions are stated to be unalterable – the parties cannot derogate from them – such as the duties of the parties. Others cannot be derogated from to the detriment of the agent, such as the compensation provisions. Others simply use the word 'shall' – the agent shall be entitled to commission. Does this mean they can be varied by contract? The DTI go into this issue in some depth in their guidance note on the regulations and conclude that probably where there is no proscription of derogation it is permitted. In other words the contract can change the provision unless the regulations say it cannot. This makes sense.

One example is when commission is due. This regulation contains provisions some of which cannot be derogated from and one other which uses the word 'shall'. It is the view of the writer that each provision should be looked at separately, but that in general terms the 'shall' provisions could be modified by contract.

Commission will also be payable to the agent after termination of the agency contract where the transaction was mainly attributable to the agent's efforts during the period of the contract and the transaction was entered into within a reasonable amount of time after the contract terminated, or where the order reaches the agent or principal before the contract terminated (Art. 8, Reg. 8). What is a reasonable time and what is 'mainly attributable' is not clear. Commission will be shared with a new agent only where this is just and equitable. Such a phrase is likely to lead to litigation. This provision, it seems, can be contracted out of, but it is essential that contracts cover the issue in some way, even if in clearer terms.

Requiring the agent to keep details of when he or she receives orders should assist a principal who is trying to determine to whom commission is payable. Commission is payable after termination where the order is received by either principal or agent before the contract is terminated.

When commission is due and payable

The directive also provides when commission becomes due. This must be at the latest when the third party customer executes their part of the transaction, which presumably means when the customer pays, or where the customer would have done so had the principal executed his or her part of the transaction. Others argue that executing the transaction on the part of the customer could mean ordering the goods or taking possession of them: this is much earlier than when payment is made and has a major impact on the commission arrangements for many agents throughout the country. Commission must be paid no later than the last day of the month following the quarter in which it became due. These provisions cannot be modified to the detriment of the agent.

The right to commission is extinguished where it is established that the contract will not be executed (that is, where the customer refuses to pay), *unless the principal is to blame*. The agent can be obliged to return commission in those circumstances. Where the principal has supplied substandard goods and the customer refuses to pay, it would be unlawful to require the agent to repay commission where the principal is 'to blame' for the defects in the goods supplied.

There is much doubt about certain commission issues in the regulations: for example, must the principal pay commission before he or she is paid? Regulation 10 states that commission is payable at the earliest of where the principal has executed his or her part of the transaction – that is, sent the goods – where the principal should have or where the third party has executed the transaction. This suggests that the agent must be paid as soon as the principal has sent the goods – the right to reclaim commission may still arise – as discussed above. However, Regulation 10(2) provides a *latest* date at which commission is payable: when the third party executes the transaction. This probably means when the third party pays (but this could mean when the customer accepts the goods: see above). This contradicts Regulation 10(1). The position is even more complicated by Regulation 10(4) which says that paragraphs 2 and 3 cannot be derogated from, but presumably paragraph 1 can. So the position must be that by contract the parties can provide that the commission is due when the customer pays, not when the principal sends the goods. If there is nothing in the contract, then commission is due when the goods are sent.

Statements

Agents are given the right to be supplied with commission statements and to be sent relevant extracts from the books of the principal to check the commission due. Any contractual provision derogating from these rights will be void.

Conclusion and termination of the agency contract

The most important provisions of the directive are those concerning the termination of the agency agreement. Agents and principals may demand from each other a written document setting out the terms of the agreement. Note that there is no obligation to supply a written statement at all, only on demand; and the principal can demand it from the agent as well as vice versa. Any contract concluded for a fixed period which is operated by the parties *after the contract is over* is treated as a contract for an indefinite term. This makes it crucial to ensure that dates for expiry of agency contracts are clearly noted in diaries and the agreement not extended by oversight, by even one day, after it comes to an end.

Are fixed term contracts better?

Some principals have entered into new fixed term contracts with agents – say for a year – to see how the law develops through case law and to give them a right to be rid of the agent after twelve months. Do they work? A series of one year contracts each renewed may be regarded by the courts as a device to get round the compensation provisions. Such devices are used to ensure that the agent could not claim to have lost commission which he or she would have received had he or she worked until reaching retirement age. It is certainly worth trying this approach, particularly if the principal is really going to assess the agent and his or her performance each year.

In commercial terms it gives the agent less security and allows the principal to negotiate new sales 'targets' each year, though such agreed targets can be written into a contract which is indefinite too. Targets should not be described as such unless the principal does not want the agent to be bound by them. A clear statement that the agent must be responsible for sales of a certain figure, should ensure that if the agent is in breach, the contract can be terminated without a right to compensation. However, such a provision should be treated carefully: see below.

Notice periods

Indefinite contracts may be terminated by at least one month's notice in the first year, two months' in the second and three months' in the third and subsequent years. Member states may specify longer periods, but the UK has followed those periods set out in the directive. The period of notice must coincide with the end of a calendar month. Fixed term contracts can be terminated on any period of notice which the parties agree. This is not always appreciated.

Compensation and indemnity

On termination of the agency contract the agent is entitled to compensation or an indemnity under the Directive. Member states were given the freedom to choose either option and most have chosen to provide that the agent is given the benefit of an indemnity as was seen earlier. The indemnity is payable where the agent has brought the principal new customers or increased the volume of business substantially. Presumably if the agent has done none of these things then an indemnity is not payable. An indemnity is payable only provided that the principal continues to derive substantial benefits from the business with the 'agent's' customers and the payment of an indemnity is equitable.

The indemnity must not exceed one year's commission, averaged over the previous five years. Agents are also allowed to seek damages. No detail on such damages is given. Presumably, if, for example, the agent were not given proper notice under the contract he or she could claim commission which would have been earned during the notice period in addition to benefiting from the indemnity. In the UK an indemnity will be payable only where the contract specifies.

The other alternative is 'compensation' for the damage the agent suffers as a result of the termination. In the UK compensation will generally be payable unless the parties have chosen the indemnity in the agreement. Damage is deemed to occur for the purposes of compensation particularly where the agent is deprived of commission which he or she would have earned but for the termination and/or where the agent has incurred costs and expenses; for example, purchasing a vehicle or computer system to perform the agency contract, on the advice of the principal. To minimise the compensation payable, a clause should be inserted in contracts where a lawyer is advising a principal, restricting the agent from incurring expenses without consent of the principal .

The directive and the regulations do not specify how much compensation will be payable and this will be left to the courts to determine. This statement is of no use to clients, whose principal concern in connection with the regulations is to know what liability they might be responsible for. In Europe payments of a year's commission and more have been ordered, but that is under the indemnity. The DTI have suggested to the writer that the English courts will look to European case law. If that case law relates to the indemnity and not compensatory damages, it is difficult to see how it can be relevant. In May 1996 in *Graham Page v. Combined Shipping and Trading Company Limited* (24.5.96 not yet reported) the Court of Appeal, in the first UK case at that level, held that the directive substantially changed English law and large amounts of compensation would be payable in many cases; several years' commission.

If an agent has his or her contract terminated because the principal wishes to appoint someone else and proper notice is given, what loss has the agent suffered under English law? Arguably nothing, if he or she has incurred no expenses. The contract has been properly performed so the agent has not suffered loss through failure to perform the contract properly. The example is given of an indefinite or, say, five-year contract. The principal gives notice. Had the contract run its term the agent would have earned, say, four years' commission. Is that what the agent receives? There will be the usual obligation to mitigate the loss; that is, get other employment or take on other agencies. There should also be allowance for accelerated receipt; and, with compensatory damages, evidence of how easy or otherwise it is to replace the lost money through other agencies is also relevant.

When compensation/indemnity is payable

There is no obligation to pay the agent compensation or an indemnity. The obligation to pay arises only if the agent makes a claim within one year of termination. Where a claim is made, but not met, the agent would have a cause of action in the national courts for damages, which could result in the principal being obliged to make the payment due. There is no obligation to mention compensation in agency agreements and any clause which limits or excludes the right will be unenforceable where the directive applies. The writer's preference is to leave any mention of compensation out of the contract, unless the client is so concerned about an unquantified cost that it wants the *comfort* of the indemnity, which must be included and can be limited to a year's commission.

Any limit imposed in the contract could be overturned by the courts for compensatory damages, and it is probably unwise to specify that the parties have agreed a certain sum as compensation as a reasonable pre-estimate of their loss in the event of termination, though the DTI suggest this in their guidance note on the regulations.

Compensation/an indemnity is payable where:

1. The agency contract is terminated on notice.
2. The agent dies.
3. The agent terminates the contract on grounds of age, infirmity or illness in consequence of which the agent cannot reasonably be required to continue.
4. The agent terminates the agreement due to circumstances attributable to the principal, for example, this might arise where the principal refuses to pay commission due.

No compensation is payable where:

1. The contract is terminated by the principal for breach of contract by the agent; for example, where the agent fails to meet binding sales targets or deals in competing products when forbidden to do so. The regulations state that compensation [and indemnity (omitted from the first attempt by the DTI to produce the SI: see correcting SI)] are

not payable where, 'the principal has terminated the agency contract because of default attributable to the commercial agent which would justify immediate termination of the agency contract pursuant to Regulation 16 above.' Regulation 16 states that the regulations shall not affect the application of any enactment or rule of law which provides for immediate termination of the agency contract because of the failure of one party to carry out all or part of his (or her) obligations under that contract or where exceptional circumstances arise. Does this mean that an agent in breach of contract does not get compensation?

Under English law the parties may specify any clause, breach of which will entitle the other to terminate. Often one party requires that termination be activated only where there is material breach, but there is no rule of law preventing termination for any sort of breach, however immaterial. The difficulty is that there is no 'rule of law' which allows termination, but just general English law of freedom of contract.

If an agent fails to meet a sales requirement by, say, £2, even if the contract gives a right to terminate, it would be foolish to use that as an excuse to be rid of the agent without paying compensation, because of the uncertainty over whether there is a right of immediate termination. This requirement also means that giving agents a right to remedy remediable breaches is not advisable.

2. The contract is assigned by the agent; that is transferred to another agent. It has been suggested that obliging the agent to assign might avoid the compensation provisions.

If the agent is too ill to perform the duties, where the *principal* terminates for breach of contract no compensation or indemnity is payable, whereas if the *agent* terminates on the grounds of illness compensation/indemnity must be paid. It appears that compensation/indemnity is payable when a fixed term contract expires, rather than terminates, though the directive is unclear. Regulation 19 of the regulations refers to 'expiry' as if it were synonymous with 'terminate'. Where an agent reaches retirement age compensation/indemnity may be payable too where the agent terminates on grounds of age.

Agents can be required to take out life insurance and permanent health insurance at their own expense to protect the principal, as has already been seen, as there is no provision in the directive forbidding such a requirement.

Insurance and death

It is possible to mitigate liability under these rules. There is no problem under the regulations or the directive in requiring an agent to take out insurance cover against his or her own death or liability, and requiring the agent to hold the proceeds payable under such a policy for the benefit of the principal. Some principals may be able to include agents under their group cover which protects employees. The level of cover required is difficult to predict. A year's commission might be a good starting point. The directive requires that agents be entitled to compensation or an indemnity on death.

It is very difficult to assess levels of compensation on death. The writer had a case recently under English law where the executors of an agent had written to the client claiming compensation. In jurisdictions where the indemnity provisions apply, the agent is compensated for the goodwill and clientele which he or she has built up over the years and from which the principal continues to derive substantial benefits. This is fixed at a maximum of a year's commission averaged over the previous five years. However, the indemnity provisions will *not* apply in the UK unless the contract says so.

This means that the alternative basis for compensation applies: compensatory damages for the damage the agent has suffered through termination of the agreement. Leaving aside the issue of whether a 'termination' of the contract has occurred at all where the agent dies, the issue then is what loss has been suffered. If anything, the loss has been suffered by the principal not the agent. There must be an argument under English law that no compensation is payable on death where the indemnity provisions do not apply. Damage is deemed to occur for the purposes of compensation under the regulations, particularly where the agent is deprived of commission which proper performance of the agency agreement would have procured for him or her.

However, the UK regulations in paragraph 17(8) refer to compensation being payable on death and refer to the contract being terminated as a result of the death of the agent. In practice, the writer has had to draft contracts to cover death, particularly in relation to agents who operate in partnership. If one agent dies the other can carry on and perhaps, if the contract allows it, take on a new partner. It is probably the case, though not yet settled in any court decision, that if only one of two partners who are agents dies then 'the agent' as a whole is not dead, and the compensation provisions do not apply. There may be many other provisions, however, that the company wants to include to cover such circumstances. For example, if one partner does the selling and the other the accounts, the principal may not want the 'dormant' partner to have the right to take over the agency.

Even more interesting considerations occur when death is applied to a corporate agent. The DTI take the view that death of an agent cannot be equated with a limited company going into liquidation. The rights of corporate agents are even harder to assess under the UK Regulations because, looking forward at the commission of which the corporate agent has been deprived through termination of the agreement, there is no limit to the number of years over which period the agent might have continued to earn commission had the contract carried on.

Where the agent has died it is difficult to see where the principal has failed properly to perform the contract and thus how the compensatory damages could be calculated. On the other hand, in jurisdictions where an indemnity is payable, then on death the agent is effectively being paid for the asset of goodwill which he or she has built up over the years.

It would be difficult to insure against liability where the agent is simply *dismissed*, because the amount of compensatory damages are much harder to assess. Insurance can be effected against an agent falling ill. The directive gives agents rights to claim compensation or an indemnity (depending on national law) where the agent terminates the contract because he or she is too old or ill reasonably to be expected to carry on with his or her duties.

Other means of mitigating the effects of the directive

The ability to insure an agent's life or health can ensure that principals reduce some of the risks they run in using agents. However, it is not possible to insure against having to pay compensation to an agent whose contract is terminated. Many UK businesses are still not aware that there is an obligation to pay compensation to agents even when proper notice has been given under the contract and the terms of the contract followed to the letter. The compensatory damages provisions are similar to UK unfair dismissal payments. If an employee's contract is terminated and no notice of termination is given, the agent can claim the wages he or she would have earned in the notice period under common law – wrongful dismissal. It is under such provisions that directors with fixed term contracts (usually between two and five years) are able to claim massive compensation payments in the high profile cases reported in the newspapers. In addition, where the employee is not in breach of contract unfair dismissal damages may have to be paid (limited to about £11,000 for employees under English law, unless there is sex discrimination in which case there is no limit on the size of claim if the employee can prove the relevant loss).

The directive's provisions are similar. This means that a company wishing to cease to use an agent simply because the agent is 'making too much money in commission', or where the agent is simply not very good but is not so poor that there is a breach of contract justifying immediate termination, will find it is liable to make a compensation payment to an agent.

To reduce this risk it is crucial to have written agency agreements which contain clear obligations on the agent, breach of which justifies termination without compensation. Most important amongst such obligations would be minimum sales requirements; not unclear 'targets' which both parties hope the agent will meet, but a legal requirement for the agent to generate turnover of a particular level, a failure in relation to which entitles the company to terminate the agreement for breach of contract without being required to pay compensation.

In addition, companies should ensure that they always give the period of notice required by the relevant national law to terminate the agreement. Any agent in their second year of an agency is entitled throughout the EU to at least three months' notice which must end at the end of a calendar month unless the contract says otherwise, so notice given on, say, 2 January 1996 would have to expire on 30 April 1996.

Agents may not contract out of their rights under agency agreements. Clauses which the writer has seen such as 'The Commercial Agents (Council Directive) Regulations 1993 do not apply to this agreement' are pointless and wholly ineffective. The law is quite clear that compensation cannot be removed. However, the DTI suggest that a genuine pre-estimate of the losses the agent might incur could be included in a contract as payment on termination. However, the problem with such an approach is that if, in fact, the agent's losses are higher he or she could later go to court for more. It is probably better in the UK to make no reference to compensation in contracts. That simply draws the attention of the agent to the provisions. Instead simply wait for claims, if any, to be made. There is no obligation to make payments until a claim is made and the claim must be made within twelve months of termination.

Agents can contract out of their entitlement once the agreement is over so an agent could be offered a cheque of, say, three months' commission, provided he or she signs a waiver of all future claims once the contract is over.

The writer's firm has advised many companies and agents under the directive in the UK (Singletons, tel. 0181 864 0835, fax 0181 248 3810, e-mail essingleton@link.org). There is no doubt that careful drafting of agency agreements can reduce the risks for companies under the directive. All companies contemplating terminating an agent's contract should consider seeking advice in the local law to which the contract is subject.

Which option is best?

The advantage of the indemnity, which will apply only where the contracts specifies, is that there is a limit, whereas compensatory damages have no statutory limit. However, in practice, compensatory damages are likely to result in smaller awards anyway, as the damages are to compensate the agent for commission he or she would otherwise have earned were the contract properly performed, or to recover costs and expenses incurred. The difficulty is that in the absence of case law it is hard to estimate what damages might be paid. In May 1996 only one case in the Court of Appeal had been heard, so little guidance is available. Under the indemnity the agent can claim 'damages' too, so on balance it is probably preferable not to opt for the indemnity.

There is no requirement to refer to compensation in agreements, and any attempt to limit the agent's claims will be void where the regulations apply. If the indemnity is desired, the contract must make a reference to this. Neither an indemnity nor compensation has to be paid unless the agent makes a claim. Agents have twelve months in which to make a claim.

Restraint of trade clauses

Finally, the regulations provide (Reg. 20) that restraint of trade clauses will be valid only where they last for no more than two years after the end of the agency agreement, and relate only to the geographical area or group of customers entrusted to the agent and to the type of goods covered under the agreement. The directive applies to restraint of trade clauses only after the expiry of the contract. A clause restricting the agent from carrying competing products, or indeed any other products, is unaffected by the directive. However, such clauses need to accord with national restraint of trade and competition law (both EC and national) in the relevant jurisdiction.

Action

Companies using agents should:

- Revise existing agency contracts to comply with the new law.
- Consider replacing agents with distributors or employed representatives, though 'sacking' agents now could leave companies open to compensation claims.
- Consider requiring agents to take out life and health insurance policies.
- Take advice before terminating agency contracts.

Implementation abroad

In practice, it is essential for UK companies to look beyond English law. Many agency agreements relate to other territories and issues of jurisdiction and choice of law can be crucial. The summary below of implementation of the directive and what the position is on compensating agents and distributors in those territories is a reasonably up to date description, but local law advice should always be sought and an English lawyer cannot summarise all foreign laws in depth without experience of the relevant jurisdiction. The principal provisions of English law in connection with distribution agreements, however, are addressed in the next chapter.

Member states

Austria

Since 1 January 1993 the Trade Agents Act 1992 has implemented the directive in Austria. It provides for an indemnity payment with compensation limited to one year's commission, but it is not clear when compensation might be payable to a distributor as well as an agent for loss of clientele.

Belgium

The Belgian government compensates agents by way of an indemnity rather than by compensatory damages. In addition, under Belgian law an indemnity must be paid to distributors on termination of·distribution agreements.

Denmark

Since 4 May 1990 the directive has been in force in Denmark and an indemnity must be paid to an agent on termination of the contract for loss of goodwill or clientele. Distribution agreements should not be terminated on less than six months' notice. An indemnity must be given to distributors where they have acted for at least ten years and their arrangement is terminated.

Finland

On 1 November 1992 Finland implemented the directive by its Act on commercial representatives and salesmen. On termination of the contract, compensation is payable for loss of goodwill which must not exceed one year's commission. For distribution agreements, compensation is not payable on termination.

France
The French have chosen the indemnity option for loss of goodwill and clientele (though the DTI guidance note on the UK Regulations refers to one category of French agents receiving compensation). There is generally no compensation for distributors on termination of agreements.

Germany
Since 1 January 1990 the directive has been implemented in Germany. The Germans were instrumental in getting the directive in place and it largely mirrors German law of agency. Agents may claim an indemnity on termination of their agreement. There is case law to the effect that distributors, where they are very close in their relationship with the supplier, may have to be paid compensation on termination of the arrangement in Germany, but not otherwise.

German law was the model for the agency directive and some assistance in construing the more obscure provisions of the directive can be obtained by examining the German commercial code that deals with these issues. There have been many cases under German law and payments of compensation to Germany agents have applied since the 1900s. In assessing payments, the courts look at whether the agent has substantially increased the business of the principal and whether new business has been brought in by the agent or whether the agent has simply serviced customers of the principal who were not recruited by him or her.

Under German law, if an agent's contract is terminated and the agent continues to service the same customers but for a new principal then the agent is barred from claiming compensation because the agent cannot argue he or she has suffered any loss of customer base if he or she has taken all the customers with him or with her. If an agent has immediately replaced one agency with another, under English law it will be hard for the agent to show what loss he or she has suffered: this is similar to these provisions of German law.

Under German law, the courts try to assess, in assessing any damages payment on termination, how much longer an agency agreement would have continued but for the termination by the principal. Often the German courts look at a four-year projection or what the agent would have earned had the contract continued. If the agent has worked for a lengthy period of time for the principal, this is likely to result in more compensation being payable. Many agents are able to claim up to three years' commission under German case law. German law allows for a discount because of early payment: in other words, if the agent is paid three years' commission at once as compensation, this will be reduced to take account of the fact that the agent has received the money ahead of when he or she would otherwise have earned it.

If part of the payments to the agent are not for obtaining new customers, but simply for administrative tasks involving no risk, that element of the commission is not taken into account under German law in assessing compensation. However, any attempt in contracts to load commission on to this element unfairly, out of proportion to the time the agent will spend on such tasks, will be ineffective.

English lawyers have had considerable difficulties in interpreting the obscure wording in the UK Regulations and the directive, particularly in relation to compensation and have looked abroad – particularly to Germany – for guidance. However, the German rules refer to the indemnity provisions which do not usually apply in the UK, so the assistance available from foreign case law is limited.

One useful point required by some German companies, is to require a new agent taking over from an old to make a lump sum payment which is then used to pay the indemnity due to the old agent under the directive. In such a manner the principal is able to avoid having to fund the compensation payment itself.

Greece
Greece implemented the directive by law PD219/1991. An indemnity may be payable on termination of the agency arrangement. Recent decisions have resulted in some distributors being paid compensation for recovery of expenses, such as purchase of stock.

Ireland
Eire implemented the directive by SI 1994 No.33 and so is similar to English law.

Italy
Italy's legislative decree No. 303 of 10 September 1991 implemented the directive. It provides for payment of an indemnity on termination. Generally there is no right to compensation on termination of a distribution agreement unless the contract says so.

Luxembourg
It seems that Luxembourg has not yet implemented the directive and no compensation under existing law is payable on termination of a distribution or agency agreement.

The Netherlands
The Netherlands implemented the directive by statute on 5 July 1989:

Staatsblad 312 provides for an indemnity on termination of an agency agreement. There are no rights to compensation for distributors.

Portugal
Portugal has implemented the directive by decree – Law No. 118/93 – in April 1993, and amended its laws so that an indemnity for loss of clientele is payable. This is no longer payable where the contract is terminated through the fault of the agent, which was the case before the directive was implemented. A distributor may also be entitled to a client indemnity.

Spain
Spain's law 12/1992 of 27 May implements the directive and provides for an indemnity for loss of clientele or for compensation by way of damages instead, where the contract was for an indefinite period. It is understood that the Spanish law applies to agents for the supply of *services* as well as for goods, whereas the directive requires that the new law be applied to agents only for the supply of goods. There is nothing, legally, to stop member states having extended laws applying to types of agents not covered by the directive. This makes it all the more necessary to check the local law position in each case. There may be circumstances where a distributor will also obtain compensation.

Sweden
On 1 January 1992 Sweden's Act on commercial agency implemented the directive. An indemnity is payable for loss of goodwill and clientele on termination of an agency agreement. Generally a distributor is not entitled to compensation on termination.

EFTA (European Free Trade Association) countries

Norway
The Norwegian Act on commercial agency came into force on 1 January 1993 and implements the Commercial Agents directive in Norway. In certain circumstances, agents are entitled to an indemnity on termination of the agreement, but distributors are entitled to compensation only where the supplier has been negligent. There is a duty to mitigate loss, as there will be in many other jurisdictions.

Switzerland
As already mentioned, Switzerland has not joined the EEA (European Economic Area) nor has it implemented the directive. An agent may be entitled to an indemnity under Swiss law for loss of clientele where

various conditions are satisfied. On termination of a distribution agreement in Switzerland, there is generally no right to compensation where proper notice has been given.

This whistle-stop tour of EC agency law cannot summarise fully the laws in those other jurisdictions. *Commercial agency and distribution agreements: Law and practice in the member states of the EC and EFTA*, Graham and Trotman (2nd edn, 1993, £95) provides a more detailed account, written by lawyers in the relevant territories.

Do other laws matter?

There are two separate major issues to consider with each non-UK agency agreement: choice of law and jurisdiction. The best starting point is the UK implementing regulations themselves. Regulation 2(5) provides that the regulations do not extend to Northern Ireland.

More importantly the UK Regulations apply only 'in relation to activities of commercial agents in Great Britain' (Reg. 1(2)). A UK company appointing an agent for France would not be subject to the UK Regulations. Regulation 1(3) states that the regulations do not apply 'where the parties have agreed that the agency contract is to be governed by the law of another member state'. Notice that this does not provide that the regulations do not apply where any other law is chosen, only the laws of another member state. The DTI guidelines on the regulations obtainable from the DTI) go into this topic and other areas in depth.

Examples assist in interpreting this provision. UK company A appoints a UK individual to be its agent in south London. It stipulates English law in the contract. The regulations obviously apply. May company A choose the laws of some other country, where there is no right to compensation, to avoid the new law? The answer is 'no' although this may make it harder for the agent to make a claim and an impoverished agent may not have the funds to argue issues of choice of law in court.

It would not work for the same reason that UK companies appointing agents for European Countries under English law agency agreements have over the years had to pay large amounts of compensation. It is not that the choice of law clause is inapplicable. It is that national courts, when litigating these issues or even just enforcing a judgement under the Brussels Convention on Jurisdiction and Enforcement of Judgements, have regard to matters of public policy. Paying compensation to agents, or enforcing competition law, are regarded as matters of public policy which cannot be avoided by judicious choice of law. In this area note the effect of the *Chiron v. Organon* patent decision at the end of 1993, where s44 of the Patents Act 1977 (outlawing *tying* clauses in patent licences) was held to apply, even though the parties had chosen the law of the state of New Jersey.

Company A appoints an agent for France. They choose English law. The principal suspects that the English courts would pay less in compensatory damages under the UK Regulations than the French courts would pay by way of an indemnity under the French provisions. Are the regulations avoided? Regulation 1(2) states that the regulations govern the relations of the parties as to the activities of the agent in GB. The parties have not chosen French law, but the UK provisions appear not to apply. In practice, if the agent sued in France the French courts would regard their agency law as a public policy issue and, despite the English law choice of law provision, apply the French rights. It, therefore, seems difficult to exploit national differences throughout the EC in the way the legislation has been implemented.

Company A appoints a French or even UK agent and chooses French or German law to apply. The UK Regulations would not apply, but the French or German laws would, even where the agent is operating in the UK.

Company B is a US corporation. All its contracts are subject to the laws of the State of New York. It appoints a UK agent to operate in the UK. The regulations will still apply as this law is not that of another member state. In the same way, companies could not appoint employees in the UK under the laws of some unregulated state to avoid the requirement to pay compensation where an employee is wrongfully or unfairly dismissed.

The examples given above are relatively straightforward. Recent examples on which the writer has been asked advice include an instance where an agent appointed by a German company carried out agency activities in three jurisdictions – where three sets of implementing regulations applied. There was no written contract and the agent was a limited company earning £1m per annum in commission. The first issue was which country's laws applied. This was very material to the case. Under German law the agent appeared to be entitled to a year's commission under the indemnity provisions of the directive. *In the UK the indemnity provisions virtually never apply.* They apply only if the contract says so and few contracts contain such provisions. Under English, Scottish and Northern Ireland law compensation for termination would be by way of compensatory damages.

If there is no choice of law in a contract then the position is more complicated and the courts will look at with which state the closest connection exists. In the example given above, the agent carried on his activities in various countries without a written agreement. In practice, there may be advantages in having separate contracts for separate EU states, particularly where there are such differences between the bases for compensation under the implementing laws made by different states under the regulations.

Local law advice

It can thus be seen that carefully drafted provisions in contracts with agents can be swept aside by national laws. Companies do not like to have to pay for lawyers in various jurisdictions to vet their agreements, but it can save money later, and, before terminating an agency agreement where the agent is appointed under non-English law or where the agent operates in another country, local law advice should be sought.

Timing

The UK Regulations apply to all contracts, not only to those made after 1 January 1994 (for the UK). There are no transitional provisions, and clauses will be implied into contracts which are not amended to reflect the law.

Previous position

Finally, a short summary of the previous position under English law is useful in setting the regulations in context. English freedom of contract principles have entitled companies to determine freely the terms and conditions which they wish to impose on agents. It was down to the parties to agree what period of notice, for example, should be given to an agent on termination of the agreement; and termination could lawfully be effected simply by giving the notice, even where the agent was not at fault.

Agents could be hired and fired at will, without any requirement to set the terms out in writing. The only circumstances in which an agent might claim compensation would be where he or she was not given the period of notice set out in the agreement. If no period of notice was specified, the agent was entitled to *reasonable notice* which would depend on the length of time the agent had worked for that principal, and all the other circumstances. There were no rights to claim compensation for the goodwill which the agent had built up for the principal over the years: the agent had been paid commission for this, and that was his or her reward. The new regulations sweep that approach aside, interfering substantially with the freedom of contract principles which served British business so well.

In practice, they have to some extent backfired on agents. In theory the position of agents is vastly improved: they are protected and cannot be dismissed without good reason. However, many companies simply dismissed their agents before the regulations came into force and either took on employed representatives, who are not covered by the regulations, or used distributors. Large companies can afford to do this; others cannot.

Termination in anticipation of the law's coming into effect

Some companies were sufficiently prepared to terminate agency agreements well in advance of the new law. Those agents had no rights to claim compensation under English law. Agents dismissed right at the end of 1993 may have had claims to compensation. Even if the courts hold that the *dismissal* took effect before the new rules came in, where the agent was not given the proper period of notice of termination, and had he or she been given proper notice, the contract would have been terminated after 1 January 1994, the English courts, under English law agency agreements will compensate an agent for lost rights to which he or she would have been entitled had a proper period of notice been given.

8 Distribution agreements

This chapter looks at formalised buying and selling of goods under a distribution agreement. Companies which buy and sell goods from each other on a one-off basis will not need a distribution agreement. The terms and conditions of sale or purchase of one or other party will be sufficient. However, where one party intends to supply products exclusively to one dealer or require the dealer to purchase all its requirements of such products from the purchaser then a formal distribution agreement is needed. There is no English distribution law as such: parties are free to set the terms they wish. This chapter, therefore, concentrates on commercial, rather than legal issues, and the EU competition rules which have a substantial impact on agreements of this type.

Commercial issues

This section addresses some of the commercial points to look out for in drafting a distribution agreement. Every company secretary will have different commercial requirements in practice, so the issues raised here are not necessarily exhaustive. In addition, within the EU the competition rules in Article 85 have a substantial impact and these are addressed separately below in the latter part of this chapter.

Parties

The contract should make it clear who is contracting. It is almost always the supplier who prepares a distribution agreement, but there is no legal requirement that this be the case. (Chapter 5, above, sets out some of the advantages in obtaining control of documents by being responsible for production of the first draft.) If an individual is contracting, ensure that his or her personal name as well as his or her trading name appears. Where a company is concerned, it is safest to include the registered number as well as the full address. Where the distributor is abroad it may not be clear what the legal status of the company is and for important contracts an appropriate company search or other investigation by local lawyers or agents should be undertaken, as mentioned above. No matter how well a contract has been drafted, if the other party cannot be traced, substantial legal problems can arise.

Some suppliers require that the distributor nominate an agent for service of proceedings in the UK and that can be very useful in practice if litigation follows, although it is not always practical. Always consider whether, where a small company is concerned, the individual who owns the company should also sign the agreement and therefore be contractually bound by its terms; whether a parent company should be involved; or whether there should be some sort of guarantee.

Dating the agreement

The agreement should be dated when the last party signs and that will be the date when it comes into force. Agreements should not be back-dated, although it is permitted to specify a date within the agreement from which the provisions will take effect; for example, this might be a month in advance, by which time the parties will have sorted out various other arrangements. Whenever there is a reference to a 'year of the agreement' it should be clear from when that period runs and whether a calendar year is intended. Some individuals, in drafting contracts of this sort, prefer both parties to add a date when they sign the contract. The advantage of this is that it makes it clear when the agreement was signed. Some distribution agreements are despatched abroad and never signed or returned. It is important to ensure that the distributor returns a signed copy. It can, however, be confusing if there are a number of dates on the agreement, adding a date by each party on signature is not the writer's preferred practice.

Another issue to consider is whether the distribution agreement should be by way of letter or a more formal contract document. Legally there is very little difference provided the distributor returns and countersigns the letter. Many companies operate by way of letters. An agreement is probably more straightforward and there is a greater chance that both parties will sign it. It can be better if a representative of the supplier travels abroad with the agreement to the distributor for signature (if commercially he or she can justify such a trip), ensuring that the distributor has had the opportunity to look at the agreement in advance, so that all parties can sign it simultaneously.

Definitions

There is little to say about definitions except that exactly what products are to be distributed should be clear, particularly if there are exclusivity obligations or if commercial restrictions are to be imposed in relation to those products. Some companies, to avoid claims for compensation on termination, simply reserve a right to withdraw some of the products which the distributor is entitled to sell, thus ensuring that the contract continues and no compensation claim can be made, but removing most of its commercial effect from the distributor. Such arrangements have yet to be tested in the English courts.

If the distributor is given a territory in which to operate, this should be clearly set out in the contract. Including a map where boundaries are fluid can assist. Some countries have quite lucrative islands which are arguably within their geographical scope and it should be set out whether the definition of a territory covers such peripheral areas. For example, there may be significant duty free sales of alcohol in various outposts of the old empires. Are they within the territory or not?

Appointment

It is surprising in practice how many commercial agreements omit the principal operative clause, such as 'A appoints B as its distributor' or 'A agrees to provide services to B'. It is wise to have a number of sub-provisions describing any restrictions on the extent of the parties' activities – such as that the supplier will not make sales into the territory or will not appoint other distributors there – rather than putting all the provisions in one clause. The reason for this is that if a judge is severing void provisions, which may well occur in connection with distribution agreements which infringe the EU competition rules, it can be advantageous that provisions are in separate clauses. Also it is not enough simply to say that the agreement is exclusive as the definition of this term is not always clear to individuals operating an agreement. Most company secretaries will know that 'exclusive' means to the exclusion of everyone including the supplier and 'sole' means that the distributor will be the only distributor in the relevant area, but the supplier may compete with the distributor. However, it is much better to define the meaning in the agreement.

Saying that the company agrees to supply the products for re-sale within the territory only to the distributor and, also (if the agreement is exclusive) that the company agrees not to supply the products for use in the territory should ensure that it is clear what is intended. Competition issues are very relevant in the EU (see below).

Terms of business

It is good practice to attach at the back of the distribution agreement the current version of the supplier's terms and conditions of sale and not repeat in the agreement all those conditions about, for example, retention of title in the goods until payment is made and whether a delivery is FOB or CIF (see Chapter 3, above). It is then possible to provide that it will be the terms and conditions of the supplier from time to time which apply. This gives the supplier the flexibility to update the conditions without having to obtain the permission of each of its distributors.

Statements about the conditions prevailing over any conditions of the distributor should also be included in the agreement to help with the so-called 'battle of the forms' when it may not be clear whose terms apply.

It should be clear at what prices the products are supplied, perhaps listing prices which could be varied over time. This is an obvious commercial point which requires little additional elaboration. Suppliers usually reserve the right to increase prices on a fixed period of notice, and the contract should address issues of currency fluctuation, value added or other sales taxes, any relevant double tax treaties between two jurisdictions which have an impact on whether the distributor must pay net of tax, interest on late payment, if any. The distributor must not be told his or her resale prices in the EU as this will infringe Article 85 though generally *recommended* prices are allowed provided that they do not become a de facto minimum price. From a competition law point of view it can be wise to say that the distributor is free to fix its own prices in the EU. The parties need to decide whether payment will be by letter of credit or other means. Often banks reject letters of credit if they are not entirely correct. The supplier may include a term in the distribution agreement stating that the distributor must pay the costs, including bank charges, associated with such errors. Payment by letter of credit removes the risk that the payment will not be made, particularly if it is clear that the letter of credit must be irrevocable. However, this means of payment cannot always be agreed.

The contract should state which of the Incoterms are relevant, such as ex works or DDP. Incoterms are a convenient shorthand means of incorporating conditions into the contract, and deal with issues such as who is responsible for shipment and by what means, who insures the goods and who pays any delivery charges. They are considered in Chapter 3, above.

It is wise to provide that the supplier is not obliged to accept any one order. This will protect the supplier where the distributor puts in an extremely large order which cannot be met, although a requirement to supply forecasts should to some extent overcome the commercial concern behind proposing such a provision. *Forecasts* are crucial to the proper working of the distribution agreement. In practice, contracts vary as to the extent to which a distributor is held to his or her forecasts. Many exclusive contracts require the distributor to place a *minimum* order each year.

The requirement for the distributor to send regular forecasts in writing, in the format approved by the supplier, should be as detailed as the supplier can achieve. Some suppliers require such information to be sent electronically or on disk and require the dealer to use computer software compatible with the requirements of the supplier. The distributor could also be required to send regular information on the state of the local market and its proposals for *advertising and promotion* in the territory.

Obligations of the distributor

What the distributor's role will be will depend on the commercial terms which the parties have agreed. Obviously if the company secretary is not involved with the detail of how the distributor will operate, he or she needs to have instructions from the manager responsible for arranging the appointment. It is dangerous to draw up a distribution agreement, however standard, without reference to the particular facts. The distributor may be obliged to purchase its requirements of the products exclusively from the company and undertake sales promotions. They may be required to advertise or may have some assistance from the supplier in this respect. They may be required to attend trade fairs. Much depends on the nature of the products. It is assumed here that the product concerned is quite clearly goods. However, this is not always the case. In *computer software* distribution agreements there will be a licence of copyright to the distributor who is given a right to grant sub-licences to users and other special concerns. Where the distributor will be combining the software with other software or hardware in a *VAR* (value added reseller) or *OEM* (original equipment manufacturer) type agreement, additional contractual provisions are required addressing issues such as quality, the terms and limits of what is licensed, and the extent to which the software distributor is entitled to decompile software to write interoperable programs. In the EU under the software directive very limited rights to decompile to write interoperable programs apply, and legal advice should be sought before exercising this decompilation right.

Where the distributor is to undertake some processing or incorporation of the goods into other goods before reselling them, other issues apply. The exemption from the competition rules for exclusive distribution and exclusive purchasing agreements will not apply, so fewer restrictions are permitted in such contracts, though only in relation to the EU. The supplier may want quality control provisions to ensure that any finished product incorporating the goods sold is to a standard which will reflect the quality of the supplier's original product, particularly if the supplier's trade mark will appear on the goods.

A restriction on the distributor warranting the products or offering any representation in connection with them should also be included in case the distributor makes untrue statements which result in the manufacturer being sued.

A distributor can be obliged to keep stocks of the products to meet demand in the territory, and to take a full range of the products offered by the supplier. Requirements concerning distributors employing qualified sales personnel and whether the distributor can in any way subcontract his or her obligations should also be included. Suppliers should ensure that the distributor does not incur any liability on the part of the supplier and there should be a restriction on the distributor holding itself out as agent of the supplier.

The distributor should be responsible for dealing with export and import controls, customs duties and any regulatory requirements, depending on the nature of the products and which Incoterms (see above) are used. Licences may need to be obtained from statutory bodies and the distributor should notify the supplier of any infringements of intellectual property rights of which it becomes aware.

The contract should make it clear whether or not the distributor provides any after sales or guarantee service and that depends on the nature of the products. An interaction with the supplier's warranty, if any, in relation to the goods should also be ensured here.

A restriction on the distributor supplying outside the territory should not be imposed in the EU or EEA, but the distributor can be restricted from soliciting customers outside the territory. A restriction on the distributor selling the products to people outside the EU and EEA may be acceptable, provided there is no possibility of those goods working their way back into the EU/EEA. The distributor can also be restricted from dealing in competing products (see the competition law section below).

Obligations of the supplier

The obligations of the supplier are largely a matter of common sense and much depends on the nature of the products and the commercial position of the parties. The supplier may give advertising material or assist with advertising or trade fairs, agree to spend a certain amount on advertising generally and perhaps train the employees of the distributor. The supplier may reimburse the distributor its costs of providing guarantee services to customers, though this is by no means universally agreed.

Intellectual property rights

There should be a statement that all intellectual property rights in the products remain the property of the supplier and, as mentioned above, it is useful if the distributor is obliged to notify the supplier of any infringements and assist in that litigation at the supplier's expense. There should be no restriction on the distributor challenging the validity of the intellectual property rights: such a ban is forbidden under EU competition law. Such restrictions are usually void under Article 85.

If the distributor is given a right to apply a trade mark, it is sensible to ensure that the supplier's trade mark is registered in the country of export (the distributor could be required to pay for such registration) and that the licence granted to the distributor is registered too with the relevant trade marks registry. The contract should state that the distributor will not acquire any goodwill in the trade marks of the supplier, and that it will not register the trade marks in its own name in the territory.

The extent to which the distributor may use the trade name in advertising of the supplier should be addressed too. Some suppliers will want to vet all advertising material which the distributor proposes to use.

Confidentiality

Some distributors will receive no confidential information, so it is probably satisfactory to rely on the general obligations under common law of confidence. However, where the distributor is to be supplied information, whether it is secret technical or financial or other information, a clause restricting use and disclosure should be imposed which will survive the termination of the agreement. There may be technical product information and secret knowhow imparted to the distributor, and express confidentiality provisions should be included into any contract. Where a prospective distributor is shown secret information in advance of a contract being signed, the distributor should be required to sign a deed of confidentiality in advance. Without a confidentiality obligation there is no means of protecting ideas. Copyright protects only the *expression* of an idea (such as in a literary work, a product specification etc.) not the idea itself.

Exclusion and limitation of liability

Not everyone includes exclusion of limitation and liability clauses in distribution contracts, but when acting for a supplier it is recommended. The clause should be in block letters, in particular excluding all indirect and consequential loss and loss of profit and other liability which the supplier might suffer through the operation of the agreement or the sale by the distributor of the products. This can be backed up by an indemnity from the distributor to the supplier against all the losses, costs and expenses including legal fees of the supplier incurred through the operation by the distributor of the agreement. There should also be a general limit of liability making sure that the provision complies with the Unfair Contract Terms Act 1977 for the UK. This provision should, like confidentiality, be expressed to survive the termination of the agreement. There is more detail on exclusion clauses and the law regulating these in Chapter 5, above.

Termination

Many distributors are appointed for a fixed term. The term may continue after the contract is over until terminated by notice in writing by either party. If the distributor is in breach or liquidation, the contract can be terminated. Under English law there is no reason why a distributor should be paid compensation when the agreement is simply terminated on notice, but this is not always the case in other EU countries.

Even where the contract is specified to be under English law, it can be necessary to pay compensation to a distributor on termination. In the drafting stage there is little that can be done to assist with this except to have the contract vetted by a local lawyer to ensure that the right period of notice of termination is expressed in the contract. It may be necessary to specify a slightly longer period for termination on notice than might otherwise have been included and commercially negotiated between the parties for particular countries. Some countries may require a period of four months.

The consequences of termination, such as what happens to orders that have already been placed and to stocks of the products, should be well spelt out. A supplier may want to have a right to buy back stocks of the products; and it might be wise to include an express agreement that no compensation will be payable for loss of profits or loss of goodwill arising from termination of the agreement.

Some distributors will also perform a servicing role in relation to the products. There may be independent servicing contracts in place between the distributor and customers in the territory, or if the distributor is supplying software there may be sub-licence contracts in place for continuing licensing to customers. The contract between the supplier and the distributor may provide that the distributor is obliged to ensure that such contracts are assignable and that if the distribution agreement terminates, the contracts with customers are assigned or transferred either to the supplier or to a new distributor.

Other clauses

A *force majeure* provision could be included. In the decision of the European Court of Justice – *Anbord Baine Co-operative Limited and Compagnie Inter-Agra SA v. Intervention Board for Agricultural Produce* (EUJ 13.10.93, case reference C-124/92) – it was held that it is normal to expect in dealing with a former Eastern Bloc country or a 'command economy' that the rules for acceptable qualities for butter oil might change, and, therefore, it was not an event of *force majeure* that such change did occur even though it was completely outside the hands of the original supplier. This case illustrates the importance of setting out in the contract what is a *force majeure* event rather than leaving it to the vagaries of a court decision.

Whether the agreement can be assigned should be specified; how notices are to be given should appear, as should the choice of law and jurisdiction. Provisions about waiver, severance (important from a competition law point of view), the entire agreement and whether other existing agreements are terminated by virtue of this one could all usefully be included.

Other laws: EU competition law

Most of the points mentioned above are commercial issues to consider in drafting distribution agreements and they will be relevant throughout the world whenever a distribution agreement is drawn up. However, for distribution agreements within the EU the competition rules of Article 85 of the Treaty of Rome will also apply. These rules prohibit anti-competitive agreements and render certain restrictions void. In addition, fines of up to 10% of worldwide group turnover can be imposed for infringements; and third parties have a right to sue for damages where they have suffered through the application of a restrictive agreement. Such provisions include exclusivity clauses, export bans, bans on handling competing products and so on. However, many such provisions are common in exclusive distribution, purchasing and franchise agreements. For that reason, the European Commission issued general exemptions for certain types of such agreements. These regulations set out in detail which provisions are exempted by the regulation and which are banned, and close attention to such regulations should be given by any company secretary drawing up such a contract. Indeed, much of the standard wording common today in distribution agreements is taken directly from these block exemption regulations. The provisions will apply wherever the effects of an agreement will be felt within the EU. In cases of doubt, legal advice should be sought from a firm specialising in competition, such as the writer's own (Singletons, tel. 0181 864 0835).

Companies entrusting another entity with the sale of their goods often do so on a non-exclusive basis, in many cases simply under their standard terms and conditions of sale. Even where standard terms are used a restrictive agreement contrary to Article 85 can arise. An example would be where the terms prohibit the export of the goods sold from the EU member state in which the sale was made or which require the distributor to resell the goods on conditions or at prices stipulated by the supplier.

Restrictions in exclusive distribution agreements, where the supplier agrees to refrain from selling in the territory given to the distributor, are capable of exemption under the Commission's block exemption regulation 1983/83, considered below. However, in all distribution agreements restrictions may appear and this section looks at typical restrictions in distribution agreements both under, and outside of, the block exemption.

Where the block exemption does not apply it will be necessary to examine the distribution agreement to determine whether it contains restrictions which infringe Article 85(1). If it does not, there is no need to use the exemption, in any event. If there are restrictions which are exempted in the block exemption (such as a restriction on the dealer handling competing goods or soliciting sales outside the territory), the agreement may be modified to remove the restrictions or may be notified to the Commission for individual exemption.

When drafting a distribution agreement which does not benefit from block exemption protection it is wise to draft the clauses as close to the provisions of the exemption as possible.

In drafting or negotiating a distribution agreement where there is a potential effect on interstate trade, or in drafting terms and conditions of supply of goods or services, the clauses considered below may infringe EU competition law: the most frequently appearing restrictions found in agreements of this sort are discussed.

Exclusive territory

A restriction on a supplier not to sell in the exclusive territory granted to the distributor has been held by the Commission to infringe Article 85. However, where there are no other provisions which have the effect of giving the distributor absolute territorial protection, some decisions of the court suggest that such a restriction on the supplier would not infringe Article 85. In practice, many exclusive distribution agreements fall within the block exemption regulation for distribution agreements.

Where this regulation applies, a restriction that a supplier will sell goods for resale only to one other company in the whole of the EU or a defined area of the EU is exempted from Article 85. The exemption applies only where the goods are sold to the other party for resale.

This point illustrates immediately one of the most frequent problems in attempting to apply these block exemptions – that many agreements do not fall neatly within their terms. Some purchasers will be using the goods purchased merely as a component in some other product which may or may not be resold. Where there is substantial manufacturing, there will be no resale and the exemption will not apply.

Proposed changes to the law

In 1995 the DTI undertook a limited consultation exercise in connection with the EU competition rules and Article 85, because the distribution block exemption regulation expires on 31 December 1997. The Commission announced in October 1996 that the regulations in this field would be extended to 31 December 1999 and it was not clear whether the Commission's Green Paper in this area would emerge in 1996 or 1997. For further information contact the DTI (tel. 0171 215 6815, fax 0171 215 6726).

Notice on the regulations

The Commission has issued a notice explaining the application of the exclusive purchasing and distribution block exemptions (published at OJ 1984 C101/2, obtainable from HMSO (tel. 0171 873 0011) and reproduced as an Appendix to this book). Resale does not occur where the goods are transformed or processed into other goods or where the purchaser uses or consumes the goods in manufacturing other goods: 'The criterion is that the goods distributed by the reseller are the same as those the other party has supplied to him for that purpose'. The purchaser is able to break up and package the goods in smaller quantities and still fall within the block exemption definition of resale.

Another difficulty with the exemption is that it applies only to goods or agreements where the charge for goods is higher than any service charge. This means that in a mixed goods and services agreement, where the charge for services is high, the parties cannot benefit from the block exemption, and if restrictions are to be included then an individual notification for clearance/exemption is necessary.

Where the block exemption does not apply, as in cases of this type, the agreement should mirror the provisions in the block exemption as far as possible to minimise the risk of infringing EU competition law; and a notification for exemption can be made to the Commission or a commercial risk taken of infringement of Article 85.

Under the distribution block exemption regulation the *only* restriction which can be imposed on the supplier is to supply the goods for resale only to the distributor in the territory granted under the agreement. If the agreement contains any other restrictions on the supplier of the type caught by Article 85, protection under the block exemption will not be available. The supplier may reserve to himself or herself the right to serve certain end users in the territory without losing the benefit of the block exemption.

Export bans

A ban on a distributor exporting goods outside his or her territory will almost always have an effect on trade between EU member states. Export bans of this sort are regarded as one of the worst forms of anti-competitive practice by the Commission and should be avoided.

The leading European Court of Justice case of *Consten and Grundig* (Case C-56, 58/64, [1966] EUR 299, [1966] CMLR 418), decided in July 1966, established that an exclusive distribution agreement which gives the distributor absolute territorial protection will infringe Article 85. It will only be in rare cases that an exemption under Article 85(3) will be granted by the Commission for an agreement containing an export ban. Fines are often levied by the Commission for export bans and companies need to consider the risks carefully before imposing an absolute ban.

The distribution block exemption allows a restriction on the distributor seeking customers, establishing a branch or maintaining a distribution depot outside the territory in relation to the contract products. The distributor can, thus, be restricted from advertising and soliciting sales in territories outside his or her own, but only provided that the goods can be sold in the territory by parallel importers, or users have a real possibility of obtaining the goods outside the territory.

The difficulty which many companies have is that, because single European pricing is not always possible, parallel importation of products continues and can seriously undermine the business of an exclusive distributor.

Export bans imposed on EU distributors restricting sales to non-EU countries may infringe EU law only where there is a possibility that the goods, but for the ban, would have been sold abroad and then re-imported into the EU. Since 1 January 1994 Article 53 of the EEA Agreement has imposed similar laws in relation to EFTA states which have joined the EEA but not the EU (Norway and Liechtenstein). In determining whether or not the goods would have been likely to have been re-imported into the EEA the Commission will look at the following factors:

- Are there customs duties in operation in relation to the type of goods under consideration between the EU/EFTA and the third state?
- Are the goods light and easy to transport, such that if they were exported out of the EU/EFTA they would be likely to find their way back on to the EU/EFTA market?
- Is the country of export geographically distant from the EU/EFTA? An export of books to Australia is unlikely to result in the goods being capable of economic re-import into the EU and still leave a margin of profit for the parallel importer.

Preventing parallel imports: indirect export bans

Most large companies have abandoned express export bans, knowing that these will infringe EU competition law and leave the company at risk of large Commission fines. Many have attempted less obvious methods of preventing parallel imports.

- The best method is to remove the incentive for the parallel importer to operate in the first place, by charging the same price for goods throughout the EU/EFTA. However, this may not always be possible.
- Buying up all parallel imported products which find their way on to the exclusive distributor's market can infringe Article 85, as Konica and Dunlop found to their cost in separate decisions of the European Commission (*Konica*, December 1987, OJ 1987 L78/34 and *Newitt/ Dunlop*, OJ 1992 L131/32). The *Konica* decision was concerned with the sale of Konica film for cameras. The price of film was 20% more in Germany than in the UK. Konica pursued a policy of isolating the German market and preventing UK dealers exporting there. Konica regularly bought Konica film that was on sale in Germany in non-specialist outlets and which had been imported from countries such as the UK. Konica also sent a telex to dealers informing them that

shipments to the UK would be individually coded so that batch numbers could be traced and the companies concerned identified. This was, in fact, a bluff. The Commission found that Konica infringed EU competition law by entering into a commitment with its German dealers to prevent the resale of parallel imported film in Germany and by buying up any such film which entered the German market. It was also an infringement to ban UK dealers from exporting Konica film to the rest of the EU.

- Other methods include monitoring where products are resold. In *Tipp-Ex* (July 1987, OJ 1987 L222/1, [1989] 4 CMLR 425) distributors were required to state to whom goods were resold, and pressure was put upon them not to supply parallel importers. The Commission held that requiring a detailed proof of identity of the final recipients of goods and carrying out post-delivery checks was simply a means of ensuring absolute territorial protection and infringed Article 85.

- Marking products can assist in determining where they are resold and in many cases can be justified on grounds other than attempting to prevent parallel imports. Companies have to mark certain types of products in order to carry out safety checks. Where there is a possibility that there may need to be product recall on safety grounds, being able to identify products by a particular batch number or special mark can be invaluable in effecting the recall. However, where the mark is used simply to prevent parallel imports, it could infringe Article 85. This was held to be the case in the *Newitt/Dunlop* decision, referred to above, concerning methods used to prevent the parallel importation of tennis balls.

- Packaging can be used legitimately to prevent parallel imports. Individual purchasers in EU member states feel comfortable purchasing goods in quantities with which they are familiar, and with instructions in their own language. Suppliers can exploit these national characteristics and, to an extent, lawfully partition the market. Examples include national differences attributable to different temperatures throughout the EU. Products will have to withstand much higher temperatures in Italy than they will in Scotland. Safety instructions will need to be in the language familiar to users.

- Parallel importers often repackage goods to make the products look familiar to users. Such action may involve infringement of trade marks or copyright. Restrictions in a distribution contract on repackaging goods may infringe Article 85 where the repackaging does not affect the original state of the product. In *Bayer Dental* (November 1990, OJ 1990 L351/46, [1992] 4 CMLR 61), a distribution contract provided that the original packaging of the supplier, which carried a registered trade mark, might be supplied to a third party only in unopened form. As this did not make it clear that repackaging would be allowed when this did not interfere with the goods, the Commission held that there was an infringement of Article 85.

- A policy of affording absolute territorial protection through product differentiation is an infringement of Article 85. In *Zera/Montedison* (OJ 1993 L272/28) it was found that the registration in Germany and other EU countries of different formulations of a herbicide was aimed at preventing parallel imports into Germany to protect the exclusive distributor there, and an infringement of Article 85 was found.

- A statement that a guarantee offered for a product will be available only in the country of first purchase will infringe Article 85. Such use of guarantees to prevent parallel imports should therefore be avoided. Guarantees must be available throughout the EU, wherever the goods were first purchased. However, it is permissible for a retailer to offer an additional guarantee for his or her own customers.

In practice, national packaging, quantities and product specifications, combined with zealous enforcement against parallel importers who infringe intellectual property rights, can all assist in cutting down the quantity of parallel imports. Parallel importers are in business to make a quick profit and where such methods are used, they will quickly turn their attention to less difficult targets. The best protection, however, must be single European pricing and many companies are moving quickly to achieve this.

Competing products

Where a distributor is granted an exclusive territory, the supplier will often insist that the distributor does not sell competing products. Even where no exclusivity is granted to the distributor, such a restriction may be imposed. The Commission regard such a restriction as an infringement of Article 85. Therefore, unless the distribution block exemption applies, such clauses should be avoided. If the provision is commercially essential, an individual notification to the Commission should be made for exemption.

Exclusive purchase

A requirement that the distributor purchase his or her requirements for the contract products from the supplier will infringe Article 85, except where the block exemption applies. Under the block exemption such a restriction is exempted.

Restriction on customers

A restriction on a distributor as to the persons to whom he or she may sell the goods will infringe Article 85. Distributors must be free to serve whichever customers they choose within the territory granted to them. In practice, companies often want to divide a market not just geographically (which may be permitted in the limited circumstances set out above) but also by types of customer. For example, a product may have a number of potential markets. There may be the duty free and duty paid markets or specialist shops, department stores and supermarkets or the market served by schools and educational institutions as against the usual retail market. Market division may be on the basis of the applications or fields of use of the products concerned: a food product may be sold to humans and animals.

Selective distribution agreements, where certain outlets only – perhaps meeting quality specifications – are able to provide substantial and essential after-sales services, are discussed later in this chapter; but market division or field of use restrictions will infringe Article 85(1). Only limited market division by geographical territory is allowed under the block exemption. The Commission states in its guidelines to the regulation:

> It would be incompatible with the regulation for the exclusive distributor to be restricted to supplying only certain categories of customers (e.g. specialist retailers) in his contract territory and prohibited from supplying other categories (e.g. department stores), which are supplied by other resellers appointed by the supplier for that purpose.

Many companies wish to impose restrictions on the customers to whom the distributor may sell the goods. The only safe course of action is to notify the Commission of the agreement for a specific exemption. If a patent licence is granted to a company to manufacture the goods, under the block exemption for patent licences the licensee *may* be restricted from selling the finished product outside a stated technical field of use. This is allowed where there is no restriction on the customers who may be served, such as a restriction on sale to a specified class of user.

If there are separate products for different markets, market division by customer may be permitted, provided that the products sold are not the same; for example, one formulation for animals and one for human use.

Companies wishing to restrict sales to particular customers or fields of use may be able to effect changes to the products, which will need to be more than an alteration of the trade mark on the goods, before imposing such restrictions, or consider a specific notification to the Commission.

Price restrictions

Any restriction on a distributor as to the prices at which he or she resells the goods will infringe Article 85. Always exercise caution where proposing to cease supplying a distributor whose retail prices are unacceptable, as a refusal to supply can be held to be a breach of Article 86 which prohibits an abuse of a dominant position. It is lawful to recommend resale prices provided that no measures are taken to enforce the recommended price. In 1995 the UK competition authorities examined the last two remaining forms of resale price maintenance in the UK – book pricing (the Net Book Agreement collapsed) and pricing for resale of pharmaceuticals when the supermarket ASDA began discounting drug prices.

Seeking to influence resale pricing by requiring the distributor to supply details of the prices at which he or she resells the goods is regarded with suspicion by the Commission. For this reason, it is best to avoid price notification requirements in distribution agreements; but if there are no attempts by the supplier to misuse the information to stop parallel imports, divide markets or police resale price maintenance, the obligation will not infringe Article 85. A supplier will always have an influence over the resale price, simply by virtue of setting the price at which the dealer will acquire the goods, but it should be for the dealer to set his or her own margin. Setting the prices charged to a dealer by reference to the supplier's list prices to customers and applying an agreed discount is standard practice in many industries. Where this arrangement is agreed, there should be complete freedom for the purchaser to resell the goods at prices other than the list price of the supplier.

Suppliers wishing to maintain a high price for their goods, to preserve their premium image for a product, need to be extremely careful. The European Commission and national competition authorities frequently receive complaints in this area, either from cheap superstore type chains refused supplies or from dealers required to charge prices specified by the supplier.

Setting up a selective distribution system, as discussed later in this chapter, may assist suppliers interested in maintaining retail prices. Another method is simply to appoint *agents* rather than distributors. An agent sells goods on behalf of his or her principal, being paid a percentage commission for his or her efforts. The agent arranges a sale between the supplier and the ultimate purchaser on the prices and terms of the supplier. (Agency agreements were examined in the previous chapter.) Under competition law there is no restriction on an agent being obliged to sell at stipulated prices.

Permitted provisions

Banned restrictions have been considered above. Provisions which would *not* infringe competition law are set out below.

Terms and conditions

Under the distribution block exemption a distributor can be required to resell the goods under trade marks or packed and presented as specified by the supplier. These provisions are unlikely to infringe Article 85. However, the supplier cannot otherwise stipulate the terms and conditions on which the goods will be resold. It is unlikely that a requirement that the dealer exclude liability or offer a particular warranty would amount to a restriction.

Suppliers seeking to require their dealers to use a set of conditions of sale for the dealers' resale of the products should ensure that those conditions do not contain any restrictive measures, such as export bans, and that imposing such terms does not result in resale price maintenance.

Other restrictions

A supplier may impose the following restrictions on a dealer under the block exemption:

- To purchase a complete range of goods.
- To purchase minimum quantities of goods.
- To promote sales by advertising, maintaining a sales network or stock of the products, and to employ staff with specialised or technical training.

Non-application of the block exemption

The block exemption for distribution agreements will not apply where manufacturers of identical or competing goods enter into reciprocal exclusive distribution agreements between themselves for those goods. However, where the turnover of competing manufacturers is under Ecu100m they are permitted to enter into a non-reciprocal distribution agreement. Where the parties' total worldwide group turnover does not exceed Ecu200m *and* their total market shares are 5% or under, the

Commission suggests, in its notice on agreements of minor importance, the competition rules may not apply.

Where users in the territory are able to obtain the contract products only from the distributor and cannot obtain supplies from outside the territory, then the block exemption will not apply. Similarly, the exemption will not apply where one party takes measures to hinder parallel imports. The block exemption applies where an exclusive distributor is appointed for the whole EU or part of the EU. Where a worldwide exclusive licence is granted, excluding the EU the block exemption will not apply, but the agreement may still affect trade between EU member states. It would need to be considered under Article 85.

Exclusive purchasing agreements

Exclusive purchasing agreements are agreements under which a purchaser agrees to purchase supplies of a particular product solely from one source. Such agreements have many features in common with the distribution agreements examined in the previous section. However, they are given separate treatment here because the Commission has issued a separate block exemption for agreements of this sort (Regulation 1984/83). The regulation also addresses the special competition law problems arising in relation to beer supply agreements and service station agreements. Exclusive purchasing agreements deprive the purchaser of the freedom to purchase goods from other sources and, as such, restrict competition. One example of the application of the law in this area arose in the *Mars v. Langnese* (OJ 1993 OJ L183/19, [1994] 4 CMLR 51) case, where suppliers of ice cream seeking to impose exclusive purchasing obligations on retailers were held to have infringed Article 85. The Commission held that exclusive purchasing agreements prevent intra-brand competition as the retailer is constrained from selling competing products. Inter-brand competition is also impeded as any company seeking to set up a new network or to consolidate its existing market position finds it harder to set up an independent distribution structure. In *Langnese-Iglo and Scholler Lebensmittel v Commission* (Cases T-7/93 and 9/93, 8 June 1995) the Commission's decision was upheld, though the Court held that the Commission was not entitled to prohibit Langnese from entering into similar agreements of only five years in length: five-year agreements are permitted under the exclusive purchasing regulation, but not agreements of longer duration.

Many such restrictive agreements exist and the block exemption removes the need for many of them to be individually notified to the Commission.

Exclusive purchase obligation

Under Regulation 1984/83 a supplier may impose a restriction on a purchaser of goods for resale only to purchase such goods from the supplier, a connected company or another company which has been entrusted by the supplier with the supply of the goods. There is no requirement that the purchaser be given a defined geographical territory.

Competing goods

The supplier may be restricted from supplying competing goods in the purchaser's principal sales area and at the purchaser's level of distribution. As no exclusive territory is granted in agreements of this type, the Commission therefore allows protection to the purchaser only at his or her level of supply. The supplier cannot be restricted from supplying goods, say, to wholesalers, where the purchaser operates at retail level. The purchaser may be restrained from manufacturing or distributing competing goods.

Other restrictions

Regulation 1984/83 permits obligations to be imposed on the purchaser (as under the distribution block exemption, considered above) that the purchaser should buy complete ranges of goods; purchase minimum quantities (but only of the goods which are subject to the exclusive purchasing obligation); sell the goods under trade marks of the supplier or packed and presented as specified by the supplier; and take measures to advertise, maintain sales networks and stocks, provide customer and guarantee services and employ trained staff.

There are similar exclusions from the application of the regulation, as under the distribution block exemption, for reciprocal agreements between competitors and non-reciprocal agreements between large competitors.

There are additional grounds on which this regulation will not apply, where exclusive purchasing obligations are imposed for types of goods which are not connected with each other, and also where the agreement lasts for an indefinite period or for a period of more than five years. Agreements for under five years that automatically continue beyond the expiry of the initial term are deemed to be of indefinite duration.

Beer supply agreements

Regulation 1984/83 also exempts certain forms of beer supply agreement. It is common in the brewing industry to sell beer through tied houses. The regulation exempts agreements whereby a purchaser agrees to purchase from a company, a connected company or a company nominated by the supplier, beers (or beers and other drinks) specified in the agreement for resale in premises used for the sale and consumption of drinks and designated in the agreement.

In the leading European Court of Justice case of *Delimitis v. Henniger Bräu* (Case C-234/89, [1991] 1 EUR 935, [1992] 5 CMLR 219) the court had to consider whether the exemption applied where the drinks, in relation to which there was an exclusive purchasing obligation, were not specified in the agreement. The purpose of requiring that drinks be specified is 'to prevent the supplier from unilaterally extending the scope of the exclusive purchasing obligation.' The court held that a contract which refers to a list of products which can be unilaterally altered by the supplier will fall outside the benefit of the block exemption. The offending clause in this case stated that the products were specified in a price list of the brewery and its subsidiaries, as amended from time to time.

This decision illustrates the importance of taking seriously the often detailed requirements for block exemption protection under the various regulations in all areas. To ensure compliance, there can be no substitute for a line-by-line examination of agreements against the relevant block exemption.

In 1992 the Commission issued a notice (OJ 1992 C121/2) setting out the circumstances in which it would regard small breweries as not being caught by the competition rules. The exemption for beer supply agreements, however, is only of relevance to those involved in that industry, so is not considered in detail here. The *Delimitis* case also described how the Commission treats networks of agreements, which, although each agreement may itself be small, are examined as to their overall effect under the competition rules.

Service station agreements

Agreements under which a supplier sells petroleum or petroleum- based motor vehicle fuels for resale in a service station frequently restrict the purchaser from dealing in other companies' products. This type of agreements is known as a petrol solus agreement. Such a restriction will infringe Article 85. Regulation 1984/83 exempts that type of restriction, provided no other goods are tied and the tie does not last longer than a period of ten years. Where the supplier provides the premises to the purchaser, the purchaser may be restricted for the whole period in which the purchaser operates the premises.

Suppliers may impose a restriction on the purchaser not to use lubricants or related petroleum-based products supplied by other undertakings, but only where the supplier has made available to the reseller, or financed, a lubrication bay or other motor vehicle lubricant equipment.

The purchaser may be restricted from advertising goods supplied by other companies at the premises, but only in proportion to the share of such competing goods which the purchaser sells at the premises. The agreement may require that the purchaser has equipment which is supplied by the supplier serviced only by the supplier.

The regulation blacklists a restriction on the purchaser buying other types of products from third parties. The benefit of the block exemption will be lost where, for example, a purchaser is obliged to purchase, say, milk, bread or fresh flowers only from the supplier.

When contemplating entering into any exclusive purchasing agreement, whether for general goods or in the special categories of beer supply or service station agreements, there is no substitute for examining the proposals against Regulation 1984/83 to ensure compliance with EU competition law.

Selective distribution agreements

Selective distribution is the sale of goods through approved outlets only. Sale of the products may require significant technical expertise to enable proper initial advice to be given, or customers may need after sales service. Many products are sold through selective distribution networks to maintain the premium brand image of the product and avoid its sale in discount stores. These agreements have in common a restriction on admission to the dealership network. Only those companies which satisfy certain defined qualitative standards are allowed to become dealers and obtain supplies of the product from the seller.

Selective distribution is common in a wide range of industries, including

- Electrical equipment, such as computers and hi-fi.
- Cosmetics and perfumes.
- Cameras and films.
- Clocks and watches.
- Motor vehicles.

Selective distribution of motor vehicles is addressed by the Commission in a special block exemption in this area, discussed later in this section.

The Commission's attitude to selective distribution has largely been favourable, provided that companies are admitted to the network on objective qualitative criteria. There have been a number of cases where the Commission and European Court of Justice have examined selective distribution agreements under Article 85(1).

Case example

AEG, a German manufacturer of consumer electronic products, notified its selective distribution agreements to the Commission for approval. Dealers were selected on the basis of whether they regularly bought the contract goods for their own account for resale and whether they would undertake to keep a record of serial numbers and not infringe competition law. They also had to satisfy various objective conditions concerning technical competence and the training of staff. The contract goods were not to be supplied to dealers not subject to the selective distribution system. The agreements were approved by the Commission but over the years the Commission received complaints from traders in the consumer electronics sector. The Commission came to believe that AEG was not applying its system in accordance with the agreements and launched raids on AEG's premises. The Commission determined that AEG had discriminated against certain distributors and influenced dealers' resale prices. The aim had been to exclude certain forms of distribution and maintain resale prices.

The court held, in the decision *AEG/Telefunken* (Case 107/82, of October 1983, [1983] EUR 3151, [1984] 3 CMLR 325), that AEG's systematic conduct in the 'improper application' of selective distribution was proved and the fine imposed by the Commission upheld. The court stated:

> It is common ground that agreements constituting a selective system necessarily affect competition in the Common Market. However, it has always been recognised in the case law of the Court that there are legitimate requirements, such as the maintenance of a specialist trade capable of providing specific services as regards high-quality and high-technology products, which may justify a reduction of price competition in favour of competition in relation to factors other than price. *Systems of selective distribution, in so far as they aim at the attainment of a legitimate goal capable of improving competition in relation to factors other than price, therefore constitute an element of competition which is in conformity with Article 85(1)* (emphasis added).

The court went on to state that it is necessary that there is an improvement in competition along these lines. In setting up a selective distribution system or considering the compatibility with EU competition law of an existing system the questions that follow should be answered.

1. What are the products or services concerned? Do those products truly require technical competence on the part of staff or special trade premises, which not all dealers will have? If not, it may be hard to justify a selective distribution system. Perfume manufacturers argue that their product, which is hardly technically complicated, needs to be sold in suitable conditions having the right ambience. Systems which exclude potential dealers on quantitative grounds, as was found to be the case in the *Yves Saint Laurent* decision, (December 1991, OJ 1992 L12/24), will infringe Article 85. Restricting the number of outlets on any grounds except grounds of quality will infringe.
2. What is the basis on which new members of the selective distribution system are chosen? Is this clearly set out? Are the criteria objective? If not, the system is likely to infringe Article 85.
3. Is there any discrimination in choosing new dealers? Are all applicants in the same position treated in the same way?
4. Is the system operated to ensure that dealers sell at resale prices required by the supplier or that only certain forms of distribution are operated? If so, Article 85 will be infringed.
5. Is there competition from other brands? In *Metro II* (Case C-75/84, October 1986, [1986] EUR 3021, [1987] 1 CMLR 118) the court held that a selective distribution system would infringe EU competition law where there was no competition from other brands or competition from products of the same brand sold through other channels.
6. Is the selective distribution system operated in the same way throughout the EU? In *Vichy* (January 1991, OJ 1991 L75/57) the Commission found that cosmetics were sold in France through a number of different types of outlet, while sold outside France only through retail pharmacists operated by a qualified pharmacist. This distinction made it difficult to justify the restriction outside France.

Where there is doubt, a notification to the Commission should be made for individual exemption.

Motor vehicle distribution and servicing agreements

Cars have been treated differently by the Commission in the field of selective distribution. This is an example of competition law being as much a political/policy tool as an objective statutory principle. In this field, the Commission has allowed quantitative restrictions, limiting the number of dealers to a network.

The justification for this favourable treatment is that consumers benefit from a system which provides proper maintenance and repairs. Regulation 1475/95 (OJ 1995 L145/25) of 29 June 1995 (replacing 123/85) grants block exemption protection for motor vehicle distribution and servicing agreements which satisfy the requirements of the regulation.

Franchising

Distribution and service franchises have received favourable treatment by the EU competition authorities. Many sale of goods transactions are effected through franchises. In October 1995 the DTI issued a short booklet on the pros and cons of franchising, called *An introduction to franchising for small firms* which provides some outline information. More detailed books include *Franchising* by John Adams (Butterworths, 3rd edn, 1990), which examines the competition law side of franchising. There are no other special UK legal rules which affect a franchise arrangement, but those drawing up franchise agreements should check whether their agreement is likely to comply with the Code of Ethics of the British Franchise Association, if they intend to apply for membership at a later date.

In the important EU competition law decision of *Pronuptia* ([1986] ECR 353, [1986] 1 CMLR 414), the European Court of Justice had to consider a franchise agreement for wedding dress shops, where the franchisee sought to avoid paying royalties by alleging that the franchise agreement contained restrictions which infringed Article 85. The court determined which typical restrictions in a franchise agreement infringed Article 86. This decision and subsequent cases which looked at franchise agreements in areas such as computer shops, clothes and service franchises led to the formulation of a block exemption for franchise agreements.

The franchise block exemption Regulation 4087/88 (OJ 1988 L359/46), which came into force for ten years on 1 February 1989, allows more restrictive provisions than those permitted under the exclusive distribution and purchasing block exemptions. In some cases, depending on the nature of the restrictions desired, it can be advantageous to distribute goods in the EU through a franchise network for this reason alone.

However, not every distribution network can be dressed up as a franchise. The block exemption defines a franchise as, 'a package of industrial or intellectual property rights relating to trade marks, trade names, shop signs, utility models, designs, copyrights, know-how or patents, to be exploited for the resale of goods or the provision of services to end users.' The agreement must include obligations concerning the use of a common name or shop sign and a uniform presentation of premises and/or means of transport, the passing of know-how from franchisor to franchisee, and continuing provision of technical or commercial assistance by franchisor to franchisee.

The first stage in assessing any franchising type arrangement is to ascertain whether or not it is a franchise within the block exemption. Many distribution arrangements do not contain these requirements for a franchise arrangement. As with other block exemptions, Regulation 4087/88 sets out those provisions or restrictions which are permitted and those which are not. Agreements containing black-listed provisions will not benefit from the block exemption and will infringe Article 85(1). Unless there is a good case for an individual exemption and a notification is made, the parties are at risk of Commission fines and restrictions in their agreements being void.

Permitted restrictions

The *franchisor* may be restricted from granting rights to third parties to exploit the franchise in the territory; from exploiting the franchise itself in the territory or marketing the goods or services the subject matter of the franchise in the territory; and from supplying its goods to third parties in the territory.

The *franchisee* may be restricted from seeking customers outside the territory and from making or selling competing products (except spare parts).

The following provisions are not regarded as restrictive and are thus permitted:

- Minimum objective quality specifications.
- A tie, requiring the franchisee to purchase goods from the franchisee or its nominee, where it is impracticable, owing to the subject matter of the franchise to set objective quality specifications for such goods where purchased from third parties.
- A restriction on competing with the franchisor, which should extend after termination of the agreement only for a reasonable period; in any event, that period must not exceed twelve months after termination.
- Restriction on acquiring an influential financial stake in the capital of a company competing with the franchisor.
- Restrictions on resales to end-users, other franchisees and resellers within manufacturer supplied distribution channels.
- A best endeavours obligation on the franchisee to effect sales, a

minimum range obligation and obligations as to minimum turnover, planning of orders, minimum after-sales support, customer and warranty services.
- A requirement to pay the franchisor a proportion of the advertising revenue.

All these permitted obligations are allowed only in so far as they are necessary to protect the intellectual property rights of the franchisor (principally the franchisor's trade or service mark) or maintain a common identity for the network.

In addition, the franchisee may be obliged to keep know-how confidential after termination of the franchising agreement and grant a licence back to the franchisor of improvements to the technology licensed, though this must be on a non-exclusive basis. Obligations such as those to undertake training, use the franchisor's commercial methods and intellectual property rights and comply with standards for equipment are permitted. Restrictions on the franchisee changing location or assigning the franchise without consent are allowed.

The franchisee must remain free to purchase goods from other franchisees. Where a franchisor requires that a franchisee honour guarantees for goods of the franchisor, such obligation is required to apply in relation to goods supplied by any member of the network or other distributors of the goods who offer a similar guarantee throughout the EU. Franchisees should state that they are independent undertakings.

The following provisions are blacklisted; that is, their appearance in a franchise contract will have the effect that the agreement will not benefit from block exemption protection and thus infringe Article 85.

- Agreements between competitors: companies producing similar competing goods cannot enter into franchise agreements with each other.
- Third-party goods: the franchisee should be free to obtain goods from a third party where they are of similar quality to those supplied by the franchisor, unless it is impracticable to set out objective quality specifications.
- Unjustified ties: a clause will be void which prevents the franchisor from purchasing goods from other persons where the franchisor has not authorised another source, unless the franchisor is merely protecting his or her intellectual property rights or maintaining a common identity for the franchised network.
- Know-how after termination: after termination of the agreement the franchisor must be free to use know-how licensed under the

agreement, provided that it has entered the public domain otherwise than through the action of the franchisee.

- Prices: although the franchisor is allowed to recommend resale prices, the franchisee must remain free to set its own retail prices.
- No-challenge clauses: the franchisee should not be restricted from challenging the franchisor's intellectual property rights. Where there is a challenge, the franchisor is allowed to terminate the agreement. It is, therefore, usual to include a clause in the franchise agreement, providing that if there is a challenge to the intellectual property rights of the franchisor, the franchisor may terminate the agreement.
- Residence of end-users: the franchisee should not be obliged to refuse to supply end users on the grounds of their geographical location.

The Commission has powers to withdraw the benefit of the block exemption; for example, where there is no competition for the goods in a particular part of the EU.

In practice, most industry standard franchise agreements have been drafted to ensure compliance with the block exemption. There is also an opposition procedure in the regulation, under which an agreement which does not contain any of the blacklisted provisions, but which contains additional restrictions to those expressly permitted, may be sent to the Commission. If no response or objection from the Commission is received within six months, the restrictions are exempted from Article 85. The opposition procedure has much to recommend it over full blown notification, where it is usually only after a period of several years that a letter is received from the Commission as to whether or not the agreement notified can be exempted or declared non-infringing; though the Commission is attempting to reduce its backlog of cases.

UK competition law and distribution agreements

The Restrictive Trade Practices Act 1976 applies, in addition to EU competition law though not where the parties' joint UK group turnover is under £20m (since 19 March 1996). This exception does not apply to price restrictions. As with Article 85, provisions offending the Act will be void and third parties have a right to sue for damages. Fines may, however, be levied only where there is contempt of court: that is, after a court order under the Act has been made and there is a subsequent breach of such order. In August 1995 over £8m in fines were levied against seventeen ready-mixed concrete companies, together with fines of up to £20,000 against individual directors for breach of such orders. The 1976 Act should be regarded as equally as important as the EU competition rules. There is an exemption in Schedule 3 paragraph 2 of the 1976

Act for distribution agreements where the only restriction on the supplier is in relation to the supply of goods of the same description and the only restriction on the purchaser is as to the purchase of such goods. So an agreement which restricted the supplier from supplying the contract goods in the distributor's exclusive territory would be exempt, as would a restriction on the distributor buying similar goods from third parties. Any additional restrictions of the type caught by s6 of the Act must not be included, otherwise the exemption cannot be used. In cases of doubt, advice should be sought in advance from the OFT or a competition law solicitor . Details of competition law solicitors regarded as expert in this field can be obtained from the annual *Chambers & partners directory 'The legal profession'* (tel. 0171 606 2266); see under European Union/Competition.

In August 1996 a new UK Competition Bill was published which will abolish the 1976 Act and bring UK law more into line with EU law.

Practice point

From 19 March 1996, by regulations made under the Deregulation and Contracting Out Act 1994, an agreement exempt by an EU competition regulation does not need to be notified under the Restrictive Trade Practices Act 1976. Various free guides on the 1976 Act may be obtained from the OFT (tel. 0171 242 2858).

9 Intellectual property rights

This chapter describes the law of intellectual property rights relevant to those buying and selling goods. Intellectual property rights are: copyright, trade marks, patents, unregistered design rights and design rights, with additional rights in special sectors such as semi-conductor topography rights and plant variety rights. The law relating to such rights is complex and this chapter does not seek to describe the law over the whole of this area. It simply summarises the principal issues which are relevant to those who buy and sell goods.

The following sections provide some practical advice to sellers and buyers on how to ensure rights are properly protected and respected.

Sellers

1. Ensure registerable rights, such as patent and registered designs and trade marks, are properly registered and renewal fees are paid on time in all countries where goods will be sold or are likely to be sold.
2. Ensure written agreements exist with everyone except employees stating who will own works produced for the company. Except for design rights the author of a work owns the rights, not the company paying for or commissioning the work, unless a contract says otherwise.
3. Before beginning sales in another state, check the position on rights there. Does someone else own the rights there? Must a licence be sought from them? Does the state provide no proper protection for such rights such that sales in that area may be commercially suicidal?
4. Place copyright, trade mark and other notices of ownership on goods and their marketing materials as a deterrent to infringers.
5. Take advice on technical and other devices, such as using holograms, to minimise the risk of copying.
6. Follow the EU free movement of goods rules: do not seek to prevent

parallel imports of your own products within the EU or Commission fines may follow.

7. Ensure licence agreements exploiting the rights comply with national and EU competition rules.
8. As far as possible, pass liability to the manufacturer and the purchaser for rights infringement, and back such obligations up with indemnities.
9. Vigorously pursue infringers.

Buyers

1. Check whether the goods infringe the rights of third parties.
2. Ensure contracts deal with intellectual property rights, including issues such as ownership of improvements made by the buyer and what rights there are to modify or repackage goods.
3. The manufacturer should be legally and financially responsible if the buyer is sued for intellectual property infringement. Ensure a written contract says so and have this backed up with an indemnity.
4. Ensure the manufacturer is obliged to litigate against infringers at its expense, to keep registered rights in force and not to assign the rights to a third party.
5. In the contract deal with which party will own any goodwill in the rights and what happens on termination.

Copyright

Copyright is divided into specific descriptions of works under the Copyright, Designs and Patents Act 1988 which is the principal consolidating statute. Works are divided into:
1. Literary, dramatic, musical or artistic works.
2. Sound recordings, films, broadcasts or cable programmes.
3. The typographical arrangement of published editions.

Originality

Literary, dramatic, musical and artistic works will be protected by copyright only where they are original. This does not apply to the other categories of copyright, such as broadcasting rights. In the *Ladbrokes (Football) Limited v. William Hill (Football) Limited* decision ([1964] 1 WLR 273) it was held that 'original' requires 'only that the work should not be copied but should originate from the author'. In order to be protected by copyright, a reasonable amount of effort must have been used by the creator of the work before protection will be available.

Works

To be capable of copyright protection there must be something substantial to the copyright work. One word is unlikely to merit copyright protection and advertising slogans, such as the title of a song 'The Man Who Broke The Bank At Montecarlo', are highly unlikely to be capable of protection by copyright. In *Francis Day & Hunter Limited v. 20th Century Fox Corporation Limited* ([1940] AC 112) it was held that copyright would not be available for such a phrase as that. Names are not entirely without protection, however. Names can be registered as a company name and also, in many cases, as trademarks in their own right and where they are written in a special form. Trade marks are dealt with later in this chapter.

A copyright work does not have to be a literary work showing artistic merit. Copyright protection has been held to apply to all sorts of works such as tables and charts of fairly mundane material.

Ideas and expression

There is no copyright in ideas. If an individual comes up with a very interesting idea for a play and she informs a friend there is nothing she can do to stop that friend using the idea, unless there is some obligation of confidentiality or some contractual agreement to the contrary between those two parties. It is only when the idea has been expressed that copyright protection will apply. The expression does not only have to be in writing. A work might be expressed on a computer program or a compact disc. Works are protected when they are recorded as literary works 'in writing or otherwise'.

Literary works

What is a literary work? It has already been seen it will include not only novels but also computer programs, letters, tables and compilations, balance sheets, mileage charts and directories, as long as they are sufficiently substantial. The name *Exxon* in the *Exxon v. Exxon decision* ([1981] 3 All ER 241) was held not to be capable of protection as an original literary work. It did not convey any information and it was not an instruction. It gave no pleasure and there was no protection for it under copyright.

Dramatic work

Dramatic works include plays, dances and mime.

Musical work

Songs are protected; the tune by protection as a musical work, and the words as a literary work. This illustrates one of the most important points to bear in mind in connection with copyright protection and that is that any particular item may well be protected by a number of different copyrights. The song may be based on a tune which is the copyright of a third person and the songwriter has obtained the permission or licence from a third person to write the song. The original copyright will continue to subsist as well as a new copyright in the new version of the song. The words may be a poem which is the copyright of someone else again.

Artistic works

Artistic works are a particularly interesting category. Under s4(1) they are:

1. A graphic work, photograph, sculpture or collage, irrespective of artistic quality.
2. A work of architecture being a building or a model for a building.
3. A work of artistic craftsmanship.

There is a further definition in s4(2) of what a graphic work is:

1. Any painting, drawing, diagram, map, chart or plan.
2. Any engraving, etching, lithograph, wood cut or similar work.

There is some doubt as to what constitutes a work of 'artistic craftsmanship', but it should be noted that graphic works and photographs, sculptures and collages are protected irrespective of their artistic quality. In the *Merlet v. Mothercare plc* decision ([1986] RPC 113) the Judge held that a cape for a baby called a 'rain cosy' was not a work of 'artistic craftsmanship'. This is an item which would not have fallen in that part of the definition of artistic work as a graphic work, photograph, sculpture or collage, so it would be capable of copyright protection under this category only where it is a work of 'artistic craftsmanship'. The maker of the garment had said that its purpose was to protect the child from the climate and therefore it was not a work of art.

Derivative works

Whilst those are the main areas for protection of copyright works, there are also what are known as 'derivative works'; that is, those which are derived from or based on other original literary, dramatic, musical or artistic works: sound recordings, films, broadcasts or cable programmes.

The definition of sound recordings in the 1988 Act in s5(1):

(a) a recording of sounds, from which the sounds may be reproduced, or
(b) a recording of the whole or any part of a literary, dramatic or musical work, from which sounds reproducing the work or part may be produced, regardless of the medium on which the recording is made or the method by which the sounds are reproduced or produced.

Films are defined as a recording on any medium from which a moving image may by any means be produced.

Under s6 of the 1988 Act a broadcast which is protected by copyright consists of visual images, sounds or other information and is a transmission by means of wireless, telegraphy or visual images. Cable programmes are also protected, the difference being that a transmission is by means of a telecommunications system other than wireless telegraphy – for example, by means of cables laid under the ground.

Typographical arrangement of published editions

The final category of protection is the typographical arrangement of published editions. This simply means the look of a book on a page. Publishers put considerable effort into selecting an appropriate typeface and designing the way the book will appear. Where a book is photocopied not only will there be infringement (assuming that there is no licence of the copyright of the author) but, also, there will be infringement of the typographical arrangement of the publisher. If, instead, someone wrote the book down by hand, there would be copying and infringement simply of the author's copyright, but not of the typographical edition.

Although the general period for copyright protection is now the life of the author plus 70 years (*The Publication Right and Duration of Copyright and Rights In Performances Regulations 1995* extended the period of copyright from the life of the author plus 50 years to the life of the author plus 70 years), this does not apply for all copyrights. For example, the copyright protection for typographical arrangements of published editions is twenty-five years from the end of the year in which the edition was first published.

Ownership of copyright

The first owner of copyright is the author under s11(1) of the 1988 Act. However, literary, dramatic, musical or artistic works which are made by an employee in the course of his or her employment will be owned by the employer unless there is an agreement to the contrary. Time and again companies need to be reminded that it is only works by employees which will be owned by the company employing them. Commissioned works produced by self-employed persons or third party companies will be owned by the company writing the work, not by the person paying for the work. It is an important misconception which appears to be widespread. It has substantial implications in industry and commerce. For example, company A needs a new computer software program and asks company B to write it for them. They do not mention copyright in their agreement. Because there is no agreement to the contrary, copyright will be owned by company B even though company A pays for the work. Companies try to argue that some sort of implied trust arises and that the work is held on trust for the company which is paying, but this is not really the law; and it is much better to have an agreement which makes it clear that copyright will be owned by the company paying for the work where that is commercially acceptable to the writer of the work.

The position is, however, reversed in relation to registered design and design right. Rights in registered designs and design rights are owned by the company commissioning the work, subject to agreement to the contrary. Another difficulty in this area is when is a work produced by an employee 'in the course of his or her employment'? Employment contracts can assist employers by spelling out exactly the duties of the employee, ensuring that they cover the production of copyright works where that is conceivable. However, it will be extremely difficult for a company to say that a secretary who writes a novel in her spare time has produced a copyright work which is owned by her employer. However, if an individual is employed by a publishing company to write books then the copyright will be owned by the company. Not all cases are as clear-cut, however, and detailed consideration should always be given to this issue.

Moral rights

Moral rights were introduced by the 1988 Act. There are four rights.

1. The right to be identified as the author of a work known as the 'paternity right'.
2. The right to object to derogatory treatment of the work, 'the integrity right'.
3. A right not to have a work falsely attributed to a person.
4. A commissioner's right of privacy in relation to a photograph or film made for private and domestic purposes.

The paternity right will not apply unless it is 'asserted'. Many copyright assignments include a standard provision waiving all moral rights.

However, that should not always be acceptable. The writer was recently advising a client who produces drawings, designs and logos for industry who was being asked to assign copyright and was happy to do so. However, it was quite clear that it was important from a business point of view that moral rights be asserted, as there was substantial kudos to be gained for that client from being associated with some of these designs and recognised as the designer. It is, therefore, a matter for commercial negotiation between the parties whether or not moral rights will apply. However, in the absence of any agreement the right to be identified as author must be asserted by the author. There are no moral rights in computer software, although there will be in computer software manuals.

Infringement of copyright

S16(1) of the 1988 Act gives the copyright owner the following exclusive rights:

1. To copy the work.
2. To issue copies of the work to the public.
3. To perform, show or play the work in public.
4. To broadcast the work or include it in a cable programme.
5. To make an adaptation of the work or do any of the above actions in relation to an adaptation.

Infringement of any of these actions is a primary infringement of copyright. The most important infringement will be copying and it is necessary to prove that copying has taken place. This is different from the position under patent law where the registered patent gives a monopoly right and it is not necessary to show that the 'infringer' was aware that the patent was in existence (except for secondary infringement). The courts will look at issues such as how similar the infringing and the original work are, and whether there are features of the allegedly infringing work which are really unnecessary and can only have appeared in the work because it was copied.

Copyright is infringed only where a substantial part of the work is taken. But it is not just a question of the quantity, but also quality. In the *Ravenscroft v. Herbert* decision ([1980] RPC 193) the defendant used the plaintiff's non-fictional work as a source. What had been copied was about 4% of the work of the defendant, but in assessing damages this was rated as 15% in terms of the value of the work.

In addition to the primary infringements of copyright there are secondary infringements too. Secondary infringement is described in ss22 to 26 of the 1988 Act. The work is infringed by someone who imports an infringing work, without consent, otherwise than for private and domestic use. However, the individual undertaking the import must know or have reason to believe that it is an infringing copy. Another category of secondary infringement is where an infringing work is possessed in the course of a business, but, again, the possessor must know or have reason to believe that it is an infringing copy.

Litigation

In advising in a case of infringement of copyright, the first question is to ask whether or not the work is protected by copyright and in what categories. The second question is who owns the copyright. It is surprising how many times it is ascertained on investigation that the copyright is not in fact owned by the client at all, but was written by some third party, or there is a complicated chain of transactions with no proper assignments. Although assignments may be obtained after the event, individuals cannot always be traced.

It is always necessary to obtain evidence of infringement. Frequently, for copyright and indeed other intellectual property right infringement actions, the *Anton Piller* order is used. This enables (sometimes without notice to the other party where it is suspected that evidence will be destroyed) the plaintiff or his or her representatives to enter the defendant's premises and to inspect and remove material. This is to prevent evidence being destroyed. Since the *Thermosensors v. Hibben* decision [1992] 1 WLR 840 it can be necessary to have a supervising solicitor with familiarity with the execution of *Anton Piller* orders present: there have been various practice directions issued clarifying the extent of supervision required.

Once it has been established that there has been copyright infringements, a civil action can be brought for damages, injunctions, an account of profits or otherwise. An account of profits is an alternative to damages for a plaintiff as the infringer may have made a profit which exceeds the value which would be awarded from the usual award of damages. What is looked at is the gain which the defendant has made. Orders may be made for delivery up of the infringing articles.

There are a considerable number of other offences under the 1988 Act including some criminal offences and offences in s107 of the Act concerning articles specifically designed to adapt or make copies.

Exceptions

The defendant may be able to allege that he or she had the licence or consent of the owner to make the copies. That will be a question of fact in each case. In addition, there are some exceptions in the Act known as 'fair dealing'. The fair dealing provisions allow the taking of a fairly substantial part of a copyright work, but not the whole of it, for the purposes of research or private study, criticism, review and reporting of current events. There are exceptions for education, libraries, archives and public administration.

EU law

The EU free movement of goods rules apply to copyright. There is no general exemption under competition law for copyright licences, which means that many licences containing restrictions must be notified to the European Commission.

UK competition law

There is an exemption for certain restrictive types of copyright licence in the Restrictive Trade Practices Act 1976 and few copyright licences are required to be registered under that Act.

Designs

Designs and registered designs are perhaps the Cinderella of intellectual property rights. There is surprising ignorance of what can be quite valuable rights. There are two entirely separate rights one of which is like copyright and the other which is a registered right. These are known as 'design right' and 'registered designs'. Design right was created by the Copyright, Designs and Patents Act 1988. Registered designs in some form have been available since the 1800s.

Designs do not have to be artistically creative. In general terms it is important to remember:

1. Purely functional objects cannot be protected as registered designs, but may attract design right.
2. Registered designs must appeal to the eye and such protection will be available for decorative items.
3. Copyright and patents may also be available in particular cases.

Design right

The unregistered design right arises when a design is made as with copyright. By s213(2) of the 1988 Act a 'design' is defined as 'the design of any aspect of the shape or configuration (whether internal or external) of the whole or part of an article'.

Like copyright, designs must be original, which means they must not be commonplace. A design for a table which consists of an ordinary square top and four legs is unlikely to attract design right. It must be recorded in some tangible form, such as a design document or an article should have been made to the design.

In many cases, designs are registrable as registered designs, but may also attract design right protection. The 1988 Act provides that both types of right might exist: see s224 where it is stated that an assignment of a registered design automatically carries with it an assignment of design right. The overlap with copyright is dealt with in ss236 and 51(2). Where a work, including a design or consisting of a design, is protected by copyright then copyright only will apply, not design right. If an article is made to a design or a copy of an article is made to a design, that design will not infringe the copyright in a design document or a model recording or embodying the design (s51).

Exceptions

Under s213(3) there is no design right in:

(a) Methods or principles of construction.
(b) Features of shape or configuration which:
  (i) enable the article to be connected to, placed in, around or against another article so that either article may perform its function (the 'must fit' exception), or
  (ii) are dependent upon the appearance of another article of which the article is intended by the designer (created by the design) to form an integral part (the 'must match' exception).
(c) Surface decoration.

Design right is available only in relation to designs for a three-dimensional article; not for a design of a T-shirt, for example, which might be protected by registered design. This is one of the main differences between design right and registered designs.

The 'must fit' and 'must match' exceptions are extremely important in industry. The design of an ink cartridge for a fountain pen will be dictated by the shape of the pen itself. Someone manufacturing cartridges without consent from the owner of any rights in the pen will make the cartridges so that they fit into the requisite hole in the pen. There may be other parts of a device, however, which are not made to fit and, therefore, design right protection may still be available. Case law in this field is considered below.

Unregistered design right lasts for fifteen years (see s216 of the 1988 Act).

Registered designs

The legislation in connection with registered designs is contained in the Registered Designs Act 1949. This, however, was substantially amended by the Copyright, Designs and Patents Act 1988 which has at its Schedule 4 a consolidated version of the Act to which reference should always be made. Registered design protection is a right which can only be obtained by applying for a registered design. Design is defined as:

> Features of shape, configuration, patent or ornament applied to an article by any industrial process, being features which in the finished article appeal to and are judged by the eye, but does not include:
> (a)   a method or principle of construction; or
> (b)   [the 'must fit/must match' exceptions seen above].

Designs where they are the same as a design which has already been registered cannot be registered as they will not be regarded as new. In addition, registration is not possible if the appearance of the article is not material. The design must really appeal to the eye, it must have aesthetic qualities.

Ownership

The author of the design will be the owner, but where it is produced pursuant to a commission then the commissioner will own the rights. This is the case with design right too, but not with copyright. Employees making designs in the course of their employment will find that the rights are owned by the employer by s2(1B).

Period of protection

Design right subsists initially for a period of five years from the date of registration (s8). The period can be extended by second, third, fourth and fifth periods of five years (that is a total of twenty-five years), provided the requisite fees are paid. As seen above, unregistered protection lasts for only fifteen years, so registered protection is better where available.

Suing for infringement

The exclusive rights which are given to the owner of a registered design are to make or import for sale or hire or for the use for the purposes of a trade or business or to sell, hire or offer or expose to sale or hire articles in respect of which the design is registered. Anyone who undertakes those activities without permission from the registered proprietor can be sued for infringement of the registered design. However, damages will not be awarded by s9(1) if the defendant can show that he or she was not aware and had no reasonable grounds for supposing that the design was registered. This is why it is important on the design to make some reference to the fact that it is registered.

Exceptions

The exceptions for designs the shape of which is dictated by the fact that they must fit or must match another design has already been considered in connection with design right, and it is the same. There are other exceptions contained in the Registered Designs Rules 1989 by Rule 26. These exclude works of sculpture, wall plaques, medals and medallions and printed matter, primarily of a literary or artistic character. Also excluded are stamps and calendars. These items are all protected by copyright, so the exclusion from registered design protection should not necessarily be a problem.

Licensing rights

Registered designs can be licensed and assigned, although the Designs Registry would need to be informed of the transfer. When drafting licences competition law should always be considered where restrictions are to be imposed on the licensor or the licensee. As with design right, following the provisions of EU competition law in connection with patent and know-how licences minimises the risk of infringing EU competition law.

In the UK the Restrictive Trade Practices Act 1976, Schedule 3 paragraph 5 contains a specific exemption for licences, not only of patents, but also of registered designs and applications for registration of a design. This applies provided that the only restrictions are in relation to paragraph 5(2)(b): 'Articles in respect of which the design is or is proposed to be registered and to which it is to be applied'. In cases of doubt licences should be registered with the OFT on a fail-safe basis before the restrictions take effect.

Some case law: the Ford decision

There have not been many reported cases on design protection. Some of the issues considered above were dealt with in the *Ford* decision. The case concerned registered design applications in the name of Ford and Fiat for the registration of twenty-four designs in total. However, it also concerned the protection for designs which were protected by design right. The companies had sought to obtain registered design protection for doors, fenders, vehicle lamps, instruments and accessory panels, steering wheels and so forth. The judge concluded that door panels were not really articles of commerce, apart from forming part of the vehicle and, therefore, could not obtain registered design protection. This divisional court decision was confirmed by the House of Lords. This decision removes from protection of registration any spare part where an applicant cannot find at least one realistic alternative use for it apart from use as a spare part.

The 'must fit' and 'must match' exceptions were also considered. These apply both to registered and unregistered designs. The judge in this decision regarded a door panel as an integral part of the vehicle. He said that a steering wheel, for example, could be substituted with an alternative wheel of a sportier design but that did not apply to a door panel. Body panels were, therefore, not capable of design right protection. It did not help the car companies concerned that when the Copyright Bill was going through the House of Lords comments were made that this 'must fit/must match' exception was specifically included to ensure that body panels would not obtain protection. Reference to ministerial and Parliamentary statements are now allowed after the leading House of Lords decision in *Pepper v. Hart*. The judge in *Ford/Fiat* held that vehicle lamps could be protected, but not rear lamps.

The relevant questions to ask in assessing whether or not a spare part for a vehicle, or indeed any other object, is capable of registered or unregistered design protection are:

1. Has the article a number of alternative uses?
2. Are there practical alternatives to the design which could be used without substantially altering the appearance of the other article of which this part is a spare?

On 24 March 1994 in *R v. Registered Designs Appeal Tribunal, ex parte Ford Motor Company Ltd* (TLR 9.3.94), the Court of Appeal upheld the earlier court's decision. The judge stated that the issues before the court were (i) whether the motor vehicle parts were *articles* within s1(1) of the 1949 Act and (ii) whether designs for such parts were excluded from registration by s1(1)(b)(ii). The judge referred to s44 of the Act which states that articles includes any part of an article if that part was 'made or sold separately'. Those words were the key.

An article must have an independent life as an article of commerce before being an article for which registered design protection can be obtained under the Act. If it is merely an adjunct to another item, no protection can be obtained. As the other court had said, the judges held that no one would buy a wing of an Escort except to replace a wing on an Escort. There was no trade in such things except for that purpose. On the second issue, designs for motor vehicle parts were excluded from registration under s1(1)(b)(ii). The House of Lords, quoting with approval the *Sifam Electrical Instrument Co Ltd v. Sangamo Weston Ltd* case [1973] RPC 899, said that main body panels, doors, the bonnet lid, the boot lid, the windscreen and the like form part of the shape and appearance of a vehicle and are not registrable. Other parts which are contributing features to the appearance of a vehicle and are subsidiary to its shape (such as wing mirrors, wheels, seats and the steering wheel) can be removed or altered without affecting the overall appearance of a vehicle. The latter can be made and sold separately and thus can be registered as designs. The House of Lords confirmed that the principal test was whether a spare part had an independent life as an article of commerce. The appeal failed and registration of many spare parts is thus not possible under registered design law.

EU law

The law concerning the protection of designs will be harmonised at EU level through the proposed Designs Directive and Regulation (OJ 1994 C29/2 and OJ 1993 C345/9). Those measures would result in a registered Community design which would apply for twenty-five years from the filing date and an unregistered Community design copyright for three years from the date of public disclosure. Rights will be harmonised throughout the EU. This is only a proposal at this stage, but is being taken forward by the Commission amongst intense lobbying from the car and other industries. The final form of the regulation and directive is not yet agreed at the date of writing.

On 12 October 1995 the European Parliament approved a controversial proposal that independent car parts manufacturers should pay a licence fee to car companies in exchange for a right to sell parts for matters such as bumpers, windscreens, lights and wing mirrors. Those items would be protected under the proposed EU designs directive. Car manufacturers would be given a monopoly over visible spare parts. The next stage is for the proposal to return to the European Commission for further work and then approval is needed by the Council of Ministers. The European spare parts industry is worth Ecu40bn a year.

Practical measures to protect designs

Companies involved in the production of design drawings can take practical measures to ensure that their legal position is enhanced if a dispute were to arise in the future:

1. Retain design drawings, date them, have the author sign them, copy them and keep the originals safe.
2. Keep a record of who thought up the ideas for a particular design. Ensure that contracts with both employees and sub-contractors make it clear who owns the rights to designs.
3. Always consider the possibility of design right and other intellectual property right protection when similar competitive products appear on the market. A company may be able to bring infringement proceedings where it holds rights capable of protection, or conversely, may be able to prevent a potential competitor from setting up in business using similar designs, where those designs infringe any design right in the company's products.

Dealing with designs

As with other rights design rights can be assigned. s222(3) requires that assignments should be in writing and signed by or on behalf of the assignor, which is standard for intellectual property rights. Licences can be granted, but by s225 exclusive licences should be in writing and signed by or on behalf of the design right owner.

Trade marks

Company secretaries involved with the buying and selling of goods need some basic knowledge of trade marks law under the Trade Marks Act 1994. The Act replaced the 1938 Act and contains a much broader definition of registered trade marks being 'any sign capable of being represented graphically which is capable of distinguishing goods or services of one undertaking from those of other undertakings'. Trade marks may comprise words, personal names, designs, letters, numerals or the shape of goods or their packaging.

Geographical names may more easily be registered under the new Act if there is evidence of prior use of the mark. They may be refused registration where they have not become sufficiently distinctive as a result of use made of the mark. A mark will not be registered where it is contrary to public policy, accepted principles of morality or would deceive the public – for example, as to the geographical origin of the goods or services.

Packaging

Distinctive packaging can be registered except where it consists exclusively of 'the shape of the goods which results from the nature of the goods themselves'.

Smells, sounds and colours

Colours have long been protected by trade marks and this continues to be the case under the 1994 Act. The 1994 Act also allows registration of sounds and smells which could not be registered as trade marks under the 1938 Act. This has led to a surge in applications for trade marks. Such marks must be capable of representation graphically.

Exploiting trade marks

The 1994 Act makes it clear that trade marks can be licensed and sub-licensed freely, and trade marks may be assigned (transferred outright) without the goodwill of a business and without the requirement to advertise.

Ensuring quality

Companies should still exercise caution in licensing trade marks and ensure the quality of goods produced under their mark. A trade mark indicates a connection in the course of trade of a trader with his or her goods. It is extremely dangerous for companies to allow third parties to use their trade marks without careful control, particularly if there is no agreement between them containing quality control provisions. If a user of a trade mark manufactures shoddy goods under the trade mark of the registered proprietor, members of the public will associate the trade mark proprietor with the production of such goods and its goodwill and business reputation will suffer drastically as a result.

Registered user agreements

Under the Trade Marks Act 1994 licensing of marks is permitted, which may be registered at the Trade Marks Registry. There are no longer many advantages in registering user agreements. Under the Act, use of a trade mark with the consent of the owner counts as 'use' under the Act in order to preserve the registration of the mark from attack for non-use. It is still possible to register licences.

Licences may be granted for all the goods or services for which the mark is registered or some only or for the use of a mark in a particular manner or a particular locality. All licensees, unless restricted by their licence, are given the right to require the licensor to sue an infringer where the matter affects the interests of the licensee, and if no action is taken for two months or more the licensee may bring the proceedings itself.

Quality and other control

There is no legal requirement to control use by a licensee, though commercial requirements make this a sensible procedure:

1. To ensure that the good reputation of the proprietor of the mark is preserved.
2. To ensure that the mark does not become subject to challenge (for example, if it becomes generic).

Registrations

S25 provides for assignments, licences and granting of fixed or floating security interests of trade marks to be registered. Until an application for registration is made, the transaction is ineffective against someone with a conflicting interest in the mark.

Assignments

The Trade Marks Act 1994 simplifies the rules on assignment of trade marks. S24 states that a registered trade mark is transmissible by assignment, testamentary disposition or operation of law 'in the same way as other personal or moveable property. It is so transmissible either in connection with the goodwill of a business or independently.'

Assignments may be partial or total, so it could apply in relation to some but not all of the goods or services for which it is registered or 'in relation to use of the trade mark in a particular manner or a particular locality'. To be valid, assignments must be in writing and signed by or on behalf of the assignor or personal representative. S24(6) provides that nothing in the Act is to be construed as affecting the assignment or other transmission of an unregistered trade mark as part of the goodwill of a business.

Period of registration

The first registration of a trade mark is for ten years (s42). (Previously it was seven years and thereafter for periods of fourteen years.) Registrations can be renewed for further periods of ten years under s43, provided renewal fees are paid.

Infringement and enforcement

The Trade Mark Act 1994 improves rights of owners of trade marks to prevent infringement, including permitting infringement proceedings to be brought where the infringer is using the trade mark in an unrelated area, provided that the trade mark has a reputation in the United Kingdom and the use of the sign, 'being without due cause, takes unfair advantage of, or is detrimental to, the distinctive character or repute of the trade mark'.

It is crucial in each case to determine whether 'use' of the trade mark has occurred and this is defined in s10(4) which provides that a person uses a sign if, in particular, he or she

1. Affixes it to goods or the packaging thereof.
2. Offers or exposes goods for sale, puts them on the market or stocks them for those purposes under the sign, or offers or supplies services under the sign.
3. Imports or exports goods under the sign.
4. Uses the sign on business papers or in advertising.

Someone who applies a registered trade mark to material intended to be used for labelling or packaging goods, as a business paper, or for advertising goods or services, is treated as a party to any use of the material which infringes the registered trade mark if, when he or she applied the mark, he or she knew or had reason to believe that the application of the mark was not duly authorised by the proprietor or a licensee.

The Act makes it clear that nothing prevents the use of a registered trade mark by any person for the purposes of identifying goods or services as those of the proprietor or a licensee; such use must be 'in accordance with honest practices in industrial or commercial matters': and the Act contains detailed provisions for revocation of trade marks, including for non-use over five years.

Offences

Criminal offences are also included in the Act and these are summarised in a Patent Office booklet on the counterfeiting provisions of the Trade Marks Act 1994, available free from the Patent Office.

Community trade mark

Since 1 April 1996 it has been possible to apply for a new right – the Community Trade Mark (CTM) – which provides EU-wide protection and will be cheaper than several national applications. National rights still continue if desired.

Patents

A patent is a registered monopoly right which protects inventions. This section describes the basic protection which is afforded by patents.

What can be patented?

The principal relevant piece of legislation is the Patents Act 1977. S1 allows the patenting of inventions only if:

1. They are new.
2. They involve an inventive step.
3. They are capable of industrial application.
4. They are not excluded by various other provisions of the Act.

Before looking at the concepts of novelty, inventive step and industrial application, it is necessary to consider in each case whether or not an exclusion applies.

Exclusions

No patent is available for an invention which consists of a discovery, scientific theory or mathematical method, a literary, dramatic, musical or artistic work or any other aesthetic creation whatsoever and, a scheme, rule or method of performing a mental act, playing a game or doing business or a program for a computer or the presentation of information. However, some inventions which fall within those defined exclusions may still be capable of patent protection as they are excluded only to the extent that the patent or application for a patent 'relates to that thing as such'. No patent is granted for an invention, publication or exploitation of which would encourage offensive, immoral or anti-social behaviour. Patents are not granted for any variety of animal or plant or any essentially biological process for the production of animals or plants which is not a micro-biological process or the product of such a process.

Novelty

A patent in the UK can be obtained only where the invention is new. It will be new only if it 'does not form part of the state of the art'. The state of the art is defined in s2(2).

> In the case of an invention shall be taken to comprise all matter (whether a product, a process, information about either, or anything else) which has at any time before the priority date of that invention been made available to the public (whether in the United Kingdom or elsewhere) by written or oral description, by use or in any other way.

An important issue here is whether or not the invention is already available to the public. Scientists unaware of the technicalities of intellectual property law often freely publish their inventions to show their colleagues in the industry concerned the advances which they have made. This is usually prejudicial and often fatal to the obtaining of patent protection. In addition, where a third party has put in a patent application before the one under consideration, if the first patent application contains information concerning the invention, that will also prejudice the claim.

What has and has not been published is often an important part of patent infringement actions. The publication does not have to be limited to the United Kingdom. Information is taken to be available to the public where the public can gain access to it on payment of a fee or free of charge (see Sacks L.J. in *General Tyre and Rubber Co v. Firestone Tyre and Rubber Co Limited* [1972] RPC 457).

Those involved in looking for prospective licensees or assignees of their rights to a new invention may need to disclose details of that invention before a patent application has been made: it is essential that a confidentiality agreement is entered into.

Inventive step

In addition to the requirement of novelty, the invention should involve an inventive step, which (by s3) is taken to mean it is 'not obvious to a person skilled in the art, having regard to any matter which forms part of the state of the art'. The state of the art for these purposes is as set out in s2(2) – that the invention has not been made public in the UK or elsewhere. Those words 'not obvious to a person skilled in the art' are important. In assessing an inventive step, publication of other patent applications is not relevant. The test involves taking a 'skilled' worker, not the man in the street. The dictionary meaning of 'obvious' is taken in determining whether such invention will be obvious to such a mythical person (see *General Tyre* above).

When might an invention be obvious? In *Parks-Cramer Co v. G. W. Thornton and Sons Limited* [1966] RPC 407 the judge said it was a question of degree as to whether or not an invention were obvious. Where a problem is known to exist with a particular product which the invention is seeking to solve the question is 'is the solution claimed by the patentee one which would have occurred to everyone of ordinary intelligence and acquaintance with the subject matter of the patent who gave his mind to the problem?' This issue was examined in the *Merrell Dow Pharmaceuticals Inc. and Another v. H N Norton and Co Ltd and v. Penn* cases (House of Lords, 26.10.95: *Times Law Reports*, 27.10.95, p.38).

Industrial application

In order to be capable of patent protection the invention should be capable of industrial application. Patent law is, after all, there to protect inventions which can be used in business. S4(1) states that an invention is taken to be capable of industrial application if it can be made or used in any kind of industry, including agriculture. However, an invention of a method of treatment of a human or an animal by surgery, therapy or diagnosis, practised on a human or animal, is not taken to be capable of industrial application. Specifically, by s4(3), drugs are taken to be capable of industrial application and, therefore, patentable.

These are the principal requirements for the patenting of an invention. Anyone who is involved in the intellectual property field dealing with patents should be familiar with the concepts of novelty, inventive step and industrial application. The next issue is who will own a patent?

Ownership

S7(2)(a) of the 1977 Patents Act provides that it is the inventor who is entitled to the patent. Applications can, however, be made jointly.

Employees
An important related issue here is that concerning inventions made by employees. Although some patents are produced by individuals, most are generated for companies by their employees. The Patents Act 1977 contains provisions in connection with employees in ss39 to 43. S39 sets

out the basic provision that inventions made by an employee will be owned by the employer where they are;

> Made in the course of the normal duties of the employee or in the course of duties falling outside his normal duties, but specifically assigned to him, and the circumstances in each case were such that an invention might reasonably be expected to result from the carrying out of his duties.

There is also an alternative provision that inventions are taken to belong to the employer where,

> The invention was made in the course of the duties of the employee and at the time of making the invention, because of the nature of his duties and the particular responsibilities arising from the nature of his duties, *he had a special obligation to further the interests of the employer's undertaking.*

Any other inventions are taken to belong to the employee.

How do these provisions apply in practice? There is a definition of employee in s130(1). An employee is a person who works (or where the employment has ceased worked) 'under a contract of employment or in employment under or for the purposes of a Government department'. This means that sub-contractors who are used to prepare inventions or freelancers will own their own inventions, unless there is an agreement to the contrary.

Disputes arise in practice over whether an invention which an employee has produced has been produced in the course of his or her normal duties. The security guard of a company, for example, who invents a new drug even when he is employed by a drug company will almost certainly own the patent rights in such invention, as it is not in his normal duties to design a drug. However, if the managing director realises that in his spare time the guard is a scientist of some competence and specifically assigns him, to use the words in s39(1)(a), with the task of preparing that drug, the rights will be owned by the company.

Some employment contracts go into some detail in relation to this provision. The first point in any clause is to define the scope of the normal duties of the employee as broadly as possible so that if he or she does produce a slightly unexpected invention it is easier to allege that the invention is owned by the employer. In addition, the contract can refer to the fact that the employee might be likely to produce inventions.

Even where employees make inventions in the course of their employment and the patent is owned by the employer, employees have a right to *compensation* where the patent is 'of outstanding benefit to the employer' and it is just that compensation should be awarded to the employee (s40). The amount of compensation is that which will secure for the employee a fair share of the benefit which the employer has derived.

Where the invention has always belonged to the employer because it was undertaken by the employee as part of his or her normal duties, the courts look at issues such as the nature of his or her duties and his or her remuneration and other advantages which he or she obtains from this employment. Other factors include the effort and skill which the employee expended in making the invention.

Any term in a contract which diminishes the employee's right to inventions is unenforceable to the extent that it diminishes his or her rights (s42(2)). It is, therefore, extremely important that employment contracts do not contain provisions which are contrary to the provisions in ss39 to 41 of the Patents Act 1977, as described above.

Applying for a patent

Anyone can apply for a patent. There is no requirement to use patent agents, although it is extremely common and cost effective so to do. A number of solicitors' firms have begun to employ patent agents, but on the whole companies will still approach independent patent agents. It would be extremely foolish to attempt to draft a patent application without technical training, although in some jurisdictions – the USA, for example – it is common for specialist lawyers to undertake such activities.

The specification for the patent is the most important document which needs to be submitted as well as the relevant form and fee. The specification will describe the invention and include drawings for illustration purposes. The application is made to the Patent Office for a UK patent and the so called 'priority date' is usually the date from which the application is received by the Patent Office. This is a crucial date as the period for patent protection, which is a twenty-year maximum, runs from the filing date. Applicants then have a period of twelve months in which to file the claims. The claims are a statement which defines the invention. They may contain claims in the alternative. Once this is done, the Patent Office begin their preliminary examination and search. The application is published and a substantive examination is undertaken by the Patent Office.

Litigating patents

The Patents Act 1977 sets out how patents can be infringed and the rights which are given through the granting of a patent. Infringement is defined in s60 and includes selling or importing patented products or using patented processes. This applies where the infringer knows, or a reasonable person would know, that use without the consent of the proprietor would be an infringement of patent.

Under s60(2) it is also an infringement if, while the patent is in force and without the consent of the proprietor, a person supplies or offers to supply in the UK a person other than the licensee with *any of the means, relating to an essential element of the invention, putting the invention into effect when he knows or a reasonable person would know that those means are suitable for putting or are intended to put the invention into effect in the UK.* However, it is not an infringement under s60(2) where there is a supply of a staple commercial product, unless the supply or offer is made for the purpose of inducing the person supplied to do an act which constitutes an infringement of patent.

The first question to consider in each case is whether the patent is for a product or a process and then to carefully go through s60 to see whether infringement can be found. The difficult cases arise where there is not an obvious taking or exact repetition of the invention, but, instead, a slight variation.

Defences

Where faced with a patent infringement action it might be possible to challenge the validity of the patent, alleging that it should be revoked for various reasons, such as that it is 'obvious'. Also the plaintiff may not have paid the patent renewal fees or the patent may have come to the end of its life. The defendant may be able to show that a third party, in fact, owns the rights or that he or she has not undertaken the "infringement" for commercial purposes.

There are also specific exemptions, such as where an act is done for experimental purposes or in relation to certain ships, aircraft or vehicles temporarily in the UK. Another area might be where the rights are said to be 'exhausted' under EU law.

Where to litigate patents

Litigants have a choice of fora in the UK in connection with the litigation of patents. The Patents County Court was set up to provide a cheaper framework than proceedings in the High Court. It was brought in under the Copyright, Designs and Patents Act 1988 and is situated in Wood Green in North London.

This court has the same patent jurisdiction as the High Court with the same powers to grant injunctions, revoke and amend patents and award damages without any financial limit. The most important differences from the High Court are in the procedure to be followed and the wider rights of audience.

The advantages of the court are that patent actions can be brought to trial more quickly and costs are saved. The abolition of automatic discovery cuts down the volume of papers required, again saving on costs. This court is particularly appropriate for smaller patent cases.

There is no upper limit on claims for damages unlike other County Courts and it has jurisdiction throughout England and Wales. There are provisions allowing transfer to the Patents County Court from the High Court and vice versa; and in considering a transfer the issue of the financial position of the parties is particularly important.

The pleadings are particularly detailed in the Patents County Court, requiring the parties to set out their arguments, not just the bare facts, upon which the parties will rely in support of their cases. In infringement proceedings the patentee (that is the owner of the patent) should construe his or her claims alleged to be infringed and explain why the alleged infringement comes within the scope of those claims. Similarly, a party alleging invalidity of a patent should identify, not only the prior art upon which he or she relies, but also the particular parts of the documents relied upon and set out any arguments he or she has in support of obviousness and so on.

There is a limitation on the number of extensions of time which can be sought in a Patents County Court case and most important of all discovery is ordered only where a party can show good cause. Rights of appeal lie directly to the Court of Appeal from the Patents County Court. To date most cases which have been appealed have subsequently been overturned.

Imports and exhaustion of rights

Under s60 of the Patents Act 1977 it is an infringement of a patent to import an article made in infringement of that patent into the UK. However, if the particular goods which are being imported were made by the proprietor of the patent or one of his or her licensees in the EU then the proprietor cannot stop those goods being imported into the UK. The rights are said to be 'exhausted' because there is one single market in the EU and goods should move freely within it.

Case example
The first case in this field was *Centrafarm v. Sterling Drug* ([1974] EUR 1147, [1974] 2 CMLR 480). Sterling Drug owned patents in the UK and the Netherlands and had given permission to use the patents to its

subsidiary company in the UK and the Netherlands. The tradename was 'Negram'. Centrafarm bought Negram in England and imported it into the Netherlands. The price at which the drug sold in England was 50% below that in the Netherlands. Sterling Drug sued for patent infringement in the Netherlands, for infringement of its Dutch patent. The European Court of Justice, which was referred the matter under an Article 177 reference, held that because Article 30 of the Treaty prohibits 'all measures having an equivalent effect to a quantitative restriction on imports' then infringement would fail here.

The rights are exhausted only in connection with the particular products which have been manufactured by the proprietor or with its consent.

Exploitation and licensing of patents

The final subject for consideration in the area of patents is their exploitation. Owners of patents have a right to grant licences of the patents to users who are given the right to manufacture products under the patent. Usually royalties will be charged on such licenses. Exclusive licences should be registered with the Patent Office. Standard provisions in licences would include a careful definition of the rights licensed and the use to which they may be put, together with provisions concerning the royalties which the patentee (the licensor) will earn. There are many other provisions included in patent licences which cannot all be set out here.

EU competition law

It is important that patent licences do not contain any restrictions which infringe competition. In drafting a patent licence it is crucial to consider the technology transfer block exemption of the European Commission regulation, 240/96.

UK competition law

In the UK, the Restrictive Trade Practices Act 1976 applies to agreements between two parties under which two restrictions relating to goods or two relating to services are accepted by two or more parties to the agreement. Many patent licences fall outside the provisions of the Act either because there are restrictions on only one party (such as the licensee), or because there is no restriction on a 'pre-existing liberty'. Under the *Ravenseft* ([1978] QB 52) doctrine it was held that a restriction on a licensee as to an activity which but for the licence he would not have been free to undertake in any event does not comprise a 'restriction' under the Act.

In addition, there is an exemption for licences of patents under Schedule 3 paragraph 5 of the 1976 Act where the only restriction is in respect of 'the invention to which the patent or application for a patent relates or articles made by use of that invention'. Each patent licence must be examined on its merits as against UK competition law legislation, unless it is exempt under EC regulation 240/96.

Of particular importance in the context of patent licensing are the draconian provisions of s44 of the Patents Act 1977. Under these provisions restrictions requiring the licensee to buy raw materials from the licensor will be void, even though such a restriction is allowed under the EU block exemption where such a 'tie' is necessary for a technically satisfactory exploitation of the licensed patent. In addition, under s44(3) there is a complete defence for a third party where such a restrictive provision is enforced. Since it is quite easy to be caught out by s44, companies should always consider it carefully.

Under s45 where a patent licence continues after the patent ceases to be in force, both parties have a right to terminate the licence on three months' notice in writing.

As well as licensing patents, patent rights can be assigned; that is, transferring ownership of the intellectual property rights entirely. The Patents Act requires that assignments should be in writing and, of course, the Patents Registry needs to be informed.

Foreign patents

Patents are a national right. The European Patent Convention, of which the UK is a signatory, permits one application to be made to the EPO office in Munich designating other contracting states in which patent protection is sought. This can save costs, but it does not result in a European Patent – simply a set of national patents.

Conclusion

Since intellectual property rights protect many of the goods sold throughout the UK and abroad, company secretaries need a basic knowledge of the law in this field. Free booklets on the various rights can be obtained from the Patent Office.

Appendix 1

Guidance notes on the use of Model One:

'General Conditions of Contract (for other than Engineering Goods)'

1 **Use**
Use for the **supply and delivery** of raw materials (whether in solid, powder, liquid or gaseous form), packaging materials, office furniture and stationery, and all similar non-engineering goods.

2 **General note on negotiation**
Always specify in the enquiry that it is a condition of the order that these Conditions are to be accepted. If the Seller raises any objections these can then be the basis for negotiation. Avoid attempting to amend Seller's conditions to meet the Buyer's requirements (see Part One, Section 1, pages 13–15).

3 **Definition of requirements**
The following information should be part of any enquiry and/or purchase order:

3.1 Quantity, description and specification (eg British, European, or International, drawing number etc) of goods. Are samples required?

3.2 Delivery date(s); be specific (see Part One Section 5 – Seller's Default).

3.3 Delivery point.

3.4 Terms of payment (see note 4.3).

3.5 Whether price is fixed or subject to a price-adjustment formula (see note 4.3).

3.6 Liquidated damages (if any) (see Part One, Section 5, page 28–29).

3.7   Whether subject to the Buyer's inspection and expediting.

3.8   Delivery programme, where deliveries are phased to production, and dates when any 'free-issue' items will be available.

3.9   Specify any material which is to be of 'free-issue' (see note 4.7).

3.10   Stipulate any restrictions to be imposed on sub-letting (see note 4.6).

3.11   Any special protection, packing or transport requirements.

4   **Notes on certain clauses**
4.1   Clauses 2 and 8 – 'Quality' and 'Acceptance':
It is advisable to specify in detail the materials and the purpose for which the goods are required, eg in the case of a chemical substance, the degree of purity; for moulding powders the temperature and flow characteristics.

4.2   Clause 5 – 'Passing of property and risk to Buyer':
Make the Seller responsible for delivery to the required site; an 'ex works' offer should not normally be agreed. In the latter case property and risk pass to the Buyer when the goods are loaded on transport at the Seller's works. The buyer will not only have to pay for transport but may also find it necessary to arrange special insurance cover against damage or loss in transit. See the provisions of Part One, Section 4, page 24 et seq., with regard to the relationship between the passing of property and stage payments.

4.3   Clause 6 – 'Terms of payment' (see Part One, Section 4, page 22 et seq.)

(a) The terms of payment are generally acceptable to most suppliers. Where different terms are negotiated for specific orders or with particular suppliers such terms must be stated on the Purchase Order.

(b) Although it is recommended practice to obtain a 'fixed price', it may be more economical in the case of long-term contracts to agree to a price subject to a price-adjustment formula. This may work out cheaper than a 'pre-loaded' firm price. When considering price-adjustment formulae it is advisable to opt for a nationally recognised system (see Part One, Section 4, page 24).

4.4   Clause 7 — 'Loss or damage in transit'
It is usual for the Seller to require notification of loss or damage in such a manner as to comply with the carrier's conditions. However, the Buyer is not party to the contract between the Seller and the carrier and cannot therefore reasonably be deemed to know of, or to have accepted, the terms of that contract. The model clause should be acceptable to the majority of suppliers.

4.5   Clause 11 — '*Force majeure*' (see Part One, Section 5.5)

(a) Costs should lie where they fall in the case of cancellation due to *force majeure*. The Buyer should not pay cancellation charges. The Seller should be covered by insurance in respect of consequential losses, eg loss of profits, loss of other contracts, interruption of business, etc., and fire or explosion at Seller's works. Negotiations should therefore be restricted to costs in respect of materials and labour actually expended up to the date of cancellation.

(b) The Seller is not entitled to impose any additional charges in respect of the storage of goods during a *force majeure* situation unless there is provision for such extra charges in the terms of the contract.

(c) Remember, a delivery extension granted under a *force majeure* situation also extends the period before which liquidated damages (if any) are payable.

(d) With regard to the imposition of supply by allocation because of *force majeure* circumstances every endeavour should be made by the Buyer to obtain an assurance from the Seller that all his customers are allocated goods on an equal basis. If any of the goods are being manufactured or processed by the Seller – whether for his own use or for sale – albeit at a reduced rate due to *force majeure*, the imposition of allocations is not itself covered by the definition of *force majeure* since the choice of customer/ user *is* under the Seller's control and at his own discretion.

(e) Where a price is established relative to a given quantity, no variation in that price basis should be allowed if the Buyer is forced to take a reduced quantity due to a declaration of *force majeure*.

4.6 Clause 12 – 'Assignment and sub-letting':
If it is anticipated that the Seller intends to sub-let a significant part of the order then the details must be discussed and agreed with the Seller before the order is placed.

4.7 Clause 16 – 'Free-issue materials':
Where the order provides for a significant amount of free-issue materials consideration should be given to the use of the Special Conditions detailed in Part One Section 7, pages 36–37, to protect the Buyer and allow him to retrieve his material, should Seller find himself in financial difficulties.

4.8 Clause 17 – 'Control of substances hazardous to health'
The Control of Substances Hazardous to Health (COSHH) Regulations 1988, made under the Health and Safety at Work etc., Act 1974, came into force in October 1989. They provide a legal framework for the control of substances hazardous to health in all types of business, including factories, farms, quarries, leisure and service activities, offices and shops. The regulations require employers to make an assessment of all work which is liable to expose any employee to hazardous solids, liquids, dusts, fumes, vapours, gases or micro-organisms. The assessment must include an evaluation of the risks to health and decisions on the action needed to remove or reduce those risks.

Guidance on the type of assessment to be made in relation to particular goods or services, and the method of undertaking the assessment can be obtained by consulting the relevant Health and Safety Executive publications, available from the local office of the HSE.

Failure to comply with the requirements of the regulations can be a criminal offence, and is subject to penalties under the Health and Safety at Work etc. Act 1974. Buyers will wish to ensure therefore that, where it is the Seller's responsibility to do so, all necessary action has been taken in relation to the requirements of the regulations, including the provision of Hazard Data Sheets where these are necessary. The clause as drafted is intended as a model clause, and can be amended as appropriate to the particular circumstances.

Draft Model Clause
Hazardous Goods and Dangerous Substances

Seller shall be responsible for complying with the requirements of COSHH Regulations 1988, and all other relevant UK and International Agreements relating to the packaging, labelling and carriage of hazardous goods, including relevant statutory regulations and codes of practice.

As soon as possible following the agreement of the contract terms all information held or reasonably available to seller regarding any potential hazards known or believed to exist in the transport, handling or use of the materials supplied shall be promptly communicated to the Buyer.

4.9   Clause 18 – 'Packages':
The use of this clause will generally only be applicable where packages are chargeable unless returned (18.1 and 18.2), or goods ae delivered in road/rail tankers (18.3). In such cases these terms would be acceptable to the majority of Sellers, however the Buyer could expect to negotiate terms with regard to delay in emptying rail tankers (ie demurrage).

4.10   Clause 19 – 'Warranty': (see Part One, Section 1, page 19)

(a) This clause defines liabilities. Sellers' liability is limited to the repair or replacement of the goods, reimbursement of the costs of dismantling, reinstallation and the making good of resulting damage to surrounding equipment and property, subject to Buyers' legal obligation to minimise his loss. Buyers' claim in damages is limited to the full value of the purchase order under which the goods were obtained, but Buyer has no claim in respect of loss of profits.

(b) Practicalities to be considered and agreed are:

- Who pays for the return of the defective goods to Seller?
- What is an acceptable time to be allowed for repair or replacement of goods?
- If service call required, are all costs covered by Warranty, ie callout, parts and labour?
- Can service be called for out of normal working hours, ie during the night, weekends and Bank Holidays?
- Is a maintenance contract (to follow the warranty period) being contemplated? – negotiate before placing the procurement contract.

4.11 Clause 20 – 'Insolvency and bankruptcy':
This clause reflects the new arrangements resulting from the Insolvency Act 1985 which changes the title of 'receiver' to 'administrative receiver' and introduces the new 'administrator' appointed by a Court. Among the reasons why an administrator might be appointed are:

(a) to continue the company in whole or in part
(b) to optimise assets for liquidation.

5 Overseas application

These model conditions may be adapted for use with overseas sources of supply by reference to Part One, Section 9, page 48 et seq.

Model One

General Conditions of Contract
(for other than Engineering Goods)

1 **Definitions**

    1.1   The term 'Buyer' shall mean the person, firm or company so named in the Purchase Order.

    1.2   The term 'Seller' shall mean the person, firm or company to whom the Purchase Order is issued.

    1.3   The word 'Goods' includes all goods covered by the Purchase Order whether raw materials, processed materials or fabricated products.

    1.4   The word 'Packages' includes bags, cases, carboys, cylinders, drums, pallets, tank wagons and other containers.

    1.5   The term 'Purchase Order' shall mean Buyer's Purchase Order which specifies that these conditions apply to it.

    1.6   'The Contract' shall mean the contract between Buyer and Seller consisting of the Purchase Order, these conditions and any other documents (or parts thereof) specified in the Purchase Order. Should there be any inconsistency between the documents comprising the contract, they shall have precedence in the order herein listed.

2 **Quality and fitness for purpose**

The Goods shall be of satisfactory quality and free from defects in material or workmanship. If the purpose for which the Goods are required is made known to the Seller expressly or by implication the Goods shall be fit for that purpose. The Goods shall conform with the specifications, drawings, descriptions and samples contained or referred to in the Contract.

    In the absence of a specification or sample, all goods supplied shall be within the normal limits of industrial quality.

3 **Delivery date**

The date of delivery of the Goods shall be that specified in the

Purchase Order unless agreed otherwise between Buyer and Seller. Seller shall furnish such programmes of manufacture and delivery as Buyer may reasonably require and Seller shall give notice to Buyer as soon as practicable if such programmes are or are likely to be delayed. Buyer has the right to instruct Seller to take such action as is required to bring the Contract to completion.

4   **Incorrect delivery**
All Goods must be delivered at the delivery point specified in the Purchase Order. If Goods ae incorrectly delivered, Seller will be held responsible for any additional expense incurred in delivering them to their correct destination.

5   **Passing of property and risk to buyer**
The property and risk in the Goods shall remain in Seller until they are delivered at the point specified in the Purchase Order.

6   **Terms of payment**
The Purchase Order shall specify the time when invoices shall become due, and the manner in which invoices shall be submitted. Unless otherwise stated in the Purchase Order, payment will be made within 28 days of receipt of a properly prepared invoice.

Value Added Tax, where applicable, shall be shown separately on all invoices as a strictly nett extra charge.

7   **Loss or damage in transit**
   7.1   Without prejudice to the rights of the Buyer under Clause 19 Buyer shall advise Seller and the Carrier (if any) in writing, otherwise than by a qualified signature on any Delivery Notice, of any loss or damage within the following time limits:

   (a) Partial loss, damage or non-delivery of any separate part of a consignment shall be advised within 7 days of date of delivery of the consignment or part consignment.

   (b) Non-delivery of whole consignment shall be advised within 21 days of notice of despatch.

   7.2   Seller shall make good free of charge to Buyer any loss of or damage to or defect in the Goods where notice is given by Buyer in compliance with this condition provided that Buyer shall not in any event claim damages in respect of loss of profits.

8 **Acceptance**

In the case of Goods delivered by Seller not conforming with the Contract whether by reason of being of quality or in a quantity measurement not stipulated or being unfit for the purpose for which they are required where such purpose has been made known in writing to Seller, Buyer shall have the right to reject such Goods within a reasonable time of their delivery and to purchase elsewhere as near as practicable to the same Contract specifications and conditions as circumstances shall permit but without prejudice to any other right which Buyer may have against Seller. The making of payment shall not prejudice Buyer's right of rejection. Before exercising the said right to purchase elsewhere Buyer shall give Seller reasonable opportunity to replace rejected Goods with Goods which conform to the contract.

9 **Variations**

Seller shall not alter any of the Goods, except as directed in writing by Buyer; but Buyer shall have the right, from time to time during the execution of the Contract, by notice in writing to direct Seller to add to or to omit, or otherwise vary, the Goods, and Seller shall carry out such variations and be bound by the same conditions, so far as applicable, as though the said variations were stated in the Contract.

Where Seller receives any such direction from Buyer which would occasion an amendment to the Contract price Seller shall, with all possible speed, advise Buyer in writing to that effect giving the amount of any such amendment, ascertained and determined at the same level of pricing as that contained in Seller's tender. The Buyer shall confirm in writing all agreed amendments to the Contract price.

If, in the opinion of Seller, any such direction is likely to prevent Seller from fulfilling any of his obligations under the Contract he shall so notify Buyer and Buyer shall decide with all possible speed whether or not the same shall be carried out and shall confirm his instructions in writing and modify the said obligations to such an extent as may be justified. Until Buyer so confirms his instructions they shall be deemed not to have been given.

10 **Patent rights**

Seller will indemnify Buyer against any claim or infringement of Letters Patent, Registered Design, Trade Mark or Copyright by the use or sale of any article or material supplied by Seller to Buyer and against all costs and damages which Buyer may incur in any action for such infringement or for which Buyer may become liable in any such action. Provided always that this indemnity shall not apply to any infringement which is due to Seller having followed any instruction furnished or given by Buyer or to the use of such article or material in a manner or for a purpose in a foreign country not specified by or disclosed to Seller, or to any infringement which is due to the use of such article or material in association or combination with any other article or material not supplied by Seller. Provided also that this indemnity is conditional on Buyer giving to Seller the earliest possible notice in writing of any claim being made or action threatened or brought against Buyer and on Buyer permitting Seller at Seller's own expense to conduct any litigation that may ensue and all negotiations for a settlement of the claim. Buyer on his part warrants that any instruction furnished or given by him shall not be such as will cause Seller to infringe any Letters Patent, Registered Design, Trade Mark or Copyright to the execution of the Purchase Order.

11 **Force majeure**
Neither party shall be liable for failure to perform its obligations under the Contract if such failure results from circumstances which could not have been contemplated and which are beyond the party's reasonable control.

12 **Assignment and sub-letting**
The Contract shall not be assigned by Seller nor sub-let as a whole. Seller shall not sub-let any part of the work without Buyer's written consent, which shall not be unreasonably withheld, but the restriction contained in this clause shall not apply to sub-contracts for materials, for minor details, or for any part of which the makers are named in the Contract. Seller shall be responsible for all work done and goods supplied by all sub-contractors.

13 **Copies of sub-orders**
When Buyer has consented to the placing of sub-contracts copies of each sub-order shall be sent by Seller to Buyer immediately it is issued.

14 **Progress and inspection**
Buyer's representatives shall have the right to progress and inspect all Goods at Seller's works and the works of sub-contractors at all reasonable times and to reject goods that do not comply with the

terms of the Contract. Seller's sub-contracts shall include this provision. Any inspection, checking, approval or acceptance given on behalf of Buyer shall not relieve Seller or his sub-contractors from any obligation under the contract.

15 Buyer's rights in specifications, plans, process information, etc.

Any specifications, plans, drawings, process information, patterns or designs supplied by Buyer to Seller in connection with the Contract shall remain the property of Buyer, and any information derived therefrom or otherwise communicated to Seller in connection with the Contract shall be kept secret and shall not, without the consent in writing of Buyer, be published or disclosed to any third party, or made use of by Seller except for the purpose of implementing the Contract. Any specifications, plans, drawings, process information, patterns or designs supplied by Buyer must be returned to Buyer on fulfilment of the Contract.

16 Free-issue materials

Where Buyer for the purposes of the Contract issues materials 'free of charge' to Seller such materials shall be and remain the property of Buyer. Seller shall maintain all such materials in good order and condition subject, in the case of tooling, patterns and the like, to fair wear and tear. Any surplus materials shall be disposed of at Buyer's discretion. Waste of such materials arising from bad workmanship or negligence of Seller shall be made good at Seller's expense. Without prejudice to any other of the rights of the Buyer, Seller shall deliver up such materials whether further processed or not to the Buyer on demand.

17 Hazardous goods

17.1 Hazardous Goods must be marked by Seller with International Danger Symbol(s) and display the name of the material in English. Transport and other documents must include declaration of the hazard and name of the material in English. Goods must be accompanied by emergency information in English in the form of written instructions, labels or markings. Seller shall observe the requirements of UK and International Agreements relating to the packing, labelling and carriage of hazardous goods.

17.2 All information held by, or reasonably available to, Seller regarding any potential hazards known or believed to exist in the transport, handling or use of the Goods supplied shall be promptly communicated to Buyer.

18 **Packages**

18.1 Where Buyer has an option to return Packages and does so, Buyer will return such Packages empty in good order and condition (consigned 'carriage paid' unless otherwise agreed) to Seller's supplying works or depot indicated by Seller, and will advise Seller the date of despatch.

Packages returned promptly in the manner aforesaid shall be subject to an allowance at Seller's standard rate operating at the time of delivery to Buyer.

18.2 Where Goods are delivered by road vehicle, available empty Packages may be returned by the same vehicle.

18.3 Where Goods are delivered by tank wagons these will be emptied and returned without delay.

19 **Warranty**

Seller shall soon as reasonably practicable repair or replace all Goods which are or become defective during the period of 12 months from putting into service or 18 months from delivery, whichever shall be the shorter, where such defects occur under proper usage and are due to faulty design, Seller's erroneous instructions as to use or erroneous use data, or inadequate or faulty materials or workmanship, or any other breach of Seller's warranties, expressed or implied. Repairs and replacements shall themselves be subject to the foregoing obligations for a period of 12 months from the date of delivery, reinstallation or passing of tests (if any) whichever is appropriate after repair or replacement. Seller shall further be liable in damages (if any) in respect of each Purchase Order up to the limit of the price of the Goods covered by that Purchase Order provided that Buyer shall not in any event claim damages in respect of loss of profits.

The foregoing states the Seller's entire statutory liability for injury in respect of Goods which are defective, other than liability arising under Clause 7 (Loss or damage in transit) and Seller shall not, save as expressly provided herein, be liable for any other claim in regard to defects in the Goods.

20 **Insolvency and bankruptcy**

If Seller becomes insolvent or bankrupt or (being a Company) makes an arrangement with its creditors or has an administrative receiver or administrator appointed or commences to be wound up (other than for the purposes of amalgamation or reconstruction), Buyer may, without prejudice to any other of his rights, terminate the Contract forthwith by notice to Seller or any person in whom the Contract may have become vested.

21 **General conditions in the tender**

No conditions submitted or referred to by Seller when tendering shall form part of the Contract unless otherwise agreed to in writing by Buyer.

22 **Applicable law**

This contract shall be subject to English law and the jurisdiction of the English High Court.

Appendix 2

Guidance notes on the use of Model Two:

'General Conditions of Contract for Services or Minor Works'

1 **Use**

Use for General Services work, (eg Office Cleaning, Window Cleaning, Gardening, Painting), Minor Repairs and Maintenance (eg Buildings, Fences, Water and Electrical Services), etc.

Note: In this form of contract the usual practice is to refer to the Buyer as the 'Employer', and to the Seller as the 'Contractor'.

2 **General note on negotiation**

Always specify in the enquiry that it is a condition of the order that these Conditions are to be accepted. If the Contractor raises any objections these can then be the basis for negotiation. Avoid attempting to amend the Contractor's conditions to meet the Employer's requirements (see Part One, Section 1.4).

3 **Definition of requirements**

The following information should be part of any enquiry and/or purchase order:

3.1 Define carefully the work to be performed.

3.2 Date by which completion is required; be specific (see Part One, Section 5 – Seller's default) or, in the case of a regular service, the period for which the contract will run.

3.3 Terms of payment (see note 4.2).

3.4 Whether price is fixed or subject to a price-adjustment formula (see note 4.2).

3.5 State what utilities and other facilities (water, electricity, canteen accommodation, welfare, etc.) will be provided by the Employer.

3.6   Define the Contractor's site responsibilities (see note 4.1).

3.7   Specify who is responsible for off-loading and storage and what notice and arrangements are required for acceptance of delivery.

3.8   Stipulate any restrictions to be imposed on sub-letting (see note 4.3).

3.9   Specify any material which is to be 'free-issue'.

4   Notes on certain clauses

4.1   Clause 3 – 'Inspection of Site':
To avoid complications at a later stage it is essential that the Contractor visits the site to discuss all aspects of the Contract. The enquiry should include such an instruction; remember to specify the person to whom the Contractor should report.

4.2   Clause 6 – 'Terms of Payment' (see Part One, Section 4)

(a) The terms of payment *must* be specified on the order. Usually the basis will be one of the following:

(i)   an 'all-in' fixed price
(ii) an 'all-in' price subject to a price-adjustment formula.
(iii) a price for equipment with separate rates for site work attendance (eg time and materials).

(b) Although it is recommended practice to obtain a 'fixed price', it may be more economical in the case of long-term contracts to agree a price subject to a price-adjustment formula. This may work out cheaper than a 'pre-loaded' firm price. When considering price-adjustment formulae it is advisable to opt for a nationally recognised system such as the BEAMA CPA formula (see Part One, Section 4).

(c) A price basis of 'time and materials', whilst satisfactory for a small repair one-off job, is almost always the most expensive for the Employer since there is no incentive for the Contractor to work quickly.

4.3 Clause 8 – 'Assignment and sub-letting':
If it is anticipated that the Contractor intends to sub-let a significant part of the work then the details must be discussed and agreed with the Contractor before the order is placed.

4.4 Clause 11 – 'Payments to site labour':
The Contractor is required to obtain the Employer's approval of his proposed arrangements for paying his labour, ie working hours, rate of pay, bonuses, etc. These proposals should be made in writing and the Employer's agreement confirmed in writing either by letter or by inserting the details in the specification or Purchase Order.

The clause is relevant in the case of long-term contracts or 'time and material' work, but it can be deleted where fixed prices are agreed.

4.5 Clauses 14-16 – 'Indemnity/Insurance/Notifications':
These clauses set out proposed wording to safeguard the Employer but guidance should be sought from one's own broker regarding the value and extent of the cover required from the Contractor under clause 15.1(a). However, make sure that the clause 15.2 is put into effect.

4.6 Clause 21 – 'Loan of Employer's plant and equipment':
Any plant and equipment on hire to the Employer from a third party must *not* be loaned to the Contractor as this may invalidate the hire agreement and put the Employer at risk. No insurance cover is available for any loss or damage that could occur whilst such plant is being used by the Contractor.

4.7 Clause 23 – 'Insolvency and bankruptcy':
This clause reflects the new arrangements resulting from the Insolvency Act 1985 which changes the title of 'receiver' to 'administrative receiver' and introduces the new 'administrator' appointed by a Court. Among the reasons why an administrator might be appointed are:

(a) to continue the company in whole or in part
(b) to optimise assets for liquidation.

Model Two

General Conditions of Contract for Services or Minor Works

1 **Definitions**

   1.1 The term 'Employer' shall mean the person, firm or company so named in the Purchase Order.

   1.2 The term 'Contractor' shall mean the person, firm or company to whom the Purchase Order is issued.

   1.3 The 'Works' shall mean all work to be undertaken, and materials to be supplied, by the Contractor in performance of the Contract.

   1.4 'The Site' shall mean the location where the Works are to be performed.

   1.5 The term 'Purchase Order' shall mean the Employer's Purchase Order which specifies that these conditions apply to it.

   1.6 'The Contract' shall mean the contract between the Employer and the Contractor consisting of the Purchase Order, these conditions and any other documents (or parts thereof) specified in the Purchase Order. Should there be any inconsistency between the documents comprising the contract, they shall have precedence in the order herein listed.

2 **Inclusions in contract**
   The Contract includes for all materials, labour, plant, equipment, transport, handling of materials and plant, tools and appliances and all other things necessary for the Works.

3 **Inspection of site**
   The Contractor is deemed to have understood the nature and extent of the Works, and to have visited the Site and shall make no claim founded on his failure to do so. The Employer shall, on request of the Contractor, grant such access as may be reasonable for this purpose.

4 **Manner of carrying out the works**

4.1 The Contractor shall make no delivery nor commence work on Site before obtaining the Employer's consent.

4.2 Access to and possession of the Site shall not be exclusive to the Contractor but only such as shall enable him to carry out the Works concurrently with the execution of work by others.

4.3 The Employer shall have the power at any time during the progress of the Works to order in writing:

(a) The removal from the Site of any materials which in the opinion of the Employer are not in accordance with the Contract.

(b) The substitution of proper and suitable materials.

(c) The removal and proper re-execution (notwithstanding any previous test thereof or interim payment therefor) of any Work which, in respect of material or workmanship, is not in the opinion of the Employer in accordance with the Contract.

4.4 No work shall be laid in excavation and no work shall be covered or hidden until approved by the Employer.

5 **Completion date**
The date of completion of the Works or, in the case of a service being performed at regular intervals, the period of the Contract, shall be that specified in the Employer's Purchase Order unless otherwise agreed between the Employer and the Contractor.

6 **Terms of payment**
Unless otherwise stated in the Contract, payment will be made within 28 days of receipt and agreement of invoices, submitted monthly, for work completed to the satisfaction of the Employer.

Value Added Tax, where applicable, shall be shown separately on all invoices as a strictly nett extra charge.

7 **Contractor's superintendence**
The Contractor shall have a competent supervisor on the Site and

any instructions given to the said supervisor (written or oral) shall be deemed to be given to the Contractor.

8 **Assignment and sub-letting**
   8.1   The Contractor shall not assign or sub-let any portion of the Contract without the prior written consent of the Employer. No sub-letting shall relieve the Contractor from the responsibility of the Contract or from active supervision of the Works during their progress.

   8.2   Where the Employer has consented to the placing of sub-contracts, copies of each sub-order shall be sent by the Contractor to the Employer immediately it is issued.

9 **Variation in contract price**
   Save as provided for under Sub-Clause 10.2 the contract price shall be a firm price unless otherwise agreed between the parties when the Purchase Order is placed.

10 **Variation of the works**
   10.1 The Contractor shall not vary any of the Works, except as directed in writing by the Employer.

   10.2 The Employer reserves the right by notice in writing to modify the quality or quantity of the Works and any alteration to the Contract price arising by reason of such modification shall be agreed between the parties.

11 **Payments to site labour**
   11.1 The Contractor and his Sub-Contractor (if any) shall pay their respective employees on the Site the rates of wages, and observe hours and conditions of working, recognised by the National Agreements for the industries or trades applicable to the Contractor's work. In the absence of such Agreements the Contractor and his Sub-Contractors shall observe rates and conditions approved by the Employer.

   11.2 Bonus and other payments outside those defined in 11.1 above shall only be made in accordance with principles agreed with the Employer.

   11.3 Hours of working, including overtime, shall be agreed with the Employer.

11.4 Before the placing of the Contract, the Contractor shall have obtained for himself and his Sub-Contractors (if any) the approval of the Employer for the arrangements covered in 11.1, 11.2 and 11.3 above. The Contractor and his Sub-Contractors shall not introduce or commence to negotiate any changes in these arrangements without the written consent of the Employer. Notice shall be given to the Employer of the implementation of any National Awards affecting these arrangements.

11.5 The Contractor shall not offer employment to any person employed by the Employer or by other contractors employed by the Employer whilst work under the Contract is taking place.

12 Statutory duties and safety

12.1 The Works shall be carried out with the proper regard to safety and the Contractor shall observe and conform to all statutory enactments and regulations and any by-laws and/or regulations of local or other authorities applicable to the Works or generally to the Site where the Works are carried out, the cost of supplying and/or doing all things required for the purpose being deemed to be included in the Contract price. Any additional expenses reasonably incurred by the Contractor in conforming with any such statutory enactments, by-laws and regulations made subsequently to the Contractor's tender shall be added to the Contract price, provided that such additional expenses were not ascertainable at the date of tender.

12.2 The Contractor shall also observe through his staff and work people the Works Rules (available on request) applicable to the Site where the Works are carried out. The Employer shall have the right to require the Contractor immediately on receipt of notice in writing to remove any of his employees on the Site who has:

(a) failed to comply with the Works Rules or

(b) in the opinion of the Employer misconducted himself, or been negligent or incompetent.

12.3   The Contractor shall be responsible for the suitability and safety of the equipment used by him and no equipment shall be used which may be unsuitable, unsafe or liable to cause damage. Without lessening the absolute responsibility of the Contractor in regard to such equipment the Employer shall have the right to inspect such equipment and if in the Employer's opinion it is unsuitable it shall not be used on the Works, no extra time or payment being allowed to the Contractor for replacement.

13 Free-issue materials

Where the Employer for the purposes of the contract issues materials free of charge to the Contractor such materials shall be and remain the property of the Employer. The Contractor shall maintain all such materials in good order and condition and shall use such materials solely in connection with the Contract. Any surplus materials shall be disposed of at the Employer's discretion. Waste of such materials arising from bad workmanship or negligence of the Contractor shall be made good at the Contractor's expense. Without prejudice to any other of the rights of the Buyer, Seller shall deliver up such materials whether further processed or not to the Buyer on demand.

14 Indemnity

The Contractor shall take every practicable precaution not to damage or injure any property or persons. The Contractor shall satisfy all claims founded on any such damage or injury which arise out of or in consequence of any operations under the Contract whether such claims are made by the Employer or by a third party against the Contractor or against the Employer, and the Contractor shall indemnify the Employer against all actions, demands, damages, costs, charges and expenses arising in connection therewith, provided, however, that nothing in this condition shall render the Contractor liable for any injury or damage resulting from any negligent act or omission of the Employer, his servants or agents, or any other contractor employed by the Employer and the Employer shall indemnify the Contractor against all demands and expenses arising in connection with any such damage or injury.

15 Insurances

15.1   The Contractor shall have in force and shall require any Sub-Contractor to have in force:

(a) Employer's Liability Insurance and

(b) Public Liability Insurance for such sum and range of cover as the Contractor deems to be appropriate but not less than £500,000 for any one accident unless otherwise agreed by the Employer in writing.

All such insurances shall be extended to indemnify the Employer against any claim for which the Contractor or Sub-Contractor may be legally liable.

15.2 The Policy of Insurance shall be shown to the Employer whenever he requests together with satisfactory evidence of payment of premiums.

15.3 The Employer shall maintain Employer's Liability and Public Liability Insurance in respect of his own liabilities.

16 Notification procedure

The Contractor shall give immediate notice in the event of any accident or damage likely to form the subject of a claim under the Employer's insurance and shall give all the information and assistance in respect thereof that the Employer's insurers may require, and shall not negotiate, pay, settle, admit or repudiate any claim without their written consent, and shall permit the insurers to take proceedings in the name of the Contractor to recover compensation or secure an indemnity from any third party in respect of any of the matters covered by the said insurance.

17 Patent rights

The Contractor shall indemnify the Employer against all claims for royalties, damages, costs and expenses claimed or incurred as a result of the embodiment of any patented invention or design or copyright in the Works or the Contract. If, however, the subject of the patented invention or design is embodied in the Works or the Contract on the express instructions of the Employer, then the responsibility thereof shall rest with the Employer.

18 Contractor's conditions

No conditions submitted or referred to by the Contractor when tendering shall form part of the Contract unless otherwise agreed to in writing by the Employer.

19 Secrecy

19.1 No photographs of any of the Employer's equipment, installations or property shall be taken without the Employer's prior consent in writing. The Contractor shall keep secret and shall not divulge to any third party (except Sub-Contractors accepting a like obligation of secrecy, and then only to the extent necessary for the performance of the sub-contract) all information given by the Employer in connection with the Contract or which becomes known to the Contractor through his performance of such work under the Contract.

19.2   The Contractor shall not mention the Employer's name in connection with the Contract or disclose the existence of the Contract in any publicity material or other similar communication to third parties without the Employer's prior consent in writing.

20 Clearance of site on completion

On completion of the Works the Contractor shall remove his plant, equipment and unused materials and shall clear away from the Site all rubbish arising out of the Works.

21 Loan of employer's plant and equipment

(The inclusion of this condition does not imply that the Employer assumes any obligations to provide 'Loaned Plant', which means plant or equipment owned by the Employer and used by or on behalf of the Contractor by agreement).

21.1   Where Loaned Plant is operated by a servant of the Employer:

(a) The Operator shall not become the servant of the Contractor but shall carry out with the Loaned Plant such work as he may be directed to do by the Contractor.

(b) The Contractor shall be liable for any damage to the Loaned Plant caused by misdirection or misuse of it due to negligence on the part of the Contractor, his servants or agents.

(c) The Employer shall be liable for any damage to the Loaned Plant caused by a defect in or faulty operation of the plant.

21.2 Where Loaned Plant is operated by a servant of the Contractor or an independent Contractor, the Contractor shall be liable for all damage to the Loaned Plant unless he can show that it was caused by a defect in the plant at the commencement of the loan and he shall be liable for any loss (including loss by theft) of the said plant.

21.3 The Employer shall have the right to withdraw Loaned Plant at any time and shall be under no liability whatever in connection with the Employer failing to lend plant at any time.

21.4 The Contractor shall satisfy himself that any Loaned Plant is suitable for the purpose intended.

22 Contractor's default

22.1 If the Contractor fails to carry out promptly any of the Employer's instructions, and fails within 10 days of notice by the Employer drawing attention to such failure to take such steps as reasonably satisfy the Employer, the Employer may, without prejudice to any other of his rights, carry out works at the risk and expense of the Contractor.

22.2 If the Contractor commits a breach of the Contract and fails within 10 days of notice by the Employer to take such steps as reasonably satisfy the Employer to rectify such breach, the Employer may, without prejudice to any other of his rights, terminate the Contract forthwith by notice to the Contractor. Thereupon, without prejudice to any other of his rights, the Employer may himself complete the Works or have it completed by a third party, using for that purpose (or making a fair and proper payment thereof) all materials, plant and equipment on the Site belonging to the Contractor, and the Employer shall not be liable to make any further payment to the Contractor until the Works have been completed in accordance with the requirements of the Contract, and shall be entitled to deduct from the Contract price (ascertained in accordance with the terms and conditions of the Contract) any additional cost incurred by the Employer. If the total cost to the Employer exceeds the said Contract price, the difference shall be recoverable by the Employer from the Contractor.

23 Insolvency and bankruptcy

If the Contractor becomes insolvent or bankrupt or (being a

Company) makes an arrangement with its creditors or has an administrative receiver or administrator appointed or commences to be wound up (other than for the purposes of amalgamation or reconstruction) the Employer may, without prejudice to any other of his rights, terminate the Contract forthwith by notice to the Contractor or any person in whom the Contract may have become vested.

24 Construction of contract

The construction, validity and performance of the Contract shall be governed by the law of England.

Appendix 3 and 4

These appendices are produced by the Chartered Institute of Purchasing and Supply who waive copyright in this material. The material may be reproduced provided acknowledgement of CIPS is given. They are taken from CIPS' book *Buying Goods and Services* by Oliver and Allwright.

They are included here for illustration only. Terms should always be carefully drafted to accommodate the needs and requirement of the party concerned. The guidance notes are also produced by CIPS in the same publication and seek to explain the clauses. Remember that in practice when drafting terms they should be modified depending on which party's position is to be enhanced. in addition material requires updating from time to time as the law changes.

The conditions are as produced by CIPS save that in relation to the conditions for goods 'satisfactory quality' replaces 'merchantable quality'.

Appendix 3

EXAMPLE OF A NON-EXCLUSIVE AGENCY AGREEMENT FOR USE BY A UK COMPANY APPOINTING AN AGENT OUTSIDE THE EU – **NOT FOR DISTRIBUTION AGREEMENTS**

Warning
No contract or precedent should be used without careful thought and amendment. This contract was drawn up for one particular set of circumstances and may not be appropriate in other cases.

Note that this agreement is for use outside the EU. Within the EU the agency directive implies certain requirements into contracts as discussed in Chapter 7.

This Agreement is made the   day of 1995 B E T W E E N :-

(1)   XXXXXX LIMITED, whose principal place of business is at [   ] ('the Principal');

(2)   [   ] of [*give company number*
if a company and say where registered] ('the Agent')

WHEREAS:-

(A)   The Principal wishes to appoint a non-exclusive agent for its products in [   ];

(B)   The Agent wishes to be appointed agent for the sale of such products in [   ];

(C)   The parties have agreed as follows:-

1.   Definitions

'Confidential Information' means information concerning the Products or the business of the Principal, including, without limitation, financial and technical information, details of customers and potential customers and other written or electronic information of the Principal.

'Connected Persons' means employees, shareholders, partners, spouses and other close family members or group companies as defined in s376 of the Companies Act 1985 (where relevant) of the Agent at the date of this Agreement and thereafter.

'Net Sales Value' means the price at which a Product is sold to a customer by the Principal, not including any shipping costs paid by the customer, value added or other sales tax, insurance, extended guarantee fees, import duties.

'The Products' means the Principal's [product line] shown in its price list as amended from time to time.

'The Territory' means [check correct title and include a map if boundaries are unclear]

2.   Appointment and Minimum Sales

2.1   the Principal appoints the Agent as its non-exclusive agent for the sale of the Products in the Territory for the duration of this Agreement.

2.2   For the duration of this Agreement the Agent undertakes to use its best endeavours to maximise sales of the Products in the Territory in accordance with the highest standards of a marketing agent and shall achieve the minimum sales requirements of the Principal set out as minimum quantities in Schedule 2 of this Agreement.

3.   Operation of the Agency

3.1   The Agent shall use its best endeavours to find customers for the Products in the Territory and shall for each potential customer complete all forms required by the Principal and forward them and any other relevant information concerning the potential customer to the Principal for consideration.

3.2   The Principal shall then visit such customer with the Agent at a time convenient to the Principal. The Principal shall decide in its absolute discretion whether to supply any potential customer.

3.3   The Principal shall despatch Products for which orders have been received and accepted to customers direct in the Territory.

3.4   The Agent shall assist the Principal with customs clearance for the Products into the Territory or regions thereof and delivery of the Products to customers as required at the Agent's expense.

3.5   The Agent shall market the Products to potential customers in the Territory on the terms and conditions of sale, and at the prices, stipulated by the Principal. The current such terms of sale and price list is attached to this Agreement as Schedule 1. The Agent has no authority to alter prices or terms under this Agreement nor to negotiate the same. Where the customer wishes to make payment in local currency and the Principal accepts this, the Principal may require the Agent to assist the Principal with obtaining payment and necessary currency conversion.

3.6   All enquiries shall be passed on to the Principal and the customer told to forward orders to the Principal, not the Agent. Any orders received by the Agent shall be forwarded forthwith to the Principal.

3.7   The Principal shall undertake servicing of the Products for its customers in the Territory.

3.8   The Agent undertakes to visit customers once every month.

4.   **Training**

4.1   The Principal shall provide training for the Agent concerning the Products and **[add other material including what form the training will take, such as where it will take place]**

5.   **Advertising and Promotion**

5.1   The Agent shall assist the Principal with advertising and promotion of the Products in the Territory and in particular shall attend shows and exhibitions of the Products as required by the Principal. The Principal shall pay the costs of such shows and exhibitions, but may require the Agent to make presentations at such events from time to time.

5.2   The Agent shall also provide advice and assistance to the Principal on advertising generally in the Territory, but shall obtain prior approval in writing from the Principal before issuing any printed material or advertisements.

5.3   The Principal shall supply the Agent with necessary information, including sales leaflets for the marketing of the Products in the Territory free of charge.

6.   Commission

6.1   The Agent shall be paid a commission of [XXXX%] on the Net Sales Value of Products sold by the Principal to customers in the Territory which have been introduced to the Principal by the Agent. The Agent shall ensure that all such introductions are made in writing and in accordance with clause 3.1.

6.2   Commission shall be paid under clause 6.2 even where after such introduction the potential customer subsequently approaches the Principal direct.

6.3   Where two agents of the Principal both pass information concerning the same potential customer to the Principal commission shall be paid to the first agent to send details to the Principal. Where such introduction is simultaneous then the agents and the Principal shall ensure an equitable division of any commission due based on the effort expended by each agent in obtaining the customer.

6.4   The obligation to pay commission under clause 6.1 on customers introduced by the Agent shall continue for so long as that customer shall place orders with the Principal from the Territory for the duration of this Agreement.

6.5   Commission shall be paid to the Agent by **[state payment form - bank transfer etc]** after payment is received by the Principal from customers for a sale of the Products once such Products have been delivered.

6.6   The Agent shall be solely responsible for all taxes and similar payments which shall be due on such commission under [XXXX] law and all bank or other charges incurred by the Agent or its bank in receiving such commission.

[6.7   The Principal shall send the Agent a [monthly] statement setting out sales for the Products in the preceding month and payments received from customers in that month. Thereupon the Agent shall within seven (7) days submit an invoice for its commission based on such payments made to the Principal by customers. Until the Principal receives such invoice it shall have no obligation to pay commission to the Agent.] **Include if monthly or quarterly commission payments will be made rather than payments every time one Product is sold.**

6.8   The Agent shall be responsible for all its own expenses in connection with the operation of this Agreement and the agency arrangement contained herein.

6.9   On termination of this Agreement as provided below the Agent shall be paid commission on any potential customer's subsequent order details of which customer have been forwarded to the Princi- pal in writing at the date of termination, provided that the Agent shall continue to offer assistance to the Principal even after termination in helping to secure the order, clear the Products through customs and deliver the Products where required.

6.10 On termination no commission, other than commission due on the date of termination, shall then be payable on any order from the Territory to the Agent.

7.   Co-operation

7.1   The Principal shall be responsible for obtaining all consents and regulatory approvals for the Products in the Territory.

7.2   The Agent shall render assistance to the Principal in connection with such consents at the Agent's expense.

7.3   The Agent shall inform the Principal on a quarterly basis in writing of local sales conditions, new and existing competitors and their products, possible infringement of the Principal's rights in the Products in the Territory and local laws and regulations which might have an effect on the Products and their sale in the Territory.

7.4   The Agent shall pass on all complaints received concerning the Products in the Territory to the Principal forthwith in writing.

7.5   The Agent shall not make contracts on behalf of the Principal nor make any promises, representations, warranties or guarantees on behalf of the Principal in relation to the Products or otherwise incur any liability on behalf of the Principal.

8. **Intellectual Property Rights and Competition**

8.1   The Principal owns all intellectual property rights, including patents, copyright, trade marks and design rights in the Products.

8.2   Nothing in this Agreement shall give the Agent any intellectual property rights in the Products.

8.3   If the Agent challenges the validity of any of the intellectual property rights in the Products the Principal shall be entitled to terminate this Agreement forthwith by written notice.

8.4   The Agent shall not undertake any modifications, developments, additions or improvements to the Products nor shall it remove the Principal's name and address or any other mark or logo on the Products or their literature. The Agent shall acquire no rights of ownership in Products sold by the Principal to its customers in the Territory.

8.5   The Agent shall describe itself as 'Agent for XXXXXX Limited' in all correspondence with customers or potential customers and discussions with them.

8.6   The Agent shall not register any trade mark or intellectual property right in respect of the Products or the Principal or any similar name or product in the Territory. The Agent shall not acquire any goodwill in such trading names or in relation to the Products. All such goodwill shall accrue to the Principal.

8.7   The Agent shall not reverse engineer the Products or otherwise deconstruct them.

8.8   The Agent shall enter into all assignments or other documents needed to ensure the Principal's ownership rights hereunder.

8.9   For the duration of this Agreement the Agent shall not, and shall ensure that its Connected Persons shall not, sell, market, manufacture or be involved in any way whether directly or indirectly with similar or competing products to the Products in the Territory.

9. **Confidentiality**

9.1   The Agent shall, and shall ensure that its Connected Persons shall, keep the Confidential Information strictly confidential and use it only for the purposes of performance of its obligations under this Agreement.

9.2   On demand, and on termination of this Agreement, the Agent shall return all Confidential Information to the Principal forthwith.

10.   Liability

10.1   In no circumstances shall the Principal be liable to the Agent for any losses, costs or other expenses for breach of contract, any implied term or in tort for a sum exceeding the total commission received by the Agent in the year of such claim save as cannot be excluded under English law.

10.2   The parties agree that the Agent is best placed to insure against all such losses and liabilities and that the level of commission has been set at a figure reflecting the limitation of liability contained in clause 10.1 above.

11.   Term and Termination

11.1   The Agent is appointed from the date of this Agreement until such Agreement is terminated as provided below.

11.2   This Agreement may be terminated by either party by written notice to the other party being at least: one month's notice in writing in the first year, two months' notice in the second year; and three months' notice thereafter.

11.3   All notices given under clause 11.2 shall expire at the end of a calendar month.

11.4   The Principal may terminate this Agreement forthwith in writing by notice to the Agent at any time for breach of contract, including, without prejudice to the foregoing generality, where the Agent fails to meet the minimum sales levels obligations in any year, contained in Schedule 2, provided, where such breach can be remedied, notice has been given to the Agent to remedy the breach and such breach has not been remedied within a period of thirty (30) days from the date of such notice.

11.5   The Principal may terminate this Agreement forthwith by notice in writing where the Agent is unable to pay its debts when they fall due, is declared bankrupt, or, if a company goes into liquidation, administration or receivership or an equivalent event in the jurisdiction to which the Agent is subject, or where the Agent is convicted of any criminal offence or otherwise involved in criminal activities or investigations by regulatory authorities.

11.6 On termination of this Agreement the Agent shall return all Confidential Information to the Principal forthwith and cease to use it nor market itself as the agent of the Principal. On such termination the Agent shall ensure a smooth handover to any new agent or the Principal.

[11.7 The Agent shall not be entitled to any compensation, payments for loss of goodwill or indemnity or other sums arising from such termination, save for payment of any commission which is outstanding at the date of this Agreement as provided under this Agreement and under clause 6.9.] **Include outside the EU only.**

12. **General**

12.1 The Agent shall perform this Agreement personally and shall not sub-contract or assign its obligations under this Agreement or assign this Agreement to a third party or Connected Person, save where the Agent is a company where it shall perform its obligations through its employees and directors.

12.2 Other than as set out in this Agreement the Agent is not empowered to bind the Principal in any way nor to enter the Principal into any commitment with a third party.

12.3 This is the entire agreement between the parties and replaces any earlier existing agreement whether in writing, by contract or arrangement.

12.4 All notices shall be sent to the parties' addresses on page one of this Agreement or such other addresses as they notify the other party in writing from time to time. Notices shall be sent by registered airmail or by fax confirmed by air mail and shall be deemed served five (5) days after despatch.

12.5 Any failure to enforce or delay in enforcing an obligation under this Agreement shall not prejudice or preclude its subsequent enforcement.

12.6 Any provision held void from this Agreement by a court or regulatory authority shall be deemed severed herefrom without affecting the validity of other provisions of this Agreement.

12.7 This Agreement shall be subject to English law and the parties agree to submit to the non-exclusive jurisdicton of the English courts in connection with any dispute arising hereunder.

12.8   Headings in this Agreement are for information only and shall not be used in its construction.

12.9   Each party shall bear its own costs in the preparation and negotiation of this Agreement.

12.10 The Principal shall not be liable for any failure to perform or delay in performing its obligations under this Agreement arising from acts of God, industrial disputes, failures on the part of sub-contractors or manufacturers or other circumstances beyond its reasonable control.

12.11 In entering into this Agreement the parties agree that they have not relied on any representation or warranty and in particular the Agent acknowledges that the Principal has not made any representation concerning the volume of transactions which the Agent should expect.

IN WITNESS THE PARTIES HAVE EXECUTED THIS AGREEMENT ON THE DATE AND YEAR ON PAGE 1

Signed by ....,) ....
for and on behalf of XXXXXXX)
Limited in the presence of:-

Witness' signature ....
           name.........................
           address......................

           ....
           occupation ....

Signed by ....,) ....
duly authorised for and on)
behalf of................)
in the presence of:-

Witness' signature ....
           name.........................
           address......................

           ....
           occupation ....

Schedule 1 Terms and Conditions of Sale of the Principal and
Current Price List of the Principal

Schedule 2 Minimum Quantities

First six months £

[Either set out figures now or state on what terms figures for subsequent years are to be reviewed and agreed between the parties]

Appendix 4

DISTRIBUTION AGREEMENT

This Agreement is made   day of
   1994

BETWEEN:

1. XXXXX LTD, registered in England, no. [   ], whose registered office is at [   ] ('the Supplier'); and

2.   , a [company] registered in ,   no. whose registered office is at   ('the Distributor')

The Supplier has agreed to appoint the Distributor as its exclusive distributor as provided below on the terms and conditions attached and the Distributor has accepted such appointment and terms by signing below.

Territory

Products

Minimum Annual Orders   Year 1:
Year 2:
Year 3:

Initial Term of the Agreement Six months from the date of this Agree-
                                 ment

Signed by   )   ....
duly authorised for   )
and on behalf of   )
XXXXXXX LIMITED   )
Signed by   )   ....
duly authorised for   )
and on behalf of   )
)

in the presence of:-

TERMS AND CONDITIONS OF DISTRIBUTION

1.   **Appointment**

1.1   The Supplier appoints the Distributor as its exclusive distributor
      for the Products in the Territory on page 1 for the duration of this
      Agreement, subject to clause 3.4.

1.2   For the duration of this Agreement the Supplier shall not supply
      the Products for resale or to customers in the Territory to any
      person other than the Distributor, subject to clause 3.4, but shall
      not be liable to the Distributor in the event that third parties,
      including other distributors, make sales in the Territory.

1.3   Any orders received by the Supplier for the delivery of Products
      in the Territory shall be referred by the Supplier to the Distribu-
      tor.

1.4   The Distributor shall not sell or market, whether directly or in-
      directly and whether itself or through connected or associated
      companies or individuals or shareholders, directors or other
      contacts, the Products outside the Territory or to those whom they
      have reasonable grounds to believe will sell the Products outside
      the Territory or sell to others who may do the same. **[EXPORT
      BANS ARE AGAINST THE LAW IN THE EU SO SHOULD**

NEVER BE INCLUDED IN AGREEMENTS OF THIS TYPE OR
COMMISSION FINES OF UP TO 10% OF TURNOVER COULD
BE LEVIED FOR BREACH OF ARTICLE 85]

1.5 The Distributor shall refer forthwith any enquiries or orders it
receives from anyone for supplies outside the Territory to the
Supplier.

1.6 The Distributor shall not copy, imitate or reproduce the Products
or their packaging, whether this comprises breach of copyright,
passing off, unfair competition or other legal wrong or not.

1.7 The Supplier shall have the option to acquire up to 30% of the
proportion of the Distributor's share capital or business which
is attributable to the sale of the Products in the Territory, at its
then current market value, by the formation of a joint venture
or other such agreement, at any time during the term of this
Agreement.

2. **Reports, Advertising and Promotion and Orders**

2.1 Within one month of the signature of this Agreement the Distributor shall send a written market survey describing in detail
the Distributor's plans for marketing in the Territory over the
first three years, including:-

(a) details of expected sales turnover, including a three to five
year forecast and marketing plan per product, to include a
product planning study, an ordering schedule, the Distributor's objectives in relation to market share to be achieved and
unit sales objectives, which shall include details of quantities which shall be ordered and order dates;

(b) an advertising and promotion proposal, which shall show
the different proposed methods of advertising broken down
into categories, such as TV, magazines and other methods of
promotion and other media and how much money will be
spent on each item (which shall comprise a minimum of 15%
of sales turnover as required by clause 2.6 below) and when
such money shall be spent, the details to be supplied on the
form contained in the software described in clause 2.5 below
(the Software);

(c) a comprehensive current market study report.

The Supplier may annually vary the formats and information to be supplied at its discretion, which changes shall be included as updates to the Software.

2.2 By the end of the last day of each month of this Agreement the Distributor shall send stock and sales statements in the format required by the Supplier as set out in the Software.

2.3 By the end of each quarter of this Agreement after commencement of sale by the Distributor in the Territory, with the monthly stock and sales statement, the Distributor shall send the Supplier (i) an advertising and promotion report setting out details of advertising and promotion in the previous quarter and proposals for the next quarter in the format required by the Supplier set out in the Software; and (ii) a customer report showing a breakdown of how many of the Products have been sold in the previous quarter to each customer. Reports under (i) and (ii) and any other reports shall be sent in the format required by the Supplier set out in the Software.

2.4 By 31 December in each year of this Agreement the Distributor shall send the supplier, with the monthly stock and sales statement and quarterly advertising and promotion and customer reports, a comprehensive, written annual report including, amongst other matters, details of levels of stock held and sales, advertising budgets, report on customers and survey of the market, including details of market share gained by the Distributor and product positioning and its plans for marketing in the next year of this Agreement, and details of the competition in the Territory including the information concerning competitors and their products, all such information under this clause to be supplied in the format required by the Supplier set out in the Software.

2.5 All reports supplied to the Supplier under clauses 2.1–2.4 above shall be supplied on the first day of the following month either (a) by modem or, if the Distributor does not have access to a modem (b) in IBM compatible diskette form and in hardcopy form both sent by courier. The Distributor shall take a licence of the Supplier's computer program and manual for £[ ] plus VAT within two weeks of the date of this Agreement and of chargeable updates thereto from time to time as required by the Supplier. Such Software is licensed to the Distributor in object code version only solely for the purposes of its performance of its obligations under this Agreement and shall not be used for any other purpose nor copied nor reverse engineered. The Supplier owns the media on which the Software is supplied and the Distributor shall acquire no rights (other than the right to use in this clause) to the Software hereby licensed. Copyright and all other rights in the Software is owned by the Supplier and the licence to use the Software shall cease when this Agreement terminates.

2.6 The Distributor shall spend a minimum of 15% of the retail sales price of Products bought from the Supplier on advertising and promotion in the Territory or whatever sum is specified by the Supplier from time to time and shall supply evidence of this on request by the Supplier and in its quarterly report to the Distributor. The Supplier shall have the right to check the books and other records of the Distributor to verify that this minimum 15% sum has been spent as required in this clause. Sales of point of sale and other marketing material to the Distributor by the Supplier shall be included in calculating the Distributor's spending on advertising and promotion under this clause. The advertising and promotion plan described in clause 2.1(b) above shall be subject to the approval of the Supplier. The Supplier may require changes to be made before the plan can be put into effect.

2.7 The Supplier shall appoint an advertising agent and shall notify the Distributor of such appointment. The Distributor shall neither appoint nor use any other such agent or marketing consultant for advertising and promotion of the Products in the Territory. The Distributor shall ensure that the Supplier has control over all advertising and marketing activities in the Territory and shall forward for prior approval by the Supplier order sheets, price lists, point of sale and other materials used in selling and marketing the products to a standard acceptable to the Supplier and ensure that its salesmen use only such approved materials.

2.8 All Products sold by the Distributor shall bear the trade name, mark and logo of XXXXX and any goodwill in such marks shall accrue to XXXXX.

2.9 The Distributor shall pay the cost of all advertising, including Product launch costs and local promotion. The Supplier shall be under no obligation to pay for local advertising and advertising materials. Advertising materials supplied by the Supplier shall be charged to the Distributor, as the Supplier is required to pay for these by the manufacturer of the Products.

2.10 The Distributor shall inform the Supplier of all relevant exhibitions and trade fairs in the Territory, and shall participate at such trade fairs and exhibit the Products there at the Distributor's cost after obtaining the prior approval of the Supplier.

2.11 The Distributor shall market the Products in accordance with the Guidelines of the Supplier which the Supplier shall supply to the Distributor in writing.

2.12 When the Supplier visits the Territory the Distributor shall ensure that it makes itself available to show the Supplier its premises and the outlets where the Products are sold by retailers and others in the Territory. The Distributor shall supply the Supplier with any information the Supplier requires on such visits at the time of the visit. The Distributor shall ensure that it allows sufficient time at the Distributor's expense to give the Supplier a comprehensive overview of customers in the Territory, the state of the market and the competition.

2.13 The Distributor shall within two weeks of the date of this Agreement register the Supplier in local trade registries or similar bodies and ensure that all necessary licences to trade are obtained for the Supplier and itself within such two week period at the expense of the Distributor. The Distributor shall also within such two week period make an application to register the trade name 'XXXXX' and the Supplier's logo as notified to the Distributor, in the Territory at the Distributor's expense, but in the name of the Supplier, with the Distributor registered as a user of such trade mark. The Distributor shall pay all renewal fees in connection with registration of such trade marks, user agreement and business registration for the duration of this Agreement and ensure that renewals are effected on time as required under local law. The Distributor shall acquire no rights to use such trade mark save in reselling the Products in their existing packaging. The Distributor shall send to the Supplier proof in writing of all registrations and renewals under this clause as soon as the registration or renewal is effected. The Distributor undertakes at its own expense to comply with all local legal and regulatory requirements at the date of this Agreement and thereafter and inform the Supplier of these rules. The Distributor shall notify the Supplier, keep the Supplier fully informed of and comply with any changes in such requirements.

2.14 The Distributor shall use its best endeavours to maximise sales of the Products in the Territory and shall order the minimum quantity of the Products set out on page 1 in each year of this Agreement. Thereafter minimum quantities shall be discussed in advance and stipulated in writing by the Supplier.

2.15   The Distributor shall use its best endeavours to spread orders for the Products throughout each year of this Agreement and give the Supplier appropriate notice of each order. The Distributor shall place at least three orders in each year of this Agreement. At the beginning of each year of this Agreement the Distributor shall notify the Supplier of the exact quantities which it wishes to order during the year and when those orders will be placed. The Supplier shall then decide whether such quantities are acceptable before informing the Distributor of the quantities required. Where additional orders are required the Distributor shall give the Supplier ample notice and all orders are subject to clause 2.16.

2.16   Although the Supplier will use its reasonable endeavours to fulfil any order it cannot be liable for a failure to fulfil any order placed nor to accept all orders. The Supplier reserves the right to change the design, composition or appearance of the Products and their packaging from time to time.

2.17   Orders shall be placed in writing and sent to the Supplier by courier air mail at its address on page 1 and all orders shall be subject to written approval and acceptance by the Supplier, who will indicate the estimated time of delivery.

2.18   The Distributor acknowledges that it has obtained at least two satisfactory bank references from a first class bank in relation to itself and forwarded these to the Supplier prior to the execution of this Agreement.

3.   **Supplies**

3.1   The Products shall be supplied FOB or CIF or on such other terms as the Supplier shall require from time to time. The Supplier shall endeavour to keep to delivery times but is not liable for any losses occasioned through late delivery. Property in the Products shall pass to the Distributor when payment is received by the Supplier in full. Until such time the Products shall not be resold and shall be stored in a manner so that they can be identified as the Supplier's goods.

3.2   The price paid by the Distributor for the Products shall be in accordance with the Supplier's price list as varied from time to time. The Supplier may increase prices on four weeks' notice. The Distributor shall offer whatever credit payment terms are normal for the local market in the Territory to its customers and the Supplier may, in addition to its other rights and remedies, terminate this Agreement where the Distributor does not comply with this provision.

3.3   The Distributor shall supply all willing sales outlets in the Territory which meet the Supplier's criteria. The Supplier may require that sales to customers cease where the standard of the outlet in which sales are taking place is, in the opinion of the Supplier, not in keeping with the premium image of the Products. The Distributor shall not be entitled to grant any retail, wholesale or other outlet exclusive rights to sell the Products or any of them.

3.4   Where the Supplier is of the opinion that the Distributor is unable or unwilling to supply the Products to all parts of the Territory, the Supplier reserves the right to appoint additional distributors for geographical areas or categories of outlet in the Territory.

3.5   For the duration of this Agreement the Distributor shall not sell any other [YYYY type product] without the consent of the Supplier. The market survey described in clause 2.1 shall state details of other products sold by the Distributor and the Distributor shall seek consent from the Supplier before it enters into an agreement to sell a product in the [WWWWW] field.

3.6   The Distributor shall be responsible for, shall pay and shall solely be liable for, all duties, taxes, levies or any other charges relating to the importation of the Products into the Territory, including any relevant product approvals or other regulatory requirements or registrations.

3.7   Payment for the Products shall be in UK pounds sterling and shall be made by confirmed, transferable, irrevocable without recourse letter of credit providing for payment at sight allowing partial deliveries and collections and issued by a reputable first class bank acceptable to the Supplier. The Distributor shall also pay any handling and shipping or other incidental costs and expenses the Supplier has incurred or will incur in relation to the Products. Prices are exclusive of VAT or other sales taxes which are payable in addition by the Distributor and are to be paid in full without deduction of taxes, charges or duties imposed. The parties shall collaborate to take advantage of any double taxation treaties in force. Where there is an error on the letter of credit, or for whatever reason the Supplier's bank rejects the letter of credit, the

Distributor shall pay all the bank charges and other costs of the Supplier in relation to such error and ensure that a correct letter of credit is issued forthwith. The Supplier shall not offer any credit to the Distributor. The Distributor shall not pledge the credit of the Supplier.

3.8   The Distributor shall open each letter of credit within seven (7) days after the Distributor's receipt of the Supplier's acceptance of the order and it shall remain open for at least thirty (30) days or such longer period as may be agreed by the parties in relation to individual letters of credit. The terms of the letter of credit may be specified by the Supplier from time to time and payment for Products shall be made in full without deduction, set off or counterclaim. For payment of the price as to time and amount, time shall be of the essence.

4.   Distributor's Obligations

4.1   The Distributor shall at its own expense maintain a suitable place of business and employ a sufficient number of qualified personnel to perform its obligations under this Agreement. The Distributor shall employ qualified and competent sales staff to whom adequate training must be given in relation to the Products. The Supplier may require that the Distributor increase the number of salesmen where the Supplier believes that the salesmen employed are insufficient in number to cover all outlets to which the Products may potentially be sold. Where the Distributor, in the opinion of the Supplier, does not have adequate in-house training facilities for its staff the Distributor shall use local training schools at its own expense for the training of its staff.

4.2   The Distributor shall not apply any process or carry out any modifications to the Products or rebottle them without the prior written consent of the Supplier. Nor shall the Distributor make any representations or warranties concerning the products.

4.3   The Distributor shall not contact, whether directly or indirectly or through its employees, agents, contacts or associated companies, the manufacturer of the Products or the Supplier's supplier except through the Supplier, for the duration of this Agreement and thereafter.

4.4   The Distributor shall maintain such stocks of the Products as are necessary to meet the Distributor's customers' requirements and at least a quantity sufficient to satisfy demand for two months.

4.5   The Distributor acknowledges that the recipes and ingredients of the Products are the property of the Supplier's own supplier and that it shall not use the same for any purpose whatsoever, nor disclose, sell, licence nor deal with them and shall keep them strictly confidential.

4.6   The Distributor shall, and ensure that its agents shall, keep the Products at **[special requirements for keeping products fresh]**.

5.   **Confidentiality**

5.1   The parties shall keep strictly confidential and not disclose any business, financial or product information of the other party and shall return all such information on demand and in any event on termination of this Agreement for any cause.

6.   **Liability**

6.1   All representations, agreements, warranties, terms and conditions whether express or implied by statute common law or otherwise are excluded, save that the Supplier shall not exclude liability for death or personal injury caused by negligence which cannot under English law be excluded. The Supplier shall not be under any liability for defective Products unless:-

(a)   a claim has been made in writing from the Distributor to the Supplier within one month of delivery specifying the nature of the defect;

(b)   the defective Products are returned carriage paid at the Distributor's risk to the Supplier's premises; and

(c)   the defect is due solely to defective materials or manufacture.

Where these conditions are fulfilled the Supplier's sole liability shall be to replace the defective Product.

6.2   The Supplier shall not be liable for any loss or damage or injury to any person or property however caused or arising and shall not be liable for any indirect or consequential loss whatever and however caused. Nothing in this agreement shall be construed as a warranty that the Products are free from infringement of intellectual property rights.

7.   **Term and Termination**

7.1   This Agreement is for a trial period, being the Initial Term set out on page 1. Before the expiry of the Initial Term the Supplier shall evaluate the performance of the Distributor and determine whether to offer a further term to the Distributor, whereupon this Agreement shall continue until terminated by either party on two months' prior written notice.

7.2   This Agreement may be terminated by either party forthwith by written notice where:-

(a)   the other commits a breach of this Agreement which (if capable of remedy) is not remedied within twenty-one (21) days;

(b)   the other party shall go into liquidation or otherwise be insolvent or bankrupt in accordance with the laws of the country to which it is subject;

(c)   there is a change of control of the other party;

(d)   in the case of the Distributor the minimum quantities required to be purchased under clause 2.14, set out on page 1, are not achieved;

(e)   the Supplier's contract with its supplier terminates.

7.3   On termination:-

(a)   any money due to the Supplier shall be paid forthwith;

(b)   the Distributor shall send to the Supplier a list with details of purchasers of the Products in the Territory over the previous two (2) years and copies of all orders, showing the number and type of the Products purchased by those persons;

(c)   the Distributor shall cease all use of the 'XXXXX' trade mark and join with the Supplier in cancelling any registered user agreement entered into;

(d)   the Distributor shall have no claim against the Supplier for compensation for loss of goodwill or any other loss;

(e)   the Distributor shall return any software licensed under clause 2.5 to the Supplier forthwith and cease to use the same;

(f)   the Distributor may sell off stocks of the Products which it holds; and

(g)   clauses 4.2, 4.4, 5, 6, 7 and 8 shall continue.

8.   **General**

8.1   The Distributor shall not assign or transfer its rights under this Agreement nor sub-contract its obligations or appoint sub-distributors or use agents, without the prior written consent of the Supplier.

8.2   This Agreement is the entire agreement between the parties and supersedes any prior understandings or agreements.

8.3   Notices under this Agreement shall be sent by fax confirmed by express airmail and be deemed served five (5) days after posting and shall be given to the addresses on page 1.

8.4   Failure to exercise a right or power under this Agreement will not be construed as a waiver thereof.

8.5   If any provision of this Agreement is deemed invalid or unenforceable by any court or regulatory authority the other provisions shall remain in full force and effect, provided that the Supplier may serve thirty (30) days notice to terminate this Agreement.

8.6   This Agreement shall not constitute a relationship of partnership nor shall the Distributor be deemed the agent of the Supplier for any purpose. The Distributor shall describe itself as 'distributor' not 'agent' for the sale of the Products.

8.7   The Supplier shall not be liable to the Distributor for any delay in or failure to perform its obligations as a result of any cause beyond its control, including, but not limited to, any industrial dispute, riot, Government action or act of God.

8.8   The Supplier may vary the terms of this Agreement by written notice to the Distributor where necessary to comply with the requirements of its supplier or in connection with the information to be supplied and the form in which it is to be supplied under clause 2 and otherwise by agreement with the Distributor in writing.

8.9   This Agreement is subject to English law and the parties submit to the non-exclusive jurisdiction of the English courts.

8.10 Where a translation of this Agreement is arranged, in the event of any conflict between the terms of the English and translated versions of the Agreement, the terms of the English version shall prevail. Any translation costs shall be paid by the Distributor.

Note

The EC regulations, notice and directive reproduced hereafter are reprinted from the European Commission's Official Journal with kind permission of the Commission of the European Communities who own the copyright therein.

I

(Acts whose publication is obligatory)

COMMISSION REGULATION (EEC) No 1983/83
of 22 June 1983
on the application of Article 85 (3) of the Treaty to categories of exclusive distribution agreements

THE COMMISSION OF THE EUROPEAN COMMUNITIES,

Having regard to the Treaty establishing the European Economic Community, and in particular Article 87 thereof.

Having regard to Council Regulation No 19/65/EEC of 2 March 1965 on the application of Article 85 (3) of the Treaty to certain categories of agreements and concerted practices (¹), as last amended by the Act of Accession of Greece, and in particular Article 1 thereof,

Having published a draft of this Regulation (²),

Having consulted the Advisory Committee on Restrictive Practices and Dominant Positions,

(1) Whereas Regulation No 19/65/EEC empowers the Commission to apply Article 85 (3) of the Treaty by regulation to certain categories of bilateral exclusive distribution agreements and analogous concerted practices falling within Article 85 (1);

(2) Whereas experience to date makes it possible to define a category of agreements and concerted

practices which can be regarded as normally satisfying the conditions laid down in Article 85 (3);

(3) Whereas exclusive distribution agreements of the category defined in Article 1 of this Regulation may fall within the prohibition contained in Article 85 (1) of the Treaty; whereas this will apply only in exceptional cases to exclusive agreements of this kind to which only undertakings from one Member State are party and which concern the resale of goods within that Member State; whereas, however, to the extent that such agreements may affect trade between Member States and also satisfy all the requirements set out in this Regulation there is no reason to withhold from them the benefit of the exemption by category;

(4) Whereas it is not necessary expressly to exclude from the defined category those agreements which do not fulfil the conditions of Article 85 (1) of the Treaty;

(5) Whereas exclusive distribution agreements lead in general to an improvement in distribution because the undertaking is able to concentrate its sales activities, does not need to maintain

---

(¹) OJ No 36, 6. 3. 1965, p. 533/65.
(²) OJ No C 172, 10.7. 1982, p.3.

* In October 1996 it was announced that Regulations 1983/83 and 1984/83 were extended to December 1999.

numerous business relations with a larger number of dealers and is able, by dealing with only one dealer, to overcome more easily distribution difficulties in international trade resulting from linguistic, legal and other differences;

(6) Whereas exclusive distribution agreements facilitate the promotion of sales of a product and lead to intensive marketing and to continuity of supplies while at the same time rationalizing distribution; whereas they stimulate competition between the products of different manufacturers; whereas the appointment of an exclusive distributor who will take over sales promotion, customer services and carrying of stocks is often the most effective way, and sometimes indeed the only way, for the manufacturer to enter a market and compete with other manufacturers already present; whereas this is particularly so in the case of small and medium-sized under-takings; whereas it must be left to the contracting parties to decide whether and to what extent they consider it desirable to incorporate in the agreements terms providing for the promotion of sales;

(7) Whereas, as a rule, such exclusive distribution agreements also allow consumers a fair share of the resulting benefit as they gain directly from the improvement in distribution, and their economic and supply position is improved as they can obtain products manufactured in particular in other countries more quickly and more easily;

(8) Whereas this Regulation must define the obligations restricting competition which may be included in exclusive distribution agreements; whereas the other restrictions on competition allowed under this Regulation in addition to the exclusive supply obligation produce a clear division of functions between the parties and compel the exclusive distributor to concentrate his sales efforts on the contract goods and the contract territory; whereas they are, where they are agreed only for the duration of the agreement, generally necessary in order to attain the improvement in the distribution of goods sought through exclusive distribution; whereas it may be left to the contracting parties to decide which of these obligations they include in their agreements; whereas further restrictive obligations and in particular those which limit the exclusive distributor's choice of customers or his freedom to determine his prices and conditions of sale cannot be exempted under this Regulation;

(9) Whereas the exemption by category should be reserved for agreements for which it can be assumed with sufficient certainty that they satisfy the conditions of Article 85 (3) of the Treaty;

(10) Whereas it is not possible, in the absence of a case-by-case examination, to consider that adequate improvements in distribution occur where a manufacturer entrusts the distribution of his goods to another manufacturer with whom he is in competition; whereas such agreements

should, therefore, be excluded from the exemption by category; whereas certain derogations from this rule in favour of small and medium-sized undertakings can be allowed;

(11) Whereas consumers will be assured of a fair share of the benefits resulting from exclusive distribution only if parallel imports remain possible; whereas agreements relating to goods which the user can obtain only from the exclusive distributor should therefore be excluded from the exemption by category; whereas the parties cannot be allowed to abuse industrial property rights or other rights in order to create absolute territorial protection; whereas this does not prejudice the relationship between competition law and industrial property rights, since the sole object here is to determine the conditions for exemption by category;

(12) Whereas, since competition at the distribution stage is ensured by the possibility of parallel imports, the exclusive distribution agreements covered by this Regulation will not normally afford any possibility of eliminating competition in respect of a substantial part of the products in question; whereas this is also true of agreements that allot to the exclusive distributor a contract territory covering the whole of the common market;

(13) Whereas, in particular cases in which agreements or concerted practices satisfying the requirements of this Regulation nevertheless have effects incompatible

with Article 85 (3) of the Treaty; the Commission may withdraw the benefit of the exemption by category from the undertakings party to them,

(14) Whereas agreements and concerted practices which satisfy the conditions set out in this Regulation need not be notified; whereas an undertaking may nonetheless in a particular case where real doubt exists, request the Commission to declare whether its agreements comply with this Regulation;

(15) Whereas this Regulation does not affect the applicability of Commission Regulation (EEC) No 3604/82 of 23 December 1982 on the application of Article 85 (3) of the Treaty to categories of specialization agreements (¹); whereas it does not exclude the application of Article 86 of the Treaty,

HAS ADOPTED THIS REGULATION:

Article 1

Pursuant to Article 85 (3) of the Treaty and subject to the provisions of this Regulation, it is hereby declared that Article 85 (1) of the Treaty shall not apply to agreements to which only two untertakings are party and whereby one party agrees with the other to supply certain goods for resale within the whole or a defined area of the common market only to that other.

Article 2

1. Apart from the obligation referred to in Article 1 no restriction on

competition shall be imposed on the supplier other than the obligation not to supply the contract goods to users in the contract territory.

2. No restriction on competition shall be imposed on the exclusive distributor other than:

(a) the obligation not to manufacture or distribute goods which compete with the contract goods;

(b) the obligation to obtain the contract goods for resale only from the other party;

(c) the obligation to refrain, outside the contract territory and in relation to the contract goods, from seeking customers, from establishing any branch and from maintaining any distribution depot.

3. Article 1 shall apply notwithstanding that the exclusive distributor undertakes all or any of the following obligations:

(a) to purchase complete ranges of goods or minimum quantities;

(b) to sell the contract goods under trademarks or packed and presented as specified by the other party;

(c) to take measures for promotion of sales, in particular:

   – to advertise,

   – to maintain a sales network or stock of goods,

   – to provide customer and guarantee services,

   – to employ staff having specialized or technical training.

Article 3

Article 1 shall not apply where:

(a) manufacturers of identical goods or of goods which are considered by users as equivalent in view of their characteristics, price and intended use enter into reciprocal exclusive distribution agreements between themselves in respect of such goods;

(b) manufacturers of identical goods or of goods which are considered by users as equivalent in view of their characteristics, price and intended use enter into a non-reciprocal exclusive distribution agreement between themselves in respect of such goods unless at least one of them has a total annual turnover of no more than 100 million ECU;

(c) users can obtain the contract goods in the contract territory only from the exclusive distributor and have no alternative source of supply outside the contract territory;

(d) one or both of the parties makes it difficult for intermediaries or users to obtain the contract goods from other dealers inside the common market or, in so far as no alternative source of supply is available there, from outside the common market, in particular where one or both of them:

1. exercises industrial property rights so as to prevent dealers or users from obtaining outside, or from selling in, the contract territory properly marked or

---

(^{1}) OJ No L 376, 31. 12. 1982, p. 33.

otherwise properly marketed contract goods;

2. exercises other rights or take other measures so as to prevent dealers or users from obtaining outside, or from selling in, the contract territory contract goods.

Article 4

1. Article 3 (a) and (b) shall also apply where the goods there referred to are manufactured by an undertaking connected with a party to the agreement.

2. Connected undertakings are:

(a) undertakings in which a party to the agreement, directly or indirectly:

– owns more than half the capital or business assets, or

– has the power to exercise more than half the voting rights, or

– has the power to appoint more than half the members of the supervisory board, board of directors or bodies legally representing the undertaking, or

– has the right to manage the affairs;

(b) undertakings which directly or indirectly have in or over a party to the agreement the rights or powers listed in (a);

(c) undertakings in which an undertaking referred to in (b) directly or indirectly has the rights or powers listed in (a).

3. Undertakings in which the parties to the agreement or undertakings connected with them jointly have the rights or powers set out in paragraph 2 (a) shall be considered to be connected with each of the parties to the agreement.

Article 5

1. For the purpose of Article 3 (b), the ECU is the unit of account used for drawing up the budget of the Community pursuant to Articles 207 and 209 of the Treaty.

2. Article 1 shall remain applicable where during any period of two consecutive financial years the total turnover referred to in Article 3 (b) is exceeded by no more than 10%.

3. For the purpose of calculating total turnover within the meaning of Article 3 (b), the turnovers achieved during the last financial year by the party to the agreement and connected undertakings in respect of all goods and services, excluding all taxes and other duties, shall be added together. For this purpose no account shall be taken of dealings between the parties to the agreement or between these undertakings and undertakings connected with them or between the connected undertakings.

Article 6

The Commission may withdraw the benefit of this Regulation, pursuant to Article 7 of Regulation No 19/65/EEC, when it finds in a particular case that an agreement which is exempted by this Regulation nevertheless has certain effects which are incompatible with the conditions set out in Article

85 (3) of the Treaty, and in particular where:

(a) the contract goods are not subject, in the contract territory, to effective competition from identical goods or goods considered by users as equivalent in view of their characteristics, price and intended use;

(b) access by other suppliers to the different stages of distribution within the contract territory is made difficult to a significant extent;

(c) for reasons other than those referred to in Article 3 (c) and (d) it is not possible for intermediaries or users to obtain supplies of the contract goods from dealers outside the contract territory on the terms there customary;

(d) the exclusive distributor:
1. without any objectively justified reason refuses to supply in the contract territory categories of purchasers who cannot obtain contract goods elsewhere on suitable terms or applies to them differing prices or conditions of sale;
2. sells the contract goods at excessively high prices.

Article 7

In the period 1 July 1983 to 31 December 1986, the prohibition in Article 85 (1) of the Treaty shall not apply to agreements which were in force on 1 July 1983 or entered into force between 1 July and 31 December 1983 and which satisfy the exemption conditions of Regulation No 67/67/EEC (¹).

Article 8

This Regulation shall not apply to agreements entered into for the resale of drinks in premises used for the sale and consumption of drinks or for the resale of petroleum products in service stations.

Article 9

This Regulation shall apply *mutatis mutandis* to concerted practices of the type defined in Article 1.

Article 10

This Regulation shall enter into force on 1 July 1983.
It shall expire on 31 December 1997.

This Regulation shall be binding in its entirety and directly applicable in all Member States.

Done at Brussels, 22 June 1983.

For the Commission
Frans ANDRIESSEN
Member of the Commission

_____

(¹) OJ No 57, 25. 3. 1967, p. 849/67.

COMMISSION REGULATION (EEC) No 1984/83
of 22 June 1983
on the application of Article 85 (3) of the Treaty to categories of exclusive purchasing agreements

THE COMMISSION OF THE EURO-PEAN COMMUNITIES,

Having regard to the Treaty establishing the European Economic Community,

Having regard to Council Regulation No 19/65/EEC of 2 March 1965 on the application of Article 85 (3) of the Treaty to certain categories of agreements and concerted practices (¹), as last amended by the Act of Accession of Greece, and in particular Article 1 thereof,

Having published a draft of this Regulation (²),

Having consulted the Advisory Committee on Restrictive Practices and Dominant Positions,

(1) Whereas Regulation No 19/65/EEC empowers the Commission to apply Article 85 (3) of the Treaty by regulation to certain categories of bilateral exclusive purchasing agreements entered into for the purpose of the resale of goods and corresponding concerted practices falling within Article 85 (1);

(2) Whereas experience to date makes it possible to define three categories of agreements and concerted practices which can be regarded as normally satisfying the conditions laid down in Article 85 (3); whereas the first category comprises exclusive purchasing agreements of short and medium duration in all sectors of the economy; whereas the other two categories comprise long-term exclusive purchasing agreements entered into for the resale of beer in premises used for the sale and consumption (beer supply agreements) and of petroleum products in filling stations (service-station agreements);

(3) Whereas exclusive purchasing agreements of the categories defined in this Regulation may fall within the prohibition contained in Article 85 (1) of the Treaty; whereas this will often be the case with agreements concluded between undertakings from different Member States; whereas an exclusive purchasing agreement to which undertakings from only one Member State are party and which concerns the resale of goods within that Member State may also be caught by

(¹) OJ No 36, 6. 3. 1965, p. 533/65.
(²) OJ No C 172, 10.7. 1982, p.7

the prohibition; whereas this is in particular the case where it is one of a number of similar agreements which together may affect trade between Member States;

(4) Whereas it is not necessary expressly to exclude from the defined categories those agreements which do not fulfil the conditions of Article 85 (1) of the Treaty;

(5) Whereas the exclusive purchasing agreements defined in this Regulation lead in general to an improvement in distribution; whereas they enable the supplier to plan the sales of his goods with greater precision and for a longer period and ensure that the reseller's requirements will be met on a regular basis for the duration of the agreement; whereas this allows the parties to limit the risk to them of variations in market conditions and to lower distribution costs;

(6) Whereas such agreements also facilitate the promotion of the sales of a product and lead to intensive marketing because the supplier, in consideration for the exclusive purchasing obligation, is as a rule under an obligation to contribute to the improvement of the structure of the distribution network, the quality of the promotional effort or the sales success; whereas, at the same time, they stimulate competition between the products of different manufacturers; whereas the appointment of several resellers, who are bound to purchase exclusively from the manufacturer and who take over sales

promotion, customer services and carrying of stock, is often the most effective way, and sometimes the only way, for the manufacturer to penetrate a market and compete with other manufacturers already present; whereas this is particularly so in the case of small and medium-sized undertakings; whereas it must be left to the contracting parties to decide whether and to what extent they consider it desirable to incorporate in their agreements terms concerning the promotion of sales;

(7) Whereas, as a rule, exclusive purchasing agreements between suppliers and resellers also allow consumers a fair share of the resulting benefit as they gain the advantages of regular supply and are able to obtain the contract goods more quickly and more easily;

(8) Whereas this Regulation must define the obligations restricting competition which may be included in an exclusive purchasing agreement; whereas the other restrictions of competition allowed under this Regulation in addition to the exclusive purchasing obligation lead to a clear division of functions between the parties and compel the reseller to concentrate his sales efforts on the contract goods; whereas they are, where they are agreed only for the duration of the agreement, generally necessary in order to attain the improvement in the distribution of goods sought through exclusive purchasing; whereas further restrictive obligations and in particular those

which limit the reseller's choice of customers or his freedom to determine his prices and conditions of sale cannot be exempted under this Regulation;

(9) Whereas the exemption by categories should be reserved for agreements for which it can be assumed with sufficient certainty that they satisfy the conditions of Article 85 (3) of the Treaty;

(10) Whereas it is not possible, in the absence of a case-by-case examination, to consider that adequate improvements in distribution occur where a manufacturer imposes an exclusive purchasing obligation with respect to his goods on a manufacturer with whom he is in competition; whereas such agreements should, therefore, be excluded from the exemption by categories; whereas certain derogations from this rule in favour of small and medium-sized undertakings can be allowed;

(11) Whereas certain conditions must be attached to the exemption by categories so that access by other undertakings to the different stages of distribution can be ensured; whereas, to this end, limits must be set to the scope and to the duration of the exclusive purchasing obligation; whereas it appears appropriate as a general rule to grant the benefit of a general exemption from the prohibition on restrictive agreements only to exclusive purchasing agreements which are concluded for a specified product or range of products and for not more than five years;

(12) Whereas, in the case of beer supply agreements and service-station agreements, different rules should be laid down which take account of the particularities of the markets in question;

(13) Whereas these agreements are generally distinguished by the fact that, on the one hand, the supplier confers on the reseller special commercial or financial advantages by contributing to his financing, granting him or obtaining for him a loan on favourable terms, equipping him with a site or premises for conducting his business, providing him with equipment or fittings, or undertaking other investments for his benefit and that, on the other hand, the reseller enters into a long-term exclusive purchasing obligation which in most cases is accompanied by a ban on dealing in competing products;

(14) Whereas beer supply and service-station agreements, like the other exclusive purchasing agreements dealt with in this Regulation, normally produce an appreciable improvement in distribution in which consumers are allowed a fair share of the resulting benefit;

(15) Whereas the commercial and financial advantages conferred by the supplier on the reseller make it significantly easier to establish, modernize, maintain and operate premises used for the sale and consumption of drinks and service stations; whereas the exclusive purchasing obligation and the ban on dealing in competing products imposed on the reseller

incite the reseller to devote all the resources at his disposal to the sale of the contract goods; whereas such agreements lead to durable cooperation between the parties allowing them to improve or maintain the quality of the contract goods and of the services to the customer and sales efforts of the reseller; whereas they allow long-term planning of sales and consequently a cost effective organization of production and distribution; whereas the pressure of competition between products of different makes obliges the undertakings involved to determine the number and character of premises used for the sale and consumption of drinks and service stations, in accordance with the wishes of customers;

(16) Whereas consumers benefit from the improvements described, in particular because they are ensured supplies of goods of satisfactory quality at fair prices and conditions while being able to choose between the products of different manufacturers;

(17) Whereas the advantages produced by beer supply agreements and service-station agreements cannot otherwise be secured to the same extent and with the same degree of certainty; whereas the exclusive purchasing obligation on the reseller and the non-competition clause imposed on him are essential components of such agreements and thus usually indispensable for the attainment of these advantages; whereas, however, this is true only as long as the reseller's obligation to

purchase from the supplier is confined in the case of premises used for the sale and consumption of drinks to beers and other drinks of the types offered by the supplier, and in the case of service stations to petroleum-based fuel for motor vehicles and other petroleum-based fuels; whereas the exclusive purchasing obligation for lubricants and related petroleum-based products can be accepted only on condition that the supplier provides for the reseller or finances the procurement of specific equipment for the carrying out of lubrication work; whereas this obligation should only relate to products intended for use within the service station;

(18) Whereas, in order to maintain the reseller's commercial freedom and to ensure access to the retail level of distribution on the part of other suppliers, not only the scope but also the duration of the exclusive purchasing obligation must be limited; whereas it appears appropriate to allow drinks suppliers a choice between a medium-term exclusive purchasing agreement covering a range of drinks and a long-term exclusive purchasing agreement for beer; whereas it is necessary to provide special rules for those premises used for the sale and consumption of drinks which the supplier lets to the reseller; whereas, in this case, the reseller must have the right to obtain, under the conditions specified in this Regulation, other drinks, except beer, supplied under the agreement or of the same type but bearing a different trademark;

whereas a uniform maximum duration should be provided for service-station agreements, with the exception of tenancy agreements between the supplier and the reseller, which takes account of the long-term character of the relationship between the parties;

(19) Whereas to the extent that Member States provide, by law or administrative measures, for the same upper limit of duration for the exclusive purchasing obligation upon the reseller as in service-station agreements laid down in this Regulation but provide for a permissible duration which varies in proportion to the consideration provided by the supplier or generally provide for a shorter duration than that permitted by this Regulation, such laws or measures are not contrary to the objectives of this Regulation which, in this respect, merely sets an upper limit to the duration of service-station agreements; whereas the application and enforcement of such national laws or measures must therefore be regarded as compatible with the provisions of this Regulation;

(20) Whereas the limitations and conditions provided for in this Regulation are such as to guarantee effective competition on the markets in question; whereas, therefore, the agreements to which the exemption by category applies do not normally enable the participating undertakings to eliminate competition for a substantial part of the products in question;

(21) Whereas, in particular cases in which agreements or concerted practices satisfying the conditions of this Regulation nevertheless have effects incompatible with Article 85 (3) of the Treaty, the Commission may withdraw the benefit of the exemption by category from the undertakings party thereto;

(22) Whereas agreements and concerted practices which satisfy the conditions set out in this Regulation need not be notified; whereas an under-taking may nonetheless, in a particular case where real doubt exists, request the Commission to declare whether its agreements comply with this Regulation;

(23) Whereas this Regulation does not affect the applicability of Commission Regulation (EEC) No 3604/82 of 23 December 1982 on the application of Article 85 (3) of the Treaty to categories of specialization agreements (1); whereas it does not exclude the application of Article 86 of the Treaty,

HAS ADOPTED THIS REGULATION:

TITLE I

General provisions

Article 1

Pursuant to Article 85 (3) of the Treaty, and subject to the conditions set out in Articles 2 to 5 of this Regulation, it is hereby declared that Article 85 (1) of the Treaty shall not apply to agreements to which only two undertakings

(1) OJ No L 376, 31. 12. 1982, p. 33.

are party and whereby one party, the reseller, agrees with the other, the supplier, to purchase certain goods specified in the agreement for resale only from the supplier or from a connected undertaking or from another undertaking which the supplier has entrusted with the sale of his goods.

Article 2

1. No other restriction of competition shall be imposed on the supplier than the obligation not to distribute the contract goods or goods which compete with the contract goods in the reseller's principal sales area and at the reseller's level of distribution.

2. Apart from the obligation described in Article 1, no other restriction of competition shall be imposed on the reseller than the obligation not to manufacture or distribute goods which compete with the contract goods.

3. Article 1 shall apply notwithstanding that the reseller undertakes any or all of the following obligations;

(a) to purchase complete ranges of goods;

(b) to purchase minimum quantities of goods which are subject to the exclusive purchasing obligation;

(c) to sell the contract goods under trademarks, or packed and presented as specified by the supplier;

(d) to take measures for the promotion of sales, in particular:
– to advertise,
– to maintain a sales network or stock of goods,
– to provide customer and guarantee services,
– to employ staff having specialized or technical training.

Article 3

Article 1 shall not apply where:

(a) manufacturers of identical goods or of goods which are considered by users as equivalent in view of their characteristics, price and intended use enter into reciprocal exclusive purchasing agreements between themselves in respect of such goods;

(b) manufacturers of identical goods or of goods which are considered by users as equivalent in view of their characteristics, price and intended use enter into a non-reciprocal exclusive purchasing agreement between themselves in respect of such goods, unless at least one of them has a total annual turnover of no more than 100 million ECU;

(c) the exclusive purchasing obligation is agreed for more than one type of goods where these are neither by their nature nor according to commercial usage connected to each other;

(d) the agreement is concluded for an indefinite duration or for a period of more than five years.

Article 4

1. Article 3 (a) and (b) shall also apply where the goods there referred to are manufactured by an undertaking connected with a party to the agreement.

2. Connected undertakings are:

(a) undertakings in which a party to the agreement, directly or indirectly:

– owns more than half the capital or business assets, or

– has the power to exercise more than half the voting rights, or

– has the power to appoint more than half the members of the supervisory board, board of directors or bodies legally representing the undertaking, or

– has the right to manage the affairs;

(b) undertakings which directly or indirectly have in or over a party to the agreement the rights or powers listed in (a);

(c) undertakings in which an undertaking referred to in (b) directly or indirectly has the rights or powers listed in (a).

3. Undertakings in which the parties to the agreement or undertakings connected with them jointly have the rights or powers set out in paragraph 2 (a) shall be considered to be connected with each of the parties to the agreement.

Article 5

1. For the purpose of Article 3 (b), the ECU is the unit of account used for drawing up the budget of the Community pursuant to Articles 207 and 209 of the Treaty.

2. Article 1 shall remain applicable where during any period of two consecutive financial years the total turnover referred to in Article 3 (b) is exceeded by no more than 10%.

3. For the purpose of calculating total turnover within the meaning of Article 3 (b), the turnovers achieved during the last financial year by the party to the agreement and connected undertakings in respect of all goods and services, excluding all taxes and other duties, shall be added together. For this purpose, no account shall be taken of dealings between the parties to the agreement or between these undertakings and undertakings connected with them or between the connected undertakings.

TITLE II

Special provisions for beer supply agreements

Article 6

1. Pursuant to Article 85 (3) of the Treaty, and subject to Articles 7 to 9 of this Regulation, it is hereby declared that Article 85 (1) of the Treaty shall not apply to agreements to which only two undertakings are party and whereby one party, the reseller, agrees with the other, the supplier, in consideration for according special commercial or financial advantages, to purchase only from the supplier, an undertaking connected with the supplier or another undertaking entrusted by the supplier with the distribution of his goods, certain beers, or certain beers and certain other drinks, specified in the agreement for resale in premises used for the sale and consumption of drinks and designated in the agreement.

2. The declaration in paragraph 1 shall also apply where exclusive purchasing obligations of the kind described in paragraph 1 are imposed on the reseller in favour of the supplier by another undertaking which is itself not a supplier.

Article 7

1. Apart from the obligation referred to in Article 6, no restriction on competition shall be imposed on the reseller other than:

(a) the obligation not to sell beers and other drinks which are supplied by other undertakings and which are of the same type as the beers or other drinks supplied under the agreement in the premises designated in the agreement;

(b) the obligation, in the event that the reseller sells in the premises designated in the agreement beers which are supplied by other undertakings and which are of a different type from the beers supplied under the agreement, to sell such beers only in bottles, cans or other small packages, unless the sale of such beers in draught form is customary or is necessary to satisfy a sufficient demand from consumers;

(c) the obligation to advertise goods supplied by other undertakings within or outside the premises designated in the agreement only in proportion to the share of these goods in the total turnover realized in the premises.

2. Beers or other drinks are of the same type are those which are not clearly distinguishable in view of their composition, appearance and taste.

Article 8

1. Article 6 shall not apply where:

(a) the supplier or a connected undertaking imposes on the reseller exclusive purchasing obligations for goods other than drinks or for services;

(b) the supplier restricts the freedom of the reseller to obtain from an undertaking of his choice either services or goods for which neither an exclusive purchasing obligation nor a ban on dealing in competing products may be imposed;

(c) the agreement is concluded for an indefinite duration or for a period of more than five years and the exclusive purchasing obligation relates to specified beers and other drinks;

(d) the agreement is concluded for an indefinite duration or for a period of more than 10 years and the exclusive purchasing obligation relates only to specified beers;

(e) the supplier obliges the reseller to impose the exclusive purchasing obligation on his successor for a longer period than the reseller would himself remain tied to the supplier.

2. Where the agreement relates to premises which the supplier lets to the reseller or allows the reseller to occupy on some other basis in law or in fact, the following provisions shall also apply:

(a) notwithstanding paragraphs (1) (c) and (d), the exclusive purchasing obligations and bans on dealing in competing products specified in this Title may be imposed on the reseller for the whole period for which the reseller in fact operates the premises;

(b) the agreement must provide for the reseller to have the right to obtain:

– drinks, except beer, supplied under the agreement from other undertakings where these undertakings offer them on more favourable conditions which the supplier does not meet,

– drinks, except beer, which are of the same type as those supplied under the agreement but which bear different trade marks, from other undertakings where the supplier does offer them.

Article 9

Articles 2 (1) and (3), 3 (a) and (b), 4 and 5 shall apply *mutatis mutandis*.

TITLE III

Special provisions for service-station agreements

Article 10

Pursuant to Article 85 (3) of the Treaty and subject to Articles 11 to 13 of this Regulation, it is hereby declared that Article 85 (1) of the Treaty shall not apply to agreements to which only two undertakings are party and whereby one party, the reseller, agrees with the other, the supplier, in consideration for the according of special commercial or financial advantages, to purchase only from the supplier, an undertaking connected with the supplier or another undertaking entrusted by the supplier with the distribution of his goods, certain petroleum-based motor-vehicle fuels or certain petroleum-based motor-vehicle and other fuels specified in the agreement for resale in a service station designated in the agreement.

Article 11

Apart from the obligation referred to in Article 10, no restriction on competition shall be imposed on the reseller other than:

(a) the obligation not to sell motor-vehicle fuel and other fuels which are supplied by other undertakings in the service station designated in the agreement;

(b) the obligation not to use lubricants or related petroleum-based products which are supplied by other undertakings within the service station designated in the agreement where the supplier or a connected undertaking has made available to the reseller, or financed, a lubrication bay or other motor-vehicle lubrication equipment;

(c) the obligation to advertise goods supplied by other undertakings within or outside the service station designated in the agreement only in proportion to the share of these goods in the total turnover realized in the service station;

(d) the obligation to have equipment owned by the supplier or a connected undertaking or financed by the supplier or a connected undertaking serviced by the supplier or an undertaking designated by him.

Article 12

1. Article 10 shall not apply where:

(a) the supplier or a connected undertaking imposes on the reseller exclusive purchasing obligations for goods other than motor-vehicle and other fuels or for services, except in the case of the obligations referred to in Article 11(b) and (d);

(b) the supplier restricts the freedom of the reseller to obtain, from an undertaking of his choice, goods or services, for which under the provisions of this Title neither an exclusive purchasing obligation nor a ban on dealing in competing products may be imposed;

(c) the agreement is concluded for an indefinite duration or for a period of more than 10 years;

(d) the supplier obliges the reseller to impose the exclusive purchasing obligation on his successor for a longer period than the reseller would himself remain tied to the supplier.

2. Where the agreement relates to a service station which the supplier lets to the reseller, or allows the reseller to occupy on some other basis, in law or in fact, exclusive purchasing obligations or prohibitions of competition indicated in this Title may, notwithstanding paragraph 1(c), be imposed on the reseller for the whole period for which the reseller in fact operates the premises.

Article 13

Articles 2 (1) and (3), 3 (a) and (b), 4 and 5 of this Regulation shall apply *mutatis mutandis.*

TITLE IV

Miscellaneous provisions

Article 14

The Commission may withdraw the benefit of this Regulation, pursuant to Article 7 of Regulation No 19/65/EEC, when it finds in a particular case that an agreement which is exempted by this Regulation nevertheless has certain effects which are incompatible with the conditions set out in Article 85 (3) of the Treaty, and in particular where:

(a) the contract goods are not subject, in a substantial part of the common market, to effective competition from identical goods or goods considered by users as equivalent in view of their characteristics, price and intended use;

(b) access by of other suppliers to the different stages of distribution in a substantial part of the common market is made difficult to a significant extent;

(c) the supplier without any objectively justified reason:

1. refuses to supply categories of resellers who cannot obtain the contract goods elsewhere on suitable terms or applies to them differing prices or conditions of sale;

2. applies less favourable prices or conditions of sale to resellers bound by an exclusive purchasing obligation as compared with other resellers at the same level of distribution.

Article 15

1. In the period I July 1983 to 31 December 1986, the prohibition in Article 85 (1) of the Treaty shall not apply to agreements of the kind described in Article 1 which either were

in force on 1 July 1983 or entered into force between 1 July and 31 December of 1983 and which satisfy the exemption conditions under Regulation No 67/67/EEC (¹).

2. In the period 1 July 1983 to 31 December 1988, the prohibition in Article 85 (1) of the Treaty shall not apply to agreements of the kinds described in Articles 6 and 10 which either were in force on 1 July 1983 or entered into force between 1 July and 31 December 1983 and which satisfy the exemption conditions of Regulation No 67/67/EEC.

3. In the case of agreements of the kinds described in Articles 6 and 10, which were in force on 1 July 1983 and which expire after 31 December 1988, the prohibition in Article 85 (1) of the Treaty shall not apply in the period from 1 January 1989 to the expiry of the agreement but at the latest to the expiry of this Regulation to the extent that the supplier releases the reseller, before 1 January 1989, from all obligations which would prevent the application of the exemption under Titles II and III.

Article 16

This Regulation shall not apply to agreements by which the supplier undertakes with the reseller to supply only to the reseller certain goods for resale, in the whole or in a defined part of the Community, and the reseller undertakes with the supplier to purchase these goods only from the supplier.

Article 17

This Regulation shall not apply where the parties or connected undertakings, for the purpose of resale in one and the same premises used for the sale and consumption of drinks or service station, enter into agreements both of the kind referred to in Title I and of a kind referred to in Title II or III.

Article 18

This Regulation shall apply *mutatis mutandis* to the categories of concerted practices defined in Articles 1, 6 and 10.

Article 19

This Regulation shall enter into force on 1 July 1983.
It shall expire on 31 December 1997.

This Regulation shall be binding in its entirety and directly applicable in all Member States.

Done at Brussels, 22 June 1983.

For the Commission
Frans ANDRIESSEN
Member of the Commission

———————

(¹) OJ No 57, 25. 3. 1967, p. 849/67.

Commission notice modifying the notice (^{1}) concerning Commission
Regulations (EEC) No 1983/83 and (EEC) No 1984/83 of 22 June 1983
on the application of Article 85 (3) of the EEC Treaty to categories of
exclusive distribution and exclusive purchasing agreements

(92/C 121/02)

This modification is undertaken consequent to the judgment of the Court of Justice in Case C-234/89 'Delimitis/ Henninger Bräu'.

The following passage is inserted after point 39, and beneath the heading 'V. Beer supply agreements'. Points 40 to 66 become points 41 to 67. The subheadings, under heading V, become:

– 2. Exclusive purchasing obligation

– 3. Other restrictions of competition that are exempted

– 4. Agreements excluded from the block exemption.

1. *Agreements of minor importance*

40. It is recalled that the Commission's notice on agreements of minor importance (^{2}) states that the Commission holds the view that agreements between undertakings do not fall under the prohibition of Article 85 (^{1}) of the EEC Treaty if certain conditions as regards market share and turnover are met by the undertakings concerned. Thus, it is

evident that when an undertaking, brewery or wholesaler, surpasses the limits as laid down in the above notice, the agreements concluded by it may fall under Article 85 (1) of the EEC Treaty. The notice, however, does not apply where in a relevant market competition is restricted by the cumulative effects of parallel networks of similar agreements which would not individually fall under Article 85 (1) of the EEC Treaty if the notice was applicable. Since the markets for beer will frequently be characterized by the existence of cumulative effects, it seems appropriate to determine which agreements can nevertheless be considered de minimis.

The Commission is of the opinion that an exclusive beer supply agreement concluded by a brewery, in the sense of Article 6, and including Article 8 (2) of Regulation (EEC) 1984/83 does not, in general, fall under Article 85 (1) of the EEC Treaty if

– the market share of that brewery is not higher than 1 % on the national market for the resale of beer in premises used for the sale and consumption of drinks, and

(^{1}) OJ No C 101, 13. 4. 1984, p. 2.
(^{2}) OJ No C 231, 12. 9. 1986, p. 2.

– if that brewery does not produce more than 200 000 hl of beer per annum.

However, these principles do not apply if the agreement in question is concluded for more than 7 and a half years in as far as it covers beer and other drinks, and for 15 years if it covers only beer.

In order to establish the market share of the brewery and its annual production, the provisions of Article 4 (2) of Regulation (EEC) 1984/83 apply.

As regards exclusive beer supply agreements in the sense of Article 6, and including Article 8 (2) of Regulation (EEC) 1984/83 which are concluded by wholesalers, the above principles apply *mutatis mutandis* by taking account of the position of the brewery whose beer is the main subject of the agreement in question.

The present communication does not preclude that in individual cases even agreements between undertakings which do not fulfil the above criteria, in particular where the number of outlets tied to them is limited as compared to the number of outlets existing on the market, may still have only a negligible effect on trade between Member States or on competition, and would therefore not be caught by Article 85 (1) of the EEC Treaty.

Neither does this communication in any way Pejudge the application of national law to the agreements covered by it.

Commission notice concerning Commission Regulations (EEC) No 1983/83 and (EEC) No 1984/83 of 22 June 1983 on the application of Article 85 (3) of the Treaty to categories of exclusive distribution and exclusive purchasing agreements

(84/C 101/02)

(This text replaces the previous text published in Official Journal of the European Communities No C 355 of 30 December 1983, page 7)

I. Introduction

1. Commission Regulation No 67/67/EEC of 22 March 1967 on the application of Article 85 (3) of the Treaty to certain categories of exclusive dealing agreements (¹) expired on 30 June 1983 after being in force for over 15 years. With Regulations (EEC) No 1983/83 and (EEC) No 1984/83 (²), the Commission has adapted the block exemption of exclusive distribution agreements and exclusive purchasing agreements to the intervening developments in the common market and in Community law. Several of the provisions in the new Regulations are new. A certain amount of interpretative guidance is therefore called for. This will assist undertakings in bringing their agreements into line with the new legal requirements and will also help ensure that the Regulations are applied uniformly in all the Member States.

2. In determining how a given provision is to be applied, one must take into account, in addition to the ordinary meaning of the words used, the intention of the provision as this emerges from the preamble. For further guidance, reference should be made to the principles that have been involved in the case law of the Court of Justice of the European Communities and in the Commission's decisions on individual cases.

3. This notice sets out the main consideration which will determine the Commission's view of whether or not an exclusive distribution or purchasing agreement is covered by the block exemption. The notice is without prejudice to the jurisdiction of national courts to apply the Regulations, although it may well be of persuasive authority in proceedings before such courts. Nor does the notice necessarily indicate the interpretation which might be given to the provisions by the Court of Justice.

II. Exclusive distribution and exclusive purchasing agreements (Regulations (EEC) No 1983/83 and (EEC) No 1984/83)

1. *Similarities and differences*

4. Regulations (EEC) No 1983/83 and (EEC) No 1984/83 are both concerned with exclusive agreements between two undertakings for the purpose of the resale of goods. Each deals with a particular type of such agreements. Regulation (EEC) No 1983/83 applies to

(¹) OJ No 57, 25. 3. 1967, p. 849/67.
(²) OJ No L 173, 30. 6. 1983, pp. 1. & 5.

exclusive distribution agreements, Regulation (EEC) No 1984/83 to exclusive purchasing agreements. The distinguishing feature of exclusive distribution agreements is that one party, the supplier, allots to the other, the reseller, a defined territory (the contract territory) on which the reseller has to concentrate his sales effort, and in return undertakes not to supply any other reseller in that territory. In exclusive purchasing agreements, the reseller agrees to purchase the contract goods only from the other party and not from any other supplier. The supplier is entitled to supply other resellers in the same sales area and at the same level of distribution. Unlike an exclusive distributor, the tied reseller is not protected against competition from other resellers who, like himself, receive the contract goods direct from the supplier. On the other hand, he is free of restrictions as to the area over which he may make his sales effort.

5. In keeping with their common starting point, the Regulations have many provisions that are the same or similar in both Regulations. This is true of the basic provision in Article 1, in which the respective subject-matters of the block exemption, the exclusive supply or purchasing obligation, are defined, and of the exhaustive list of restrictions of competition which may be agreed in addition to the exclusive supply or purchasing obligation (Article 2 (1) and (2)), the non-exhaustive enumeration of other obligations which do not prejudice the block exemption (Article 2 (3)), the inapplicability of the block exemption in principle to exclusive agreements between competing manufacturers (Article 3 (a) and (b), 4 and 5), the withdrawal of the block exemption in

individual cases (Article 6 of Regulation (EEC) No 1983/83 and Article 14 of Regulation (EEC) No 1984/83), the transitional provisions (Article 7 of Regulation (EEC) No 1983/83 and Article 15 (1) of Regulation (EEC) No 1984/83), and the inclusion of concerted practices within the scope of the Regulations (Article 9 of Regulation (EEC) No 1983/83 and Article 18 of Regulation (EEC) No 1984/83). In so far as their wording permits, these parallel provisions are to be interpreted in the same way.

6. Different rules are laid down in the Regulations wherever they need to take account of matters which are peculiar to the exclusive distribution agreements or exclusive purchasing agreements respectively. This applies in Regulation (EEC) No 1983/83, to the provisions regarding the obligation on the exclusive distributor not actively to promote sales outside the contract territory (Article 2 (2) (c)) and the inapplicability of the block exemption to agreements which give the exclusive distributor absolute territorial protection (Article 3 (c) and (d)) and, in Regulation (EEC) No 1984/83, to the provisions limiting the scope and duration of the block exemption for exclusive purchasing agreements in general (Article 3 (c) and (d)) and for beer-supply and service-station agreements in particular (Titles II and III).

7. The scope of the two Regulations has been defined so as to avoid any overlap (Article 16 of Regulation (EEC) No 1984/83).

2. *Basic provision*
   (Article 1)

8. Both Regulations apply only to

agreements entered into for the purpose of the resale of goods to which not more than two undertakings are party.

(a) 'For resale'

9. The notion of resale requires that the goods concerned be disposed of by the purchasing party to others in return for consideration. Agreements on the supply or purchase of goods which the purchasing party transforms or processes into other goods or uses or consumes in manufacturing other goods are not agreement for resale. The same applies to the supply of components which are combined with other components into a different product. The criterion is that the goods distributed by the reseller are the same as those the other party has supplied to him for that purpose. The economic identity of the goods is not affected if the reseller merely breaks up and packages the goods in smaller quantities, or repackages them, before resale.

10. Where the reseller performs additional operations to improve the quality, durability, appearance or taste of the goods (such as rust-proofing of metals, sterilization of food or the addition of colouring matter or flavourings to drugs), the position will mainly depend on how much value the operation adds to the goods. Only a slight addition in value can be taken not to change the economic identity of the goods. In determining the precise dividing line in individual cases, trade usage in particular must be considered. The Commission applies the same principles to agreements under which the reseller is supplied with a concentrated extract for a drink which he has to dilute with water, pure alcohol or another liquid and to bottle before reselling.

(b) 'Goods'

11. Exclusive agreements for the supply of services rather than the resale of goods are not covered by the Regulations. The block exemption still applies, however, where the reseller provides customer or after-sales services incidentally to the resale of the goods. Nevertheless, a case where the charge for the service is higher than the price of the goods would fall outside the scope of the Regulations.

12. The hiring out of goods in return for payment comes closer, economically speaking, to a resale of goods than to provision of services. The Commission therefore regards exclusive agreements under which the purchasing party hires out or leases to others the goods supplied to him as covered by the Regulations.

(c) 'Only two undertakings party'

13. To be covered by the block exemption, the exclusive distribution or purchasing agreement must be between only one supplier and one reseller in each case. Several undertakings forming one economic unit count as one undertaking.

14. This limitation on the number of undertakings that may be party relates solely to the individual agreement. A supplier does not lose the benefit of the block exemption if he enters into exclusive distribution or purchasing agreements covering the same goods with several resellers.

15. The supplier may delegate the

performance of his contractual obligations to a connected or independent undertaking which he has entrusted with the distribution of his goods, so that the reseller has to purchase the contract goods from the latter undertaking. This principle is expressly mentioned only in Regulation (EEC) No 1984/83 (Article 1, 6 and 10), because the question of delegation arises mainly in connection with exclusive purchasing agreements. It also applies, however, to exclusive distribution agreements under Regulation (EEC) No 1983/83.

16. The involvement of undertakings other than the contracting parties must be confined to the execution of deliveries. The parties may accept exclusive supply or purchase obligations only for themselves, and not impose them on third parties, since otherwise more than two undertakings would be party to the agreement. The obligation of the parties to ensure that the obligations they have accepted are respected by connected undertakings is, however, covered by the block exemption.

3. *Other restrictions on competition that are exempted*
(Article 2 (1) and (2))

17. Apart from the exclusive supply obligation (Regulation (EEC) No 1983/83) or exclusive purchase obligation (Regulation (EEC) No 1984/83), obligations defined in Article 1 which must be present if the block exemption is to apply, the only other restrictions of competition that may be agreed by the parties are those set out in Article 2 (1) and (2). If they agree on further obligations restrictive of competition, the agreement as a whole is no longer

covered by the block exemption and requires individual exemption. For example, an agreement will exceed the bounds of the Regulations if the parties relinquish the possibility of independently determining their prices or conditions of business or undertake to refrain from, or even prevent, cross-border trade, which the Regulations expressly state must not be impeded. Among other clauses which in general are not permissible under the Regulations are those which impede the reseller in his free choice of customers.

18. The obligations restrictive of competition that are exempted may be agreed only for the duration of the agreement. This also applied to restrictions accepted by the supplier or reseller on competing with the other party.

4. *Obligations upon the reseller which do not prejudice the block exemption*
(Article 2 (3))

19. The obligations cited in this provision are examples of clauses which generally do not restrict competition. Undertakings are therefore free to include one, several or all of these obligations in their agreements. However, the obligations may not be formulated or applied in such a way as to take on the character of restrictions of competition that are not permitted. To forestall this danger, Article 2(3) (b) of Regulation (EEC) No 1984/83 expressly allows minimum purchase obligations only for goods that are subject to an exclusive purchasing obligation.

20. As part of the obligation to take measures for promotion of sales and in particular to maintain a distribution network (Article 2 (3) (c) of Regulation

(EEC) No 1983/83 and Article 2 (3) (d) of Regulation (EEC) No 1984/83), the reseller may be forbidden to supply the contract goods to unsuitable dealers. Such clauses are unobjectionable if admission to the distribution network is based on objective criteria of a qualitative nature relating to the professional qualifications of the owner of the business or his staff or the suitability of his business premises, if the criteria are the same for all potential dealers, and if the criteria are actually applied in a nondiscriminatory manner. Distribution systems which do not fulfil these conditions are not covered by the block exemption.

5. *Inapplicability of the block exemption to exclusive agreements between competing manufacturers* (Articles 3 (a) and (b), 4 and 5)

21. The block exemption does not apply if either the parties themselves or undertakings connected with them are manufacturers, manufacture goods belonging to the same product market, and enter into exclusive distribution or purchasing agreements with one another in respect of those goods. Only identical or equivalent goods are regarded as belonging to the same product market. The goods in question must be interchangeable. Whether or not this is the case must be judged from the vantage point of the user, normally taking the characteristics, price and intended use of the goods together. In certain cases, however, goods can form a separate market on the basis of their characteristics, their price or their intended use alone. This is true especially where consumer preferences have developed. The above provisions are applicable regardless of whether or not the parties of the undertakings connected with them are based in the Community and whether or not they are already actually in competition with one another in the relevant goods inside or outside the Community.

22. In principle, both reciprocal and non-reciprocal exclusive agreements between competing manufacturers are not covered by the block exemption and are therefore subject to individual scrutiny of their compatibility with Article 85 of the Treaty, but there is an exception for non-reciprocal agreements of the above mentioned kind where one or both of the parties are undertakings with a total annual turnover of no more than 100 million ECU (Article 3 (b)). Annual turnover is used as a measure of the economic strength of the undertakings involved. Therefore, the aggregate turnover from goods and services of all types, and not only from the contract goods, is to be taken. Turnover taxes and other turnover-related levies are not included in turnover. Where a party belongs to a group of connected undertakings, the world-wide turnover of the group, excluding intra-group sales (Article 5 (3)), is to be used.

23. The total turnover limit can be exceeded during any period of two successive financial years by up to 10% without loss of the block exemption. The block exemption is lost if, at the end of the second financial year, the total turnover over the preceding two years has been over 220 million ECU (Article 5 (2)).

6. *Withdrawal of the block exemption in individual cases* (Article 6 of Regulation (EEC) No 1983/83 and Article 14 of Regulation (EEC) No 1984/83)

24. The situations described are meant as illustrations of the sort of situations in which the Commission can exercise its powers under Article 7 of Council Regulation No 19/65/EEC (¹) to withdraw a block exemption. The benefit of the block exemption can only be withdrawn by a decision in an individual case following proceedings under Regulation No 17. Such a decision cannot have retroactive effect. It may be coupled with an individual exemption subject to conditions or obligations or, in an extreme case, with the finding of an infringement and an order to bring it to an end.

7. *Transitional provisions*
   (Article 7 of Regulation (EEC) No 1983/83 and Article 15 (1) of Regulation (EEC) No 1984/83

25. Exclusive distribution or exclusive purchasing agreements which were concluded and entered into force before 1 January 1984 continue to be exempted under the provisions of Regulation No 67/67/EEC until 31 December 1986. Should the parties wish to apply such agreements beyond 1 January 1987, they will either have to bring them into line with the provisions of the new Regulations or to notify them to the Commission. Special rules apply in the case of beer-supply and service-station agreements (see paragraphs 64 and 65 below).

8. *Concerted practices*
   (Article 9 of Regulation (EEC) No 1983/83 and Article 18 of Regulation (EEC) No 1984/83

26. These provisions bring within the

(¹) OJ No 36, 6.3. 1965, p. 533/65.

scope of the Regulations exclusive distribution and purchasing arrangements which are operated by undertakings but are not the subject of a legally-binding agreement.

III. Exclusive distribution agreements (Regulation (EEC) No 1983/83)

1. *Exclusive supply obligation*
   (Article 1)

27. The exclusive supply obligation does not prevent the supplier from providing the contract goods to other resellers who afterwards sell them in the exclusive distributor's territory. It makes no difference whether the other dealers concerned are established outside or inside the territory. The supplier is not in breach of his obligation to the exclusive distributor provided that he supplies the resellers who wish to sell the contract goods in territory only at their request and that the goods are handed over outside the territory. It does not matter whether the reseller takes delivery of the goods himself or through an intermediary, such as a freight forwarder. However, supplies of this nature are only permissible if the reseller and not the supplier pays the transport costs of the goods into the contract territory.

28. The goods supplied to the exclusive distributor must be intended for resale in the contract territory. This basic requirement does not, however, mean that the exclusive distributor cannot sell the contract goods to customers outside his contract territory should he receive orders from them. Under Article 2 (2) (c), the supplier can prohibit him only from seeking

customers in other areas, but not from supplying them.

29. It would also be incompatible with the Regulation for the exclusive distributor to be restricted to supplying only certain categories of customers (e.g. specialist retailers) in his contract territory and prohibited from supplying other categories (e.g. department stores), which are supplied by other resellers appointed by the supplier for that purpose.

2. *Restriction on competition by the supplier*
(Article 2 (1))

30. The restriction on the supplier himself supplying the contract goods to final users in the exclusive distributor's contract territory need not be absolute. Clauses permitting the supplier to supply certain customers in the territory – with or without payment of compensation to the exclusive distributor – are compatible with the block exemption provided the customers in question are not resellers. The supplier remains free to supply the contract goods outside the contract territory to final users based in the territory. In this case the position is the same as for dealers (see paragraph 27 above).

3. Inapplicability of the block exemption in cases of absolute terrtorial protection (Articles 3 (c) and (d)).

31. The block exemption cannot be claimed for agreements that give the exclusive distributor absolute territorial protection. If the situation described in Article 3 (c) obtains, the parties must ensure either that the contract goods can be sold in the contract territory by

parallel importers or that users have a real possibility of obtaining them from undertakings outside the contract territory, if necessary outside the Community, at the prices and on the terms there prevailing. The supplier can represent an alternative source of supply for the purposes of this provision if he is prepared to supply the contract goods on request to final users located in the contract territory.

32. Article 3 (d) is chiefly intended to safeguard the freedom of dealers and users to obtain the contract goods in other Member States. Action to impede imports into the Community from third countries will only lead to loss of the block exemption if there are no alternative sources of supply in the Community. This situation can arise especially where the exclusive distributor's contract territory covers the whole or the major part of the Community.

33. The block exemption ceases to apply as from the moment that either of the parties takes measures to impede parallel imports into the contract territory. Agreements in which the supplier undertakes with the exlusive distributor to prevent his other customers from supplying into the contract territory are ineligible for the block exemption from the outset. This is true even if the parties agree only to prevent imports into the Community from third countries. In this case it is immaterial whether or not there are alternative sources of supply in the Community. The inapplicability of the block exemption follows from the mere fact that the agreement contains restrictions on competition which are not covered by Article 2 (1).

IV. **Exclusive purchasing agreements (Regulation (EEC) No 1984/83)**

1. *Structure of the Regulation*

34. Title I of the Regulation contains general provisions for exclusive purchasing agreements and Titles II and III special provisions for beer-supply and service-station agreements. The latter types of agreement are governed exclusively by the special provisions, some of which (Articles 9 and 13), however, refer to some of the general provisions, Article 17 also excludes the combination of agreements of the kind referred to in Title I with those of the kind referred to in Titles II or III to which the same undertakings or undertakings connected with them are party. To prevent any avoidance of the special provisions for beer-supply and service-station agreements, it is also made clear that the provisions governing the exclusive distribution of goods do not apply to agreements entered into for the resale of drinks on premises used for the sale or consumption of beer or for the resale of petroleum products in service stations (Article 8 of Regulation (EEC) No 1983/83).

2. *Exclusive purchasing obligation* (Article 1)

35. The Regulation only covers agreements whereby the reseller agrees to purchase all his requirements for the contract goods from the other party. If the purchasing obligation relates to only part of such requirements, the block exemption does not apply. Clauses which allow the reseller to obtain the contract goods from other suppliers, should these sell them more cheaply or on more favourable terms than the other party are still covered by the block exemption. The same applies to clauses releasing the reseller from his exclusive purchasing obligation should the other party be unable to supply.

36 The contract goods must be specified by brand or denomination in the agreement. Only if this is done will it be possible to determine the precise scope of the reseller's exclusive purchasing obligation (Article 1) and of the ban on dealing in competing products (Article 2 (2)).

3. *Restriction on competition by the supplier* (Article 2 (1))

37. This provision allows the reseller to protect himself against direct competition from the supplier in his principal sales area. The reseller's principal sales area is determined by his normal business activity. It may be more closely defined in the agreement. However, the supplier cannot be forbidden to supply dealers who obtain the contract goods outside this area and afterwards resell them to customers inside it or to appoint other resellers in the area.

4. *Limits of the block exemption* (Article 3 (c) and (d))

38. Article 3 (c) provides that the exclusive purchasing obligation can be agreed for one or more products, but in the latter case the products must be so related as to be thought of as belonging to the same range of goods. The relationship can be founded on technical (e.g., a machine, accessories and spare parts for it) or commercial grounds (e.g. several products used for

the same purpose) or on usage in the trade (different goods that are customarily offered for sale together). In the latter case, regard must be had to the usual practice at the reseller's level of distribution on the relevant market, taking into account all relevant dealers and not only particular forms of distribution. Exclusive purchasing agreements covering goods which do not belong together can only be exempted from the competition rules by an individual decision.

39. Under Article 3 (d), exclusion purchasing agreements concluded for an indefinite period are not covered by the block exemption. Agreements which specify a fixed term but are automatically renewable unless one of the parties gives notice to terminate are to be considered to have been concluded for an indefinite period.

V. Beer-supply agreements (Title II of Regulation (EEC) No 1984/83)

1. *Exclusive purchasing obligation* (Article 6)

40. The beers and other drinks covered by the exclusive purchasing obligation must be specified by brand or denomination in the agreement. An exclusive purchasing obligation can only be imposed on the reseller for drinks which the supplier carries at the time the contract takes effect and provided that they are supplied in the quantities required, at sufficiently regular intervals and at prices and on conditions allowing normal sales to the consumer. Any extension of the exclusive purchasing obligation to drinks not specified in the agreement requires an additional agreement, which must likewise satisfy the requirements of

Title II of the Regulation. A change in the brand or denomination of a drink which in other respects remains unchanged does not constitute such an extension of the exclusive purchasing obligation.

41. The exclusive purchasing obligation can be agreed in respect of one or more premises used for the sale and consumption of drinks which the reseller runs at the time the contract takes effect The name and location of the premises must be stated in the agreement. Any extension of the exclusive purchasing obligation to other such premises requires an additional agreement, which must likewise satisfy the provisions of Title II of the Regulation.

42. The concept of 'premises used for the sale and consumption of drinks' covers any licensed premises used for this purpose. Private clubs are also included. Exclusive purchasing agreements between the supplier and the operator of an off-licence shop are governed by the provisions of Title I of the Regulation.

43. Special commercial or financial advantages are those going beyond what the reseller could normally expect under an agreement. The explanations given in the 13th recital are illustrations. Whether or not the supplier is affording the reseller special advantages depends on the nature, extent and duration of the obligation undertaken by the parties. In doubtful cases usage in the trade is the decisive element.

44. The reseller can enter into exclusive purchasing obligations both with a brewery in respect of beers of a certain type and with a drinks wholesaler in respect of beers of another type and/or

other drinks. The two agreements can be combined into one document. Article 6 also covers cases where the drinks wholesaler performs several functions at once, signing the first agreement on the brewery's and the second on his own behalf and also undertaking delivery of all the drinks. The provisions of Title II do not apply to the contractual relations between the brewery and the drinks wholesaler.

45. Article 6 (2) makes the block exemption also applicable to cases in which the supplier affords the owner of premises financial or other help in equipping them as a public house, restaurant, etc., and in return the owner imposes on the buyer or tenant of the premises an exclusive purchasing obligation in favour of the supplier. A similar situation, economically speaking, is the transmission of an exclusive purchasing obligation from the owner of a public house to his successor. Under Article 8 (1) (e) this is also, in principle, permissible.

2. *Other restrictions of competition that are exempted*
(Article 7)

46. The list of permitted obligations given in Article 7 is exhaustive. If any further obligations restricting competition are imposed on the reseller, the exclusive purchasing agreement as a whole is no longer covered by the block exemption.

47. The obligation referred to in paragraph 1 (a) applies only so long as the supplier is able to supply the beers or other drinks specified in the agreement and subject to the exclusive purchasing obligation in sufficient quantities to cover the demand the reseller

anticipates for the products from his customers.

48. Under paragraph 1 (b), the reseller is entitled to sell beer of other types in draught form if the other party has tolerated this in the past. If this is not the case, the reseller must indicate that there is sufficient demand from his customers to warrant the sale of other draught beers. The demand must be deemed sufficient if it can be satisfied without a simultaneous drop in sales of the beers specified in the exclusive purchasing agreement. It is definitely not sufficient if sales of the additional draught beer turn out to be so slow that there is a danger of its quality deteriorating. It is for the reseller to assess the potential demand of his customers for other types of beer; after all, he bears the risk if his forecasts are wrong.

49. The provision in paragraph 1 (c) is not only intended to ensure the possibility of advertising products supplied by other undertakings to the minimum extent necessary in any given circumstances. The advertising of such products should also reflect their relative importance *vis-á-vis* the competing products of the supplier who is party to the exclusive purchasing agreement. Advertising for products which the public house has just begun to sell may not be excluded or unduly impeded.

50. The Commission believes that the designations of types customary in inter-State trade and within the individual Member States may afford useful pointers to the interpretation of Article 7 (2). Nevertheless the alternative criteria stated in the provision itself are decisive. In doubtful cases, whether or not two beers are clearly distinguish-

able by their composition, appearance or taste depends on custom at the place where the public house is situated. The parties may, if they wish, jointly appoint an expert to decide the matter.

3. *Agreements excluded from the block exemption*
(Article 8)

51. The reseller's right to purchase drinks from third parties may be restricted only to the extent allowed by Articles 6 and 7. In his purchases of goods other than drinks and in his procurement of services which are not directly connected with the supply of drinks by the other party, the reseller must remain free to choose his supplier. Under Article 8 (1) (a) and (b), any action by the other party or by an undertaking connected with or appointed by him or acting at his instigation or with his agreement to prevent the reseller exercising his rights in this regard will entail the loss of the block exemption. For the purposes of these provisions it makes no difference whether the reseller's freedom is restricted by contract, informal understanding, economic pressures or other practical measures.

52. The installation of amusement machines in tenanted public houses may by agreement be made subject to the owner's permission. The owner may refuse permission on the ground that this would impair the character of the premises or he may restrict the tenant to particular types of machines. However, the practice of some owners of tenanted public houses to allow the tenant to conclude contracts for the installation of such machines only with certain undertakings which the

owner recommends is, as a rule, incompatible with this Regulation, unless the undertakings are selected on the basis of objective criteria of a qualitative nature that are the same for all potential providers of such equipment and are applied in a non-discriminatory manner. Such criteria may refer to the reliability of the undertaking and its staff and the quality of the services it provides. The supplier may not prevent a public house tenant from purchasing amusement machines rather than renting them.

53. The limitation of the duration of the agreement in Article 8 (1) (c) and (d) does not affect the parties' right to renew their agreement in accordance with the provisions of Title II of the Regulation.

54. Article 8 (2) (b) must be interpreted in the light both of the aims of the Community competition rules and of the general legal principle whereby contracting parties must exercise their rights in good faith.

55. Whether or not a third undertaking offers certain drinks covered by the exclusive purchasing obligation on more favourable terms than the other party for the purposes of the first indent of Article 8 (2) (b) is to be judged in the first instance on the basis of a comparison of prices. This should take into account the various factors that go to determine the prices. If a more favourable offer is available and the tenant wishes to accept it, he must inform the other party of his intentions without delay so that the other party has an opportuniry of matching the terms offered by the third undertaking. If the other party refuses to do so or fails to let the tenant have his decision

within a short period, the tenant is entitled to purchase the drinks from the other undertaking. The Commission will ensure that exercise of the brewery's or drinks wholesaler's right to match the prices quoted by another supplier does not make it significantly harder for other suppliers to enter the market.

56. The tenant's right provided for in the second indent of Article 8 (2) (b) to purchase drinks of another brand or denomination from third undertakings obtains in cases where the other party does not offer them. Here the tenant is not under a duty to inform the other party of his intentions.

57. The tenant's rights arising from Article 8 (2) (b) override any obligation to purchase minimum quantities imposed upon him under Article 9 in conjunction with Article 2 (3) (b) to the extent that this is necessary to allow the tenant full exercise of those rights.

VI. **Service-station agreements (Title III of Regulation (EEC) No 1984/83)**

1. *Exclusive purchasing obligation* (Article 10)

58. The exclusive purchasing obligation can cover either motor vehicle fuels (e.g., petrol, diesel fuel, LPG, kerosene) alone or motor vehicle fuels and other fuels (e.g., heating oil, bottled gas, paraffin). All the goods concerned must be petroleum-based products.

59. The motor vehicle fuels covered by the exclusive purchasing obligations must be for use in motor-powered land or water vehicles or aircraft. The term 'service station' is to be interpreted in a correspondingly wide sense.

60. The Regulation applies to petrol stations adjoining public roads and fuelling installations on private property not open to public traffic.

2. *Other restrictions on competition that are exempted* (Article 11)

61. Under Article 11(b) only the use of lubricants and related petroleum-based products supplied by other undertakings can be prohibited. This provision refers to the servicing and maintenance of motor vehicles, i.e. to the reseller's activity in the field of provision of services. It does not affect the reseller's freedom to purchase the said products from other undertakings for resale in the service station. The petroleum-based products related to lubricants referred to in paragraph (b) are additives and brake fluids.

62. For the interpretation of Article 11 (c), the considerations stated in paragraph 49 above apply by analogy.

3. *Agreements excluded from the block exemption* (Article 12)

63. These provisions are analogous to those of Article 8 (1) (a), (b), (d) and (e) and 8 (2) (a). Reference is therefore made to paragraphs 51 and 53 above.

VII. *Transitional provisions for beer-supply and service-station agreements (Article 15 (2) and (3))*

64. Under Article 15 (2), all beer-supply and service-station agreements which were concluded and entered into force before I January 1984 remain covered by the provision of Regulation No 67/67/EEC until 31 December 1988.

From 1 January 1989, they must comply with the provisions of Titles II and III of Regulation (EEC) No 1984/83. Under Article 15 (3), in the case of agreements which were in force on 1 July 1983, the same principle applies except that the 10-year maximum duration for such agreements laid down in Article 8 (1) (d) and Article 12 (1) (c) may be exceeded.

65. The sole requirement for the eligible beer-supply and service-station agreements to continue to enjoy the block exemption beyond 1 January 1989 is that they be brought into line with the new provisions. It is left to the undertakings concerned how they do so. One way is for the parties to agree to amend the original agreement, another for the supplier unilaterally to release the reseller from all obligations that would prevent the application of the block exemption after 1 January 1989. The latter method is only mentioned in Article 15 (3) in relation to agreements in force on 1 July 1983. However, there is no reason why this possibility should not also be open to parties to agreements entered into between 1 July 1983 and 1 January 1984.

66. Parties lose the benefit of application of the transitional provisions if they extend the scope of their agreement as regards persons, places or subject matter, or incorporate into it additional obligations restrictive of competition. The agreement then counts as a new agreement. The same applies if the parties substantially change the nature or extent of their obligations to one another. A substantial change in this sense includes a revision of the purchase price of the goods supplied to the reseller or of the rent for a public house or service station which goes beyond mere adjustment to the changing economic environment.

COMMISSION REGULATION (EEC) No 4087/88
of 30 November 1988
on the application of Article 85 (3) of the Treaty to categories of franchise agreements

THE COMMISSION OF THE EURO-PEAN COMMUNITIES,

Having regard to the Treaty establishing the European Economic Community,

Having regard to Council Regulation No 19/65/EEC of 2 March 1965 on the application of Article 85 (3) of the Treaty to certain categories of agreements and concerted practices (¹), as last amended by the Act of Accession of Spain and Portugal, and in particular Article 1 thereof,

Having published a draft of this Regulation (²),

Having consulted the Advisory Committee on Restrictive Practices and Dominant Positions,

Whereas:

(1) Regulation No 19/65/EEC empowers the Commission to apply Article 85 (3) of the Treaty by Regulation to certain categories of bilateral exclusive agreements falling within the scope of Article 85 (1) which either have as their object the exclusive distribution or exclusive purchase of goods, or include restrictions imposed in relation to the assignment or use of industrial property rights.

(2) Franchise agreements consist essentially of licences of industrial or intellectual property rights relating to trade marks or signs and know-how, which can be combined with restrictions relating to supply or purchase of goods.

(3) Several types of franchise can be distinguished according to their object: industrial franchise concerns the manufacturing of goods, distribution franchise concerns the sale of goods, and service franchise concerns the supply of services.

(4) It is possible on the basis of the experience of the Commission to define categories of franchise agreements which fall under Article 85 (1) but can normally be regarded as satisfying the conditions laid down in Article 85 (3). This is the case for franchise agreements whereby one of the parties supplies goods or provides services to end users. On the other hand, industrial franchise agreements should not be covered by this Regulation. Such agreements, which usually

(¹) OJ No 36, 6. 3. 1965, p. 533/65.
(²) OJ No C 229, 27. 8. 1987, p. 3.

govern relationships between producers, present different characteristics than the other types of franchise. They consist of manufacturing licences based on patents and/or technical know-how, combined with trade-mark licences. Some of them may benefit from other block exemptions if they fulfil the necessary conditions.

(5) This Regulation covers franchise agreements between two undertakings, the franchisor and the franchisee, for the retailing of goods or the provision of services to end users, or a combination of these activities, such as the processing or adaptation of goods to fit specific needs of their customers. It also covers cases where the relationship between franchisor and franchisees is made through a third undertaking, the master franchisee. It does not cover wholesale franchise agreements because of the lack of experience of the Commission in that field.

(6) Franchise agreements as defined in this Regulation can fall under Article 85 (1). They may in particular affect intra-Community trade where they are concluded between undertakings from different Member States or where they form the basis of a network which extends beyond the boundaries of a single Member State.

(7) Franchise agreements as defined in this Regulation normally im-prove the distribution of goods and/or the provision of services as they give franchisors the possibility of establishing a uniform network with limited investments, which may assist the entry of new competitors on the market, particularly in the case of small and medium-sized undertakings, thus increasing interbrand competition. They also allow independent traders to set up outlets more rapidly and with higher chance of success than if they had to do so without the franchisor's experience and assistance. They have therefore the possibility of competing more efficiently with large distribution undertakings.

(8) As a rule, franchise agreements also allow consumers and other end users a fair share of the resulting benefit, as they combine the advantage of a uniform network with the existence of traders personally interested in the efficient operation of their business. The homogeneity of the network and the constant co-operation between the franchisor and the franchisees ensures a constant quality of the products and services. The favourable effect of franchising on interbrand competition and the fact that consumers are free to deal with any franchisee in the network guarantees that a reasonable part of the resulting benefits will be passed on to the consumers.

(9) This Regulation must define the obligations restrictive of competition which may be included in

franchise agreements. This is the case in particular for the granting of an exclusive territory to the franchisees combined with the prohibition on actively seeking customers outside that territory, which allows them to concentrate their efforts on their allotted territory. The same applies to the granting of an exclusive territory to a master franchisee combined with the obligation not to conclude franchise agreements with third parties outside that territory. Where the franchisees sell or use in the process of providing services, goods manufactured by the franchisor or according to its instructions and or bearing its trade mark, an obligation on the franchisees not to sell, or use in the process of the provision of services, competing goods, makes it possible to establish a coherent network which is identified with the franchised goods. However, this obligation should only be accepted with respect to the goods which form the essential subject-matter of the franchise. It should notably not relate to accessories or spare parts for these goods.

(10) The obligations referred to above thus do not impose restrictions which are not necessary for the attainment of the above-mentioned objectives. In particular, the limited territorial protection granted to the franchisees is indispensable to protect their investment,

(11) It is desirable to list in the Regulation a number of obligations that are commonly found in franchise agreements and are

normally not restrictive of competition and to provide that if, because of the particular economic or legal circumstances, they fall under Article 85 (1), they are also covered by the exemption. This list, which is not exhaustive, includes in particular clauses which are essential either to preserve the common identity and reputation of the network or to prevent the know-how made available and the assistance given by the franchisor from benefiting competitors.

(12) The Regulation must specify the conditions which must be satisfied for the exemption to apply. To guarantee that competition is not eliminated for a substantial part of the goods which are the subject of the franchise, it is necessary that parallel imports remain possible. Therefore, cross deliveries between franchisees should always be possible. Furthermore, where a franchise network is combined with another distribution system, franchisees should be free to obtain supplies from authorized distributors. To better inform consumers, thereby helping to ensure that they receive a fair share of the resulting benefits, it must be provided that the franchisee shall be obliged to indicate its status as an independent undertaking, by any appropriate means which does not jeopardize the common identity of the franchised network. Furthermore, where the franchisees have to honour guarantees for the franchisor's goods, this obligation should also apply to goods supplied by the

franchisor, other franchisees or other agreed dealers.

(13) The Regulation must also specify restrictions which may not be included in franchise agreements if these are to benefit from the exemption granted by the Regulation, by virtue of the fact that such provisions are restrictions falling under Article 85 (1) for which there is no general presumption that they will lead to the positive effects required by Article 85 (3). This applies in particular to market sharing between competing manufacturers, to clauses unduly limiting the franchisee's choice of suppliers or customers, and to cases where the franchisee is restricted in determining its prices. However, the franchisor should be free to recommend prices to the franchisees, where it is not prohibited by national laws and to the extent that it does not lead to concerted practices for the effective application of these prices.

(14) Agreements which are not automatically covered by the exemption because they contain provisions that are not expressly exempted by the Regulation and not expressly excluded from exemption may nonetheless generally be presumed to be eligible for application of Article 85 (3). It will be possible for the Commission rapidly to establish whether this is the case for a particular agreement. Such agreements should therefore be deemed to be covered by the

exemption provided for in this Regulation where they are notified to the Commission and the Commission does not oppose the application of the exemption within a specified period of time.

(15) If individual agreements exempted by this Regulation nevertheless have effects which are incompatible with Article 85 (3), in particular as interpreted by the administrative practice of the Commission and the case law of the Court of Justice, the Commission may withdraw the benefit of the block exemption. This applies in particular where competition is significantly restricted because of the structure of the relevant market.

(16) Agreements which are automatically exempted pursuant to this Regulation need not be notified. Undertakings may nevertheless in a particular case request a decision pursuant to Council Regulation No 17 (^{1}) as last amended by the Act of Accession of Spain and Portugal.

(17) Agreements may benefit from the provisions either of this Regulation or of another Regulation, according to their particular nature and provided that they fulfil the necessary conditions of application. They may not benefit from a combination of the provisions of this Regulation with those of another block exemption Regulation.

HAS ADOPTED THIS REGULATION:

Article 1

(^{1}) OJ No 13, 21. 2. 1962, p. 204/62.

1. Pursuant to Article 85 (3) of the

Treaty and subject to the provisions of this Regulation, it is hereby declared that Article 85 (1) of the Treaty shall not apply to franchise agreements to which two undertakings are party, which include one or more of the restrictions listed in Article 2.

2. The exemption provided for in paragraph 1 shall also apply to master franchise agreements to which two undertakings are party. Where applicable, the provisions of this Regulation concerning the relationship between franchisor and franchisee shall apply *mutatis mutandis* to the relationship between franchisor and master franchisee and between master franchisee and franchisee.

3. For the purposes of this Regulation:

(a) 'franchise' means a package of industrial or intellectual property rights relating to trade marks, trade names, shop signs, utility models, designs, copyrights, know-how or patents, to be exploited for the resale of goods or the provision of services to end users;

(b) 'franchise agreement' means an agreement whereby one undertaking, the franchisor, grants the other, the franchisee, in exchange for direct or indirect financial consideration, the right to exploit a franchise for the purposes of marketing specified types of goods and/or services; it includes at least obligations relating to:

  – the use of a common name or shop sign and a uniform presentation of contract premises and/or means of transport,

  – the communication by the franchisor to the franchisee of know-how,

  – the continuing provision by the franchisor to the franchisee of commercial or technical assistance during the life of the agreement;

(c) 'master franchise agreement' means an agreement whereby one undertaking, the franchisor, grants the other, the master franchisee, in exchange of direct or indirect financial consideration, the right to exploit a franchise for the purposes of concluding franchise agreements with third parties, the franchisees;

(d) 'franchisor's goods' means goods produced by the franchisor or according to its instructions, and/or bearing the franchisor's name or trade mark;

(e) 'contract premises' means the premises used for the exploitation of the franchise or, when the franchise is exploited outside those premises, the base from which the franchisee operates the means of transport used for the exploitation of the franchise (contract means of transport);

(f) 'know-how' means a package of non-patented practical information, resulting from experience and testing by the franchisor, which is secret, substantial and identified;

(g) 'secret' means that the know-how, as a body or in the precise configuration and assembly of its components, is not generally known or easily accessible; it is not limited in the narrow sense that each individual component of the know-how should be totally unknown or unobtainable outside the franchisor's business;

(h) 'substantial' means that the know-how includes information which is of importance for the sale of goods or the provision of services to end users, and in particular for the presentation of goods for sale, the processing of goods in connection which the provision of services, methods of dealing with customers. and administration and financial management; the know-how must be useful for the franchisee by being capable, at the date of conclusion of the agreement, of improving the competitive position of the franchisee, in particular by improving the franchisee's performance or helping it to enter a new market;

(i) 'identified' means that the know-how must be described in a sufficiently comprehensive manner so as to make it possible to verify that it fulfils the criteria of secrecy and substantiality; the description of the know-how can either be set out in the franchise agreement or in a separate document or recorded in any other appropriate form.

Article 2

The exemption provided for in Article 1 shall apply to the following restrictions of competition:

(a) an obligation on the franchisor, in a defined area of the common market, the contract territory, not to:

  – grant the right to exploit all or part of the franchise to third parties,

  – itself exploit the franchise, or itself market the goods or services which are the subject-matter of the franchise under a similar formula.

  – itself supply the franchisor's goods to third parties;

(b) an obligation on the master franchisee not to conclude franchise agreement with third parties outside its contract territory;

(c) an obligation on the franchisee to exploit the franchise only from the contract premises;

(d) an obligation on the franchisee to refrain, outside the contract territory, from seeking customers for the goods or the services which are the subject-matter of the franchise;

(e) an obligation on the franchisee not to manufacture, sell or use in the course of the provision of services, goods competing with the franchisor's goods which are the subject-matter of the franchise; where the subject-matter of the franchise is the sale or use in the course of the provision of services both certain types of goods and spare parts or accessories therefor, that obligation may not be imposed in respect of these spare parts or accessories.

Article 3

1. Article 1 shall apply notwithstanding the presence of any of the following obligations on the franchisee, in so far as they are necessary to protect the franchisor's industrial or

intellectual property rights or to maintain the common identity and reputation of the franchised network:

(a) to sell, or use in the course of the provision of services, exclusively goods matching minimum objective quality specifications laid down by the franchisor;

(b) to sell, or use in the course of the provision of services, goods which are manufactured only by the franchisor or by third parties designed by it, where it is impracticable, owing to the nature of the goods which are the subject-matter of the franchise, to apply objective quality specifications;

(c) not to engage, directly or indirectly, in any similar business in a territory where it would compete with a member of the franchised network, including the franchisor; the franchisee may be held to this obligation after termination of the agreement, for a reasonable period which may not exceed one year, in the territory where it has exploited the franchise;

(d) not to acquire financial interests in the capital of a competing undertaking, which would give the franchisee the power to influence the economic conduct of such undertaking;

(e) to sell the goods which are the subject-matter of the franchise only to end users, to other franchisees and to resellers within other channels of distribution supplied by the manufacturer of these goods or with its consent;

(f) to use its best endeavours to sell the goods or provide the services that are the subject-matter of the franchise; to offer for sale a minimum range of goods, achieve a minimum turnover, plan its orders in advance, keep minimum stocks and provide customer and warranty services;

(g) to pay to the franchisor a specified proportion of its revenue for advertising and itself carry out advertising for the nature of which it shall obtain the franchisor's approval.

2. Article 1 shall apply notwithstanding the presence of any of the following obligations on the franchisee:

(a) not to disclose to third parties the know-how provided by the franchisor; the franchisee may be held to this obligation after termination of the agreement;

(b) to communicate to the franchisor any experience gained in exploiting the franchise and to grant it, and other franchisees, a non-exclusive licence for the know-how resulting from that experience;

(c) to inform the franchisor of infringements of licensed industrial or intellectual property rights, to take legal action against infringers or to assist the franchisor in any legal actions against infringers;

(d) not to use know-how licensed by the franchisor for purposes other than the exploitation of the franchise; the franchisee may be held to this obligation after termination of the agreement;

(e) to attend or have its staff attend training courses arranged by the franchisor;

(f) to apply the commercial methods devised by the franchisor, including any subsequent modification thereof, and use the licensed industrial or intellectual property rights;

(g) to comply with the franchisor's standards for the equipment and presentation of the contract premises and/or means of transport;

(h) to allow the franchisor to carry out checks of the contract premises and/or means of transport, including the goods sold and the services provided, and the inventory and accounts of the franchisee;

(i) not without the franchisor's consent to change the location of the contract premises;

(j) not without the franchisor's consent to assign the rights and obligations under the franchise agreement.

3. In the event that, because of particular circumstances, obligations referred to in paragraph 2 fall within the scope of Article 85 (1), they shall also be exempted even if they are not accompanied by any of the obligations exempted by Article 1.

Article 4

The exemption provided for in Article 1 shall apply on condition that:

(a) the franchisee is free to obtain the goods that are the subject-matter of the franchise from other franchisees; where such goods are also distributed through another network of authorized distributors, the franchisee must be free to obtain the goods from the latter;

(b) where the franchisor obliges the franchisee to honour guarantees for the franchisor's goods, that obligation shall apply in respect of such goods supplied by any member of the franchised network or other distributors which give a similar guarantee, in the common market;

(c) the franchisee is obliged to indicate its status as an independent undertaking; this indication shall, however, not interfere with the common identity of the franchised network resulting in particular from the common name or shop sign and uniform appearance of the contract premises and/or means of transport.

Article 5

The exemption granted by Article 1 shall not apply where:

(a) undertakings producing goods or providing services which are identical or are considered by users as equivalent in view of their characteristics, price and intended use, enter into franchise agreements in respect of such goods or services;

(b) without prejudice to Article 2 (e) and Article 3 (1) (b), the franchisee is prevented from obtaining supplies of goods of a quality equivalent to those offered by the franchisor;

(c) without prejudice to Article 2 (e), the franchisee is obliged to sell, or use in the process of providing services, goods manufactured by the franchisor or third parties designated by the franchisor and the franchisor refuses, for reasons other than protecting the franchisor's industrial or intellectual property rights, or maintaining the common identity and reputation of the franchised network, to designate as authorized manufacturers third parties proposed by the franchisee;

(d) the franchisee is prevented from continuing to use the licensed know-how after termination of the agreement where the know-how has become generally known or easily accessible, other than by breach of an obligation by the franchisee;

(e) the franchisee is restricted by the franchisor, directly or indirecdy, in the determination of sale prices for the goods or services which are the subject-matter of the franchise, without prejudice to the possibility for the franchisor of recommending sale prices;

(f) the franchisor prohibits the franchisee from challenging the validity of the industrial or intellectual property rights which form part of the franchise, without prejudice to the possibility for the franchisor of terminating the agreement in such a case;

(g) franchisees are obliged not to supply within the common market the goods or services which are the subject-matter of the franchise to end users because of their place of residence.

Article 6

1. The exemption provided for in Article 1 shall also apply to franchise agreements which fulfil the conditions laid down in Article 4 and include obligations restrictive of competition which are not covered by Articles 2 and 3 (3) and do not not fall within the scope of Article 5, on condition that the agreements in question are notified to the Commission in accordance with the provisions of Commission Regulation No 27(¹) and that the Commission does not oppose such exemption within a period of six months.

2. The period of six months shall run from the date on which the notification is received by the Commission. Where, however, the notification is made by registered post, the period shall run from the date shown on the postmark of the place of posting.

3. Paragraph 1 shall apply only if:

(a) express reference is made to this Article in the notification or in a communication accompanying it; and

(b) the information furnished with the notification is complete and in accordance with the facts.

4. The benefit of paragraph 1 can be claimed for agreements notified before the entry into force of this Regulation by submitting a communication to the Commission referring expressly to this Article and to the notification. Paragraphs 2 and 3 (b) shall apply *mutatis mutandis.*

5. The Commission may oppose exemption. It shall oppose exemption if it receives a request to do so from a Member State within three months of

---

(¹) OJ No 35, 10. 5. 1962, p. 1118/62.

the forwarding to the Member State of the notification referred to in paragraph I or the communication referred to in paragraph 4. This request must be justified on the basis of considerations relating to the competition rules of the Treaty.

6. The Commission may withdraw its opposition to the exemption at any time. However, where that opposition was raised at the request of a Member State, it may be withdrawn only after consultation of the advisory Committee on Restrictive Practices and Dominant Positions.

7. If the opposition is withdrawn because the undertakings concerned have shown that the conditions of Article 85 (3) are fulfilled, the exemption shall apply from the date of the notification.

8. If the opposition is withdrawn because the undertakings concerned have amended the agreement so that the conditions of Article 85 (3) are fulfilled, the exemption shall apply from the date on which the amendments take effect.

9. If the Commission opposes exemption and its opposition is not withdrawn, the effects of the notification shall be governed by the provisions of Regulation No 17.

Article 7

1. Information acquired pursuant to Article 6 shall be used only for the purposes of this Regulation.

2. The Commission and the authorities of the Member States, their officials and other servants shall not disclose information acquired by them pursuant to this Regulation of a kind that is covered by the obligation of professional secrecy.

3. Paragraphs 1 and 2 shall not prevent publication of general information or surveys which do not contain information relating to particular undertakings or associations of undertakings.

Article 8

The Commission may withdraw the benefit of this Regulation, pursuant to Article 7 of Regulation No 19/65/EEC, where it finds in a particular case that an agreement exempted by this Regulation nevertheless has certain effects which are incompatible with the conditions laid down in Article 85 (3) of the EEC Treaty, and in particular where territorial protection is awarded to the franchisee and:

(a) access to the relevant market or competition therein is significantly restricted by the cumulative effect of parallel networks of similar agreements established by competing manufacturers or distributors;

(b) the goods or services which are the subject-matter of the franchise do not face, in a substantial part of the common market, effective competition from goods or services which are identical or considered by users as equivalent in view of their characteristics, price and intended use;

(c) the parties, or one of them, prevent end users, because of their place of residence, from obtaining, directly or through intermediaries, the goods or services which are the subject-matter of the franchise within the common market, or use differences in specifications concerning those goods or services in different Member States, to isolate markets;

(d) franchisees engage in concerted practices relating to the sale prices of the goods or services which are the subject-matter of the franchise;

(e) the franchisor uses its right to check the contract premises and means of transport, or refuses its agreement to requests by the franchisee to move the contract premises or assign its rights and obligations under the franchise agreement, for reasons other than protecting the franchisor's industrial or intellectual property rights, maintaining the common identity and reputation of the franchised network or verifying that the franchisee abides by its obligations under the agreement.

Article 9

This Regulation shall enter into force on 1 February 1989.
It shall remain in force until 31 December 1999.

This Regulation shall be binding in its entirety and directly applicable in all Member States.

Done at Brussels, 30 November 1988.

For the Commission
Peter SUTHERLAND
Member of the Commission

COUNCIL DIRECTIVE
of 18 December 1986
on the coordination of the laws of the Member States relating to self-employed commercial agents

(86/653/EEC)

THE COUNCIL OF THE EUROPEAN COMMUNITIES,

Having regard to the Treaty establishing the European Economic Community, and in particular Articles 57 (2) and 100 thereof,

Having regard to the proposal from the Commission (¹),

Having regard to the opinion of the European Parliament (²),

Having regard to the opinion of the Economic and Social Committee (³),

Whereas the restrictions on the freedom of establishment and the freedom to provide services in respect of activities of intermediaries in commerce, industry and small craft industries were abolished by Directive 64/224/EEC (⁴);

Whereas the differences in national laws concerning commercial representation substantially affect the condi-

tions of competition and the carrying-on of that activity within the Community and are detrimental both to the protection available to commercial agents *vis-a-vis* their principals and to the security of commercial transactions; whereas moreover those differences are such as to inhibit substantially the conclusion and operation of commercial representation contracts where principal and commercial agent are established in different Member States;

Whereas trade in goods between Member States should be carried on under conditions which are similar to those of a single market, and this necessitates approximation of the legal systems of the Member States to the extent required for the proper functioning of the common market: whereas in this regard the rules concerning conflict of laws do not, in the matter of commercial representation, remove the inconsistencies referred to above, nor would they even if they were made uniform, and accordingly the proposed harmonization is necessary notwithstanding the existence of those rules;

Whereas in this regard the legal relationship between commercial agent and principal must be given priority;

(¹) OJ No C 13, 18. 1. 1977, p. 2; OJ No C 56, 2. 3. 1979, p. 5.
(²) OJ No C 239, 9. 10. 1978, p 17.
(³) OJ No C 59, 8. 3. 1978, p 31.
(⁴) OJ No 56, 4. 4. 1964, p 869/64.

Whereas it is appropriate to be guided by the principles of Article 117 of the Treaty and to maintain improvements already made, when harmonizing the laws of the Member States relating to commercial agents;

Whereas additional transitional periods should be allowed for certain Member States which have to make a particular effort to adapt their regulations, especially those concerning indemnity for termination of contract between the principal and the commercial agent, to the requirements of this Directive,

HAS ADOPTED THIS DIRECTIVE:

CHAPTER I

Scope

Article 1

1. The harmonization measures prescribed by this Directive shall apply to the laws, regulations and administrative provisions of the Member States governing the relations between commercial agents and their principals.

2. For the purposes of this Directive, 'commercial agent' shall mean a self-employed intermediary who has continuing authority to negotiate the sale or the purchase of goods on behalf of another person, hereinafter called the 'principal', or to negotiate and conclude such transactions on behalf of and in the name of that principal.

3. A commercial agent shall be understood within the meaning of this Directive as not including in particular:

– a person who, in his capacity as an officer, is empowered to enter into commitments binding on a company or association,

– a partner who is lawfully authorized to enter into commitments binding on his partners,

– a receiver, a receiver and manager, a liquidator or a trustee in bankruptcy.

Article 2

1. This Directive shall not apply to:

– commercial agents whose activities are unpaid,

– commercial agents when they operate on commodity exchanges or in the commodity market, or

– the body known as the Crown Agents for Overseas Governments and Administrations, as set up under the Crown Agents Act 1979 in the United Kingdom, or its subsidiaries.

2. Each of the Member States shall have the right to provide that the Directive shall not apply to those persons whose activities as commercial agents are considered secondary by the law of that Member State.

CHAPTER II

Rights and obligations

Article 3

1. In performing his activities a commercial agent must look after his principal's interests and act dutifully and in good faith.

2. In particular, a commercial agent must:

(a) make proper efforts to negotiate

and, where appropriate, conclude the transactions he is instructed to take care of;

(b) communicate to his principal all the necessary information available to him;

(c) comply with reasonable instructions given by his principal.

Article 4

1. In his relations with his commercial agent a principal must act dutifully and in good faith.

2. A principal must in particular:

(a) provide his commercial agent with the necessary documentation relating to the goods concerned;

(b) obtain for his commercial agent the information necessary for the performance of the agency contract, and in particular notify the commercial agent within a reasonable period once he anticipates that the volume of commercial transactions will be significantly lower than that which the commercial agent could normally have expected.

3. A principal must, in addition, inform the commercial agent within a reasonable period of his acceptance, refusal, and of any non-execution of a commercial transaction which the commercial agent has procured for the principal.

Article 5

The parties may not derogate from the provisions of Articles 3 and 4.

CHAPTER III

Remuneration

Article 6

1. In the absence of any agreement on this matter between the parties, and without prejudice to the application of the compulsory provisions of the Member States concerning the level of remuneration, a commercial agent shall be entitled to the remuneration that commercial agents appointed for the goods forming the subject of his agency contract are customarily allowed in the place where he carries on his activities: If there is no such customary practice a commercial agent shall be entitled to reasonable remuneration taking into account all the aspects of the transaction.

2. Any part of the remuneration which varies with the number or value of business transactions shall be deemed to be commission within the meaning of this Directive.

3. Articles 7 to 12 shall not apply if the commercial agent is not remunerated wholly or in part by commisson.

Article 7

1. A commercial agent shall be entitled to commission on commercial transactions concluded during the period covered by the agency contract:

(a) where the transaction has been concluded as a result of his action; or

(b) where the transaction is concluded with a third party whom he has previously acquired as a customer for transactions of the same kind.

2. A commercial agent shall also be entitled to commission on transactions concluded during the period covered by the agency contract:

– either where he is entrusted with a specific geographical area or group of customers,

– or where he has an exclusive right to a specific geographical area or group of customers,

and where the transaction has been entered into with a customer belonging to that area or group.

Member States shall include in their legislation one of the possibilities referred to in the above two indents.

Article 8

A commercial agent shall be entitled to commission on commercial trans-actions concluded after the agency contract has terminated:

(a) if the transaction is mainly attributable to the commercial agent's efforts during the period covered by the agency contract and if the transaction was entered into within a reasonable period after that contract terminated; or

(b) if, in accordance with the conditions mentioned in Article 7, the order of the third party reached the principal or the commercial agent before the agency contract terminated.

Article 9

A commercial agent shall not be entitled to the commission referred to in Article 7, if that commission is

payable, pursuant to Article 8, to the previous commerial agent, unless it is equitable because of the circumstances for the commission to be shared between the commercial agents.

Article 10

1 The commission shall become due as soon as and to the extent that one of the following circumstances obtains:

(a) the principal has executed the transaction; or,

(b) the principal should, according to his agreement with the third party, have executed the trans-action; or

(c) the third party has executed the transaction.

2. The commission shall become due at the latest when the third party has executed his part of the transaction or should have done so if the principal had executed his part of the transaction, as he should have.

3. The commission shall be paid not later than on the last day of the month following the quarter in which it became due.

4. Agreements to derogate from paragraphs 2 and 3 to the detriment of the commercial agent shall not be permitted,

Article 11

1. The right to commission can be extinguished only if and to the extent that:

– it is established that the contract between the third party and the principal will not be executed, and

– that face is due to a reason for which the principal is not to blame.

2. Any commission which the commercial agent has already received shall be refunded if the right to it is extinguished.

3. Agreements to derogate from paragraph 1 to the detriment of the commercial agent shall not be permitted.

Article 12

1. The principal shall supply his commercial agent with a statement of the commission due, not later than the last day of the month following the quarter in which the commission has become due. This statement shall set out the main components used in calculating the amount of commission.

2. A commercial agent shall be entitled to demand that he be provided with all the information, and in particular an extract from the books, which is available to his principal and which he needs in order to check the amount of the commission due to him.

3. Agreements to derogate from paragraphs 1 and 2 to the detriment of the commercial agent shall not be permitted.

4. This Directive shall not conflict with the internal provisions of Member States which recognize the right of a commercial agent to inspect a principal's books.

CHAPTER IV

Conclusion and termination of the agency contract

Article 13

1. Each party shall be entitled to receive from the other on request a signed written document setting out the terms of the agency contract including any terms subsequently agreed. Waiver of this right shall not be permitted.

2. Notwithstanding paragraph 1 a Member State may provide that an agency contract shall not be valid unless evidenced in writing.

Article 14

An agency contract for a fixed period which continues to be performed by both parties after that period has expired shall be deemed to be converted into an agency contract for an indefinite period.

Article 15

1. Where an agency contract is concluded for an indefinite period either party may terminate it by notice.

2. The period of notice shall be one month for the first year of the contract, two months for the second year commenced, and three months for the third year commenced and subsequent years. The parties may not agree on shorter periods of notice.

3. Member States may fix the period of notice at four months for the fourth year of the contract, five months for the fifth year and six months for the sixth and subsequent years. They may decide that the parties may not agree to shorter periods.

4. If the parties agree on longer periods

than those laid down in paragraphs 2 and 3, the period of notice to be observed by the principal must not be shorter than that to be observed by the commercial agent.

5. Unless otherwise agreed by the parties, the end of the period of notice must coincide with the end of a calendar month.

6. The provisions of this Article shall apply to an agency contract for a fixed period where it is converted under Article 14 into an agency contract for an indefinite period, subject to the proviso that the earlier fixed period must be taken into account in the calculation of the period of notice.

Article 16

Nothing in this Directive shall affect the application of the law of the Member States where the latter provides for the immediate termination of the agency contract:

(a) because of the failure of one party to carry out all or part of his obligations;

(b) where exceptional circumstances arise.

Article 17

1. Member States shall take the measures necessary to ensure that the commercial agent is, after termination of the agency contract, indemnified in accordance with paragraph 2 or compensated for damage in accordance with paragraph 3.

2. (a) The commercial agent shall be entitled to an indemnity if and to the extent that:

– he has brought the principal new customers or has significantly increased the volume of business with existing customers and the principal continues to derive substantial benefits from the business with such customers, and

– the payment of this indemnity is equitable having regard to all the circumstances and, in particular, the commission lost by the commercial agent on the business transacted with such customers. Member States may provide for such circumstances also to include the application or otherwise of a restraint of trade clause, within the meaning of Article 20;

(b) The amount of the indemnity may not exceed a figure equivalent to an indemnity for one year calculated from the commercial agent's average annual remuneration over the preceding five years and if the contract goes back less than five years the indemnity shall be calculated on the average for the period in question;

(c) The grant of such an indemnity shall not prevent the commercial agent from damages.

3. The commercial agent shall be entitled to compensation for the damage he suffers as a result of the termination of his relations with the principal.

Such damage shall be deemed to occur

particularly when the termination takes place in circumstances:

– depriving the commercial agent of the commission which proper performance of the agency contract would have procured him whilst providing the principal with substantial benefit: linked to the commercial agent's activities,

– and/or which have not enabled the commercial agent to amortize the costs and expenses that he had incurred for the performance of the agency contract on the principal's advice.

4. Entitlement to the indemnity as provided for in paragraph 2 or to compensation for damage as provided for under paragraph 3, shall also arise where the agency contract is terminated as a result of the commercial agent's death.

5. The commercial agent shall lose his entitlement to the indemnity in the instances provided for in paragraph 2 or to compensation for damage in the instances provided for in paragraph 3, if within one year following termination of the contract he has not notified the principal that he intends pursuing his entitlement.

6. The Commission shall submit to the Council, within eight years following the date of notification of this Directive, a report on the implementation of this Article, and shall if necessary submit to it proposals for amendments.

Article 18

The indemnity or compensation referred to in Article 17 shall not be payable:

(a) where the principal has terminated the agency contract because of default attributable to the commercial agent which would justify immediate termination of the agency contract under national law;

(b) where the commercial agent has terminated the agency contract, unless such termination is justified by circumstances attributable to the principal or on grounds of age, infirmary or illness of the commercial agent in consequence of which he cannot reasonably be required to continue his activities;

(c) where, with the agreement of the principal, the commercial agent assigns his rights and duties under the agency contract to another person.

Article 19

The parties may not derogate from Articles 17 and 18 to the detriment of the commercial agent before the agency contract expires.

Article 20

1. For the purposes of this Directive, an agreement restricting the business activities of a commercial agent following termination of the agency contract is hereinafter referred to as a restraint of trade clause.

2. A restraint of trade clause shall be valid only if and to the extent that:

(a) it is concluded in writing; and

(b) it relates to the geographical area or the group of customers and the geographical area entrusted to the commercial agent and to the kind of goods covered by his agency under the contract.

3. A restraint of trade clause shall be valid for not more than two years after termination of the agency contract.

4. This Article shall not affect provisions of national law which impose other restrictions on the validity or enforceability of restraint of trade clauses or which enable the courts to reduce the obligations on the parties resulting from such an agreement.

CHAPTER V

General and final provisions

Article 21

Nothing in this Directive shall require a Member State to provide for the disclosure of information where such disclosure would be contrary to public policy.

Article 22

1. Member States shall bring into force the provisions necessary to comply with this Directive before 1 January 1990. They shall forthwith inform the Commission thereof. Such provisions shall apply at least to contracts concluded after their entry into force. They shall apply to contracts in operation by 1 January 1994 at the latest.

2. As from the notification of this Directive, Member States shall communicate to the Commission the main laws, regulations and administrative provisions which they adopt in the field governed by this Directive.

3. However, with regard to Ireland and the United Kingdom, 1 January 1990 referred to in paragraph 1 shall be replaced by 1 January 1994.
With regard to Italy, 1 January 1990 shall be replaced by 1 January 1993 in the case of the obligations deriving from Article 17.

Article 23

This Directive is addressed to the Member States.

Done at Brussels, 18 December 1986.

For the Council
The President
M. JOPLING

Index